THE SPARE CHANCELLOR
The Life of Walter Bagehot

WALTER BAGEHOT

THE
SPARE CHANCELLOR

THE LIFE OF WALTER BAGEHOT

Alastair Buchan

MICHIGAN STATE UNIVERSITY PRESS

1960

The Michigan State University Press
East Lansing, Michigan

Library of Congress Catalog Card Number: 60-11303

© Copyright Alastair Buchan 1959
© Copyright Alastair Buchan 1960

MANUFACTURED IN THE UNITED STATES OF AMERICA

For Hope

CONTENTS

INTRODUCTION

N O-ONE—scholar, student or common reader—can travel
very far into the history of the last hundred years without
meeting the name of Walter Bagehot. The encounter may not
be face to face, in his books or in his essays, for his aphorisms
and ideas traverse and illuminate the works of more famous
men. Yet, because what he said has been so widely quoted,
misquoted or unconsciously accepted the man has tended to
recede into a myth, behind the eyeglass and the bushy beard.
Posterity likes to place its forbears in categories, but Bagehot
refuses to play this innocent game. He was a literary critic
who was also a master of hounds, a banker and a social psychologist, an economist, a great editor, a political analyst and
a biographer. Though he never entered public life, he was
for many years regarded in Whitehall as a spare Chancellor
of the Exchequer. Whatever niche the historian attempts to
assign him to, he instantly eludes. He died at the age of fifty-
one and the fact that his life formed so brief an interlude in
an era of continuous change—his uncle was William Pitt's
secretary, one of his friends took part in an international
negotiation with John Foster Dulles—makes it even harder
to set him in his true dimension.

He was childless in more senses than the obvious, and
founded no school of thought associated with his name, no
great intellectual dynasty like the Stephens, the Huxleys,
the Darwins, the Arnolds or the Forsters. He had little
concern with posthumous fame which he compared to "a moth
going into Chancery", and he made gentle fun of Macaulay
for regarding "living men as the necessary prerequisites of
great grand children". His principal memorial is an attitude
and a style which by slow pervasion have influenced letters

and journalism throughout the English speaking world—a
compound of irony, clarity and humanity. His was not one of
the great seminal minds of one of the greatest ages of mind,
and he rightly has no niche in the long marble gallery of
the Great Victorians. Like de Tocqueville, his background
made him, in certain important respects, stand outside his
time: like de Tocqueville this both gave him a subtle observation of it and endowed his writing with a more enduring
quality than that of profounder men who were deeply immersed in the controveries of the mid-Victorian years.

This book is an attempt to portray the man himself, the
mind behind the rich diversity of talent. I first became interested in Bagehot as a journalist, and in attempting to master
the many facets of his mind, I have greatly extended my own
education, but have also ventured into fields which may, I
fear, make me the prey of scholars of greater and more specialised learning.

Bagehot has been a source of direct inspiration to many
different kinds of men, Arthur Balfour and William James,
Woodrow Wilson and James Bryce, Herbert Read and Jacques
Barzun, and a large specialist bibliography of critical essays
surrounds his work, for his reputation has grown steadily in
the eighty years since his death. In addition his own writings
cover nine large volumes—together with a host of articles in
The Economist and elsewhere. But the material with which a
biographer rather than a critic must work is much less rich.
In 1914 Bagehot's sister-in-law, Mrs. Russell Barrington, published a life of him, drawing on letters and diaries which have
since disappeared, but also containing a number of personal
recollections by those who knew him in his private and his
official life. She also published his love letters to his future
wife, Eliza Wilson, as a separate book. In addition to these
books, some of his letters as a schoolboy and as an undergraduate have been preserved, together with some of his correspondence with his lifelong friend, Richard Holt Hutton, the editor
of *The Spectator,* and with his father-in-law, James Wilson,
the founder of *The Economist.*

Bagehot was a careless man who did not bother to keep the letters of his friends or copies of letters which he wrote to them. Moreover, a great deal of the material that might have been available has been the victim of time and mischance. The original files of *The Economist* were destroyed by a fire bomb during the Second World War, and it is therefore impossible to say with complete accuracy what he wrote for it. Where I have quoted from *The Economist,* it is either from articles which Mrs. Barrington definitely assigned to him in Vol. IX of the Works or in her Life, or where the style is unmistakable. In addition, many of his letters and papers were thrown away by Mrs. Barrington and her sisters after she had been through them for her own book, presumably on the assumption that she had written a definitive biography.

This book, therefore, is not the result of any golden harvest of new material. I have been fortunate in having been able to read Eliza Bagehot's diaries in the original, and to see such of Walter Bagehot's family letters as still exist. But, in the main, it derives from a reorganization of well-known sources and it has been completed in odd moments and in several places on two continents.

Augustine Birrell wrote of Bagehot "You can know a man from his books, and if he is a writer of good faith and has the knack, you may know him very well: better it may be than did his directors or his partners in business or even his own flesh and blood. . . . Everyone who has read Mr. Bagehot's writings will agree at once that he is an author who can be known from his books", for he was "a personal author, though he tells us very little directly about himself". This is true, and it is in this spirit that I have used Bagehot's own writings as he used those of Adam Smith, Gibbon or Macaulay in the attempt to discover what manner of man it was that wrote them.

I am greatly indebted to the late Mr. G. M. Young and to Sir Geoffrey Crowther for first encouraging me to write Bagehot's life: to Mrs. Guy Barrington of Taunton for invaluable help with the history and the atmosphere of Langport: to

Mr. Robert Bagehot Porch for the opportunity to read some of Bagehot's unpublished letters of his youth: to Colonel Noel Halsey for the loan of Eliza Bagehot's diaries and Bagehot's unpublished correspondence with James Wilson: and to Mr. Eric Gibb for his help in tracing the members of the family. I am grateful to Mr. Wilfred King, the Editor of *The Banker*, for reading Chapter 9 and for the benefit of his great knowledge of the nineteenth century City: to Mr. Donald Tyerman, the Editor of *The Economist*, for reading the MS., for his comments, and his fortifying interest: and to Mr. Graham Hutton for his advice and help. In addition I have been helped by much useful advice on specific points from many correspondents which I have tried to acknowledge in the footnotes. I am most grateful to Mrs. Frances Hugill for helping me initially with research, and to Miss Elizabeth Blandy for her assistance in preparing the MS. Finally, I must thank my wife for her patience and encouragement during a period of gestation more suited to some great encyclopedic pachyderm than this modest offspring.

ALASTAIR BUCHAN

Brill, Buckinghamshire,
October, 1958

THE SPARE CHANCELLOR

The Life of Walter Bagehot

Chapter 1

BOW STREET AND CHEAPSIDE

"Before letters were invented, or books were, or gov-
ernesses discovered, the neighbours' children, the out-
door life, the fists and the wrestling sinews, the old
games—the oldest things in the world—the bare hill and
the clear river—these were education".

Essay on Oxford

I

AMONG the proud names of the shires of southern England, the county of Somerset occupies an unassuming
place. Though it has many famous places and churches and
fortresses—Glastonbury, Sedgmoor, Dunster—its name does
not immediately evoke an image or quicken the blood as
Sussex or Devon or Dorset may do. For it has always been a
frontier, dividing the old West Country from the rest of
England, dividing Roman from Celt, Briton from Saxon,
Daneland from Wessex, conformist from rebel. Like other
frontier societies its loyalties have been divided: Taunton
and the Quantocks are the forward defences of a different
and simpler pattern of life than the rest of southern England:
Frome and Wells have looked north and east towards a wider
and more sophisticated society. It has the climate and quality
of the land it guards, the West: it has the salt smell of the
Atlantic, soft lush grass and cider orchards. It has little of the
Augustan, landscaped air of Wiltshire or of Kent, for it is a
land that is hard to tame, part moorland and part marsh.
The names of its villages are the deposit of many layers of
history: Stratton-on-the-Fosse, Middlezoy and Chedzoy, Isle
Brewers and Firehead, Kingsbury Episcopi and Staple Fitzjames, Compton Pauncefoot and Brympton D'Evercy. But like
the people of other frontier societies, Tennessee or the Pays
Basque, Somerset men have a certain indifference to outward
forms, a passionate attachment to their own shaggy and untidy

maquis, and an aptitude for resisting the pretensions of those who have used their land as a battleground or taken their loyalties for granted.

The heart of Somerset is the Vale of Taunton, and at the center of the Vale there is an unpretentious town with the quiet name of Langport, at the point where two rivers, the Yeo and the Parrett, join to form a navigable channel to the sea below Bridgwater. All round it lie the "moors", the lush and treacherous marshland: the town, resting on a Roman causeway is confined to a single street which is called, in brave analogy of a larger city, at one end Bow Street and at the other Cheapside.

Langport has seen much fighting. Its causeway and its twin hills on either side of the Parrett gave it strategic importance in Saxon history and it was one of the frontier towns of Wessex. Four miles to the west of Langport lies Athelney where Alfred, as we should say, went underground, where he burnt the cakes, and where he organized his great counter-offensive against the Danes; to the north of the town rises the ridge of Aller where he took his prisoner, King Guthrun, to Christian baptism. Beyond Aller and the Polden hills stands Glastonbury; two miles to the south of Langport is the great Benedictine house of Muchelney, and beyond lies Montacute.

Langport was a royal borough in Saxon times; it has an Elizabethan Charter and was given corporate status under James I. It returned two members to the first two Parliaments of Edward I but thereafter its burgesses, with an indifference to the merits of representative government which is characteristic of Somerset, asked to be relieved of the bother and expense. (Walter Bagehot once remarked that Somersetshire would not subscribe one thousand pounds "to be represented by an archangel".) It sprang briefly to fame in July, 1645 when Goring, attempting to cover the defences of the West, drew up his forces outside Langport, only to be outmaneuvred by Fairfax and routed by a charge of Cromwell's cavalry. It was this battle, the eclipse of any Royalist hopes of holding the West country, which drew from Cromwell the cry on which his detractors have fastened, as he watched Goring's men falling back towards the burning streets of Langport: "To see this, is it not to see the face of God." Forty years later the scared and routed remnants of Monmouth's army straggled through Langport's streets or hid their arms among the thatch of its houses.

By the beginning of the second quarter of the last century Langport had become a flourishing town in the midst of a prosperous countryside. In the north of the county, in the Avon valley, the old wool and worsted trades were losing ground to Lancashire and to West Riding, and in the Mendips coal mining was disturbing the social balance of an agricultural economy. (Lord Carlingford who was attempting to retrieve the Waldegrave family fortunes from bankruptcy a little later in the century based his calculations on the assumption that Radstock would be a second Manchester and to Cobbett Frome had all the vitality of "a sort of little Manchester".) But in the Vale of Taunton the industrial revolution had as yet made little mark. It was a land of small yeoman farmers who raised their cattle and sheep on the high ground and fattened them on the moor pastures before driving them to Taunton or Smithfield. Prices were not so high or times so good as they had been during "the war", but the cattle prices had not suffered the same fall as corn prices and there was less distress in the dairy farming areas of Somerset than in the corn growing counties. The wages of the laborers were very low—averaging about seven shillings a week—and their housing was probably as bad as any in the country. But supplementary sources of income were appearing, among them the growing of osiers on Sedgmoor and Allermoor, while the sewing of gloves for the Yeovil glove-masters enabled the peasant women to support their menfolk during hard times— which accounted for the relative tranquillity of the area during the disturbances of 1830.

It was a fairly flexible community; there were no great landowners in the Vale of Taunton, although the more delectable pastures and hills were crowned by the parks and houses of

the gentry—many of them, like the Pinneys of Somerton, successful West Indian merchants from Bristol. It was a countryside in which a farm house had not infrequently been a manor
house in Elizabethan times or where "the manor" was a
promoted farm house. A yeoman by turning to trading might
set himself up as a minor country gentleman, and a small
landowner did not feel inhibited from engaging in local
commerce. The prevalence of Dissent also helped to make
this neighborhood unlike the rest of southern England.
Taunton had been "the nursery of rebellion" at the end of the
seventeenth century, and the country towns of Somerset had
been the scenes of Whitfield and Wesley's earliest triumphs.
The little towns and villages round Langport could be distinguished across the flat moor by the magnificent square
towers of their medieval churches built of the soft Ham Hill
stone from the quarries above Montacute. But as often as not
it was in the squat little red brick chapels—Methodist or Con-
gregational—that the real life of the community centered.

In the 1820s Langport was a busy place—the very reverse
of "sleepy", which is the inevitable epithet in an urban generation for all country towns. It had a population of nearly 1,200,
as against 750 in 1801 or 772 in 1951, and it had a weekly
market and an annual cattle fair. Being at the head of navigation salt, coal, millstones and general merchandise came up
by barge from Bridgwater to be distributed from the quay at
Langport to a wide hinterland of small towns and hamlets.
The most important merchants in this trade were the Bagehot
family.

It was this position on the river which gave Langport an
economic advantage, but the chief reason for its vitality was
that it was the headquarters of what was variously called "The
Langport Bank" or "The Bristol and Somersetshire Bank"
but which was known far and wide as "Stuckey's".

For a generation or more these two families had eyed each
other's business along the length of Bow Street and Cheapside,
and 1824 they made a family compact whereby Edith Stuckey
married Thomas Watson Bagehot. Within two years Thomas

had been made a partner in Stuckey's; a hale son had been born to their marriage; and the Bank had become the second of all the private banks in England to register as a joint stock company.

II

The family of Bagehot, which is now extinct in the male line, can be traced back to the seventeenth century. It used to be a legend in the family that "Bagehot" was one of the original spellings of "Bagot" but there is no certainty of this. Certainly there is a reference to a Baghott of Cambridgeshire in the Roll of Battle Abbey. In 1587 Edward Baghott was presented to the living of Prestbury in Gloucestershire (now a suburb of Cheltenham) and the family settled there.

No direct line can be traced thus far back, but from the end of the sixteenth century the Baghott family were the owners of Prestbury. Sir Thomas Baghott was Master of the Buckhounds to James I and fought for his son at Newbury. He died without issue and the lands passed to his nephew, Edward. Edward had two sons, of whom the elder William married Anne de la Bere in 1684. The family continued as Baghot and Baghot de la Bere at Prestbury until the beginning of this century. William's younger brother, Edward, on the other hand, embraced Dissent and moved to the more congenial atmosphere of Abergavenny. His grandson was born at Abergavenny in 1717 and after being educated as a Nonconformist settled in Langport in 1747. He married an Osler of Bristol, added an *e* into his name and had four children, of whom the youngest, Robert Codrington Bagehot, was the grandfather of Walter. Robert Bagehot and his sons were general traders and merchants, bringing commodities up the Parrett by barge and distributing them throughout the Vale of Taunton, a business that later became dignified by the name of The Somerset Trading Company. It was the marriage of the younger son, Thomas Watson Bagehot, with Edith

Stuckey which united the Bagehots with the other enterprising family in Langport.

The Stuckeys had no such long descended history. In the manner which was possible in Somerset they had probably risen from farm labourers to yeomen and from yeomen to merchants. About 1770 Samuel Stuckey, who was a general merchant in Langport, trading in corn and salt in much the same fashion as the Bagehots, established a banking business as an offshoot of his trading activities. It was a common practice in the country towns of England at the end of the eighteenth century for the most substantial merchant in the town to offer rudimentary banking facilities as a convenience to his customers. Samuel Stuckey took charge of his customers' gold and silver and issued in exchange vellum notes of hand which began to circulate in the area. He was a man of considerable energy and both his banking and his trading businesess flourished and expanded. In 1782 they justified the existence of an agent in London and in 1800 he took his brother George into partnership. But it was the introduction into the business in the following year of George's son, Vincent, which began the transformation of their fortunes.

Vincent Stuckey, by a mixture of character and good fortune, had had a very thorough training in finance. As a young man he had attracted the attention of Lady Chatham, the widow of the elder Pitt, who lived at Burton Pynsent close to Langport, the estate which had been left to Pitt by his admirer, Sir William Pynsent. Lady Chatham had a great regard for the Stuckey family, and, from the warmth with which on one occasion she defended their growing monopoly of banking in the area, it is probable that Vincent and his uncle had helped to underpin the chaotic finances of the Chatham family. On her introduction Vincent Stuckey was given a Clerkship in the Treasury by William Pitt, and in 1797, the year of the great panic when the Bank of England was ordered to suspend cash payments, he was the head of the Bill Department of the Treasury. In 1800 he was Private Secretary to Pitt himself, but in 1801 at the age of thirty he decided to forego a public career, returned to Langport, and married his first cousin, Julia, the daughter of Samuel Stuckey.

Thereafter the banking business, borne up partly by the agricultural prosperity of the war years, but largely by the energy and acumen of Vincent himself, began to expand rapidly. In 1806 the name of the business was changed to the Langport Bank, and branches were opened at Bridgwater and at Bristol. In 1812 Samuel Stuckey died and Vincent became the senior partner. In 1819 when the bank had extended its branches to Wells and Taunton, Vincent Stuckey was asked to give evidence before Sir Robert Peel's select committee on the resumption of cash payments, and there is no doubt that the committee regarded him as one of the leading bankers in the West Country.

Fortune had been less kind to Edith Stuckey than to her brother Vincent. In 1804 at the age of eighteen she had married Joseph Estlin of Bristol, the son of a famous Unitarian divine, John Prior Estlin. He had died ten years later leaving her with three sons. The eldest, Vincent, was half-witted from birth, the second son was killed in a coach accident at the age of twenty, and the youngest died in childhood. She was a widow of twenty-eight—lively, beautiful and tragic —when Thomas Bagehot was a boy of eighteen, but despite the difference in years he fell deeply in love with her, and in 1824 when she was 38 and he 28 they were married. On 3rd of February, 1826, their second and only surviving child, Walter, was born at the Bank House in Langport—"a large handsome fellow who can already make the nursery ring with his strong voice."

As a boy the twin influences that were to shape his character lay not only spiritually but geographically on either side of Walter. The Bank House, a roomy rather desolate dwelling of three stories with wide staircases and a pleasant garden at the back, lies in the middle of Langport. To its right at the top of the hill stood Hill House where Vincent Stuckey dwelt in considerable state. The Stuckeys were not unlike the Dodsons in *The Mill on the Floss* "the family badge was to be honest and rich, and not only rich, but richer than was supposed". Of the whole group of intertwined relationships between the two families—Stuckeys, Bagehots, Reynolds and Michells—Vincent was the unchallenged patriarch. He was in close touch with the world of affairs; he had been the lifelong friend of Huskisson, the adviser of Lord Althorp, and the valued witness before several Select Committees. Every spring his coach with its postillions was rolled out of the stable to take him to his house in Sloane Street for the season. (Characteristically, Vincent Stuckey had a town house in London while most of the Somerset country gentlemen had theirs in Bristol or Taunton.) But for all his experience of the world, he had deliberately preferred Somerset over Great George Street, and he loved to hold a kind of rural court of families and neighbors on the lawn of Hill House, or to hunt his pack of hounds over the moor. He had the "enjoying instinct" which, Bagehot suggested, is the basis of true conservatism.*

At the other end of the town Walter's grandparents, the Robert Codrington Bagehots, were building a comfortable and unpretentious country house on the summit of a round knoll called Herd's Hill. It was the Bagehots who gave to the little society in Langport its strong intellectual flavor. They were a high-minded, well-educated, intelligent family who became Nonconformists or embraced the Establishment according to the dictates of their individual conscience. Thomas Watson, Walter Bagehot's father, was an admirable example of the family tradition. In religion he was a Unitarian, in politics a Whig, in his economics a Free Trader. He was a keen landscape gardener, and a tolerable water colorist. He was widely read in history and philosophy, and the latest books, French and English, were added to his shelves as they came out. He

* Vincent Stuckey used also to tell his family that he had shot snipe on the land where Belgrave Square now stands. My own great grandfather, whose brother owned the land, used to tell his family the same thing, and I have found it as a household legend in several other families. Either Belgrave Square was built on an exceptionally fine snipe bog, before Cubitt scooped the clay out of it and dumped it in Chelsea, or else here is the spring of one of those group legends which flourish when the originators of them are in little danger of being contradicted.

took the *Edinburgh* and the *Quarterly* and was greatly interested in events and ideas. Walter Bagehot often said that
"when he wanted any detail concerning the English political
history of the last half century, he had only to ask his father,
to obtain it".

The influence of Thomas Bagehot on his son was profound.
He lived throughout the whole of Walter's lifetime and
beyond it, dying in 1881 at the age of 86. He had no ambitions
for himself, he never wished to leave Langport, and he was
content to be Vincent Stuckey's bank manager rather than a
banker. But for his son he was intensely ambitious. His "greatest treasure" was to have advantages which had been denied
to him. When Walter was an undergraduate his father wrote
to him:

> Every day I feel how much I have lost in not having had such
> an education as I wish to give you, and you need not there-
> fore fear that anything will be wanting on my part to secure
> to you its advantages. I do not repine although I feel that
> there is a world beyond my ken, and that that world of knowl-
> edge and usefulness may bring with it more happiness than
> can be mine. But thankfulness and not mere contentment is
> the deep sentiment of my heart for the blessings of my lot, and
> as I have education enough for the immediate duties of my
> station, and for growing wiser and better for that world where
> light and truth and peace reign now and forever, I must be more
> anxious to make a right use of the talent I have, than disap-
> pointed that it is not larger.

This sense of humility did not make him an indulgent
parent. Walter must take the stiffest educational fences,
must work and develop his mind, and succeed in a world
where the prizes went only to the earnest and the energetic.
But there was nothing of Mr. Fairchild in Mr. Bagehot. He
was a reserved and dignified man whose whole life centered
round his wife and boy. But he never condescended to his
son, nor gave that feel of unchallengeable parental authority
which withers a child's heart. He would play games like a boy

himself, or discuss politics as if he were conversing with a grown man.

It was from his father that Walter inherited his gentleness, his almost pantheistic feeling for natural beauty, his mastery of politics and philosophy, and his sense of reality. But it was from his mother that he acquired the sparkle of his mind and his interest in poetry and literature. Mrs. Barrington who knew her in her old age says that she had a fine speaking voice —persuasive yet emphatic, and a great gift for long letters. Her letters convey a sense of hectic and hilarious enjoyment which was in curious contrast with the gentleness of the Bagehot family or the shrewdness of her brother Vincent. She was, in the opinion of her contemporaries, a woman of considerable beauty, and certainly of great humor, vitality and charm. Unlike his father, Mrs. Bagehot was High Church, and although she had married two Unitarians, she was scornful of their creed.

But life at the Bank House or Herd's Hill was not as placid or easy as the devotion of these three might suggest. Vincent Estlin, her only surviving son by her first marriage was a gentle half wit, and although he was twenty years old when Walter was born he had the terrible longevity of the feeble minded and died only a few years before him. Walter's elder brother, Watson, died in October, 1827 at the age of three. But there was a far longer shadow over the family, for Mrs. Bagehot herself had bouts of insanity. There were many times throughout her life when her quick imaginative mind would outstrip all restraint, and she would develop fits of melancholia which only Walter could redress. Whether there was some inherent weakness of her mind, or whether the tragedy of her Estlin children had induced some form of manic disorder, her family have left no evidence to judge. These attacks came without any warning, and Walter and his father had to exercise a hawk-like vigilance over her.* This was Walter's private

* She herself depended upon this vigilance. When Walter was a schoolboy she wrote to him of a plan that she should come and see him by herself. "Papa said, 'you can go if you like', but upon my eyes sparkling, and my heart leaping, added, 'but I think you had better stay at home'. Now I

tragedy throughout his life—the knowledge that any moment he might be summoned to Langport to look after her, and the more cankerous fear that he, who so much resembled her, might go mad also. The buoyant and cheerful man of the later years had steeled himself to overcome his dread of the dark places of the mind.

In every other respect, Langport was a perfect place for childhood. It was a community of uncles and aunts and cousins, modest squires or substantial merchants, amusing, well off and tolerant. The town was full of movement; at one end of the street was the bustle and noise of the quays where the barges loaded and unloaded, and next door to the Bank House the London-Taunton-Barnstaple coach changed horses. A Bagehot cousin in the Navy had died and his little son, Watson, had been adopted by Walter's parents; and Walter and "Watty" in their tight duck trousers and postboy's caps scrambled over the rhynes and levels of the moor or explored the hills behind. Walter was always a bold horseman, and at three used to charge through the garden at Herd's Hill on a hobby horse called Friskey Pony, which gave way to a real pony called Medora. He was a headstrong boy, and a cousin who was his contemporary remembered him swarming up a great tree during one of Uncle Vincent's levees at Hill House, "and there glaring down on the assembly from the topmost bough in a surprising manner and to the detriment of his sabbath raiment". He terrified his mother by running round the coping at the top of the great memorial obelisk to Lord Chatham at Burton Pynsent.

It was a diverse and open air life in lush and pleasant surroundings, a world removed from the childhood of, say, John Stuart Mill being taught Greek by his father when he was

---

think both of us are aware that without him to take care of me and keep me together, as my imagination and feelings are so prone to travel railroad speed, my body must be kept at a more temperate pace." *Life* p. 75. In 1866, for instance, when he was writing the last chapter of *The English Constitution* he had suddenly to dash from London to Langport because she had started breaking all the windows at the bank, and must be taken to an asylum for several months.

three; or of John Morley entertained only by "narrow, un-historic, and rancorous" theology among the Evangelicals of Blackburn; or of Edmund Gosse, who never heard a children's story, reading aloud Jukes on Prophecy in his Plymouth Brethren household. The sense of happiness and security which Langport and his parents implanted in him had later a profound effect upon Walter's political thought, as a similar childhood had on Burke's, both giving him confidence and making him, as he grew older, fear developments which might disrupt familiar patterns.

But life was often a solitary affair for the only son at the Bank House, and his private world of wonder and imagination developed rapidly. When he was seven his father gave him a sword, on the anniversary of Waterloo, and the flowers in the garden at Herd's Hill did duty as Saracens. Twenty years later in his essay on Hartley Coleridge, which is in part a self-portrait, he wrote:

> All children have a world of their own, as distinct from that of the grown people who gravitate around them as the dreams of girlhood from our prosaic life; as the ideas of the kitten that plays with the falling leaves, from those of her carnivorous mother that catches mice and is sedulous in her domestic duties. But about this interior existence children are dumb. You have warlike ideas but you cannot say to a sinewy relative, "My dear aunt, I wonder when the big bush in the garden will begin to walk about; I'm sure it's a crusader, and I was cutting it all to-day with my steel sword. But what do you think, aunt, for I'm puzzled about its legs, because you see, aunt, it has only *one* stalk; and besides, aunt, the leaves." You cannot remark this in secular life; but you hack at the infelicitous bush till you do not altogether reject the idea that your small garden is Palestine, and yourself the most adventurous of knights.

III

In the 1830s and for at least another generation thereafter serious education began as soon as a child could read and write. There were few children's books, and the plunge into literature was instant and immediate. At six Walter possessed a book called *Daily Food for Christians* which he read till it fell to pieces, but thereafter he was started on Scott, Dickens and the rudiments of Latin under a governess. At eight or nine, he was sent to Langport Grammar School whose remarkable scholmaster, Mr. Quekett, had been pounding knowledge into the heads of Langport's children since the year after the French Revolution.* He had been a schoolfellow of Christopher and William Wordsworth at Cockermouth, and he must have been a teacher of a far higher order than most schoolmasters of that day for, when Walter went to Bristol College at the age of thirteen, he had already read the whole of Virgil and had some grounding in mathematics.

But is was his father who was the real guide of his studies and who taught him what to read, not only in books but in the periodical literature of the day. At twelve his father made him write in succession essays on the battle of Marathon, St. Augustine, Julius Caesar and other great subjects. His mother used sometimes to go to London for the season with her brother and sent him her version of political news, such as a sight of the Duke of Wellington at a concert "quite old and tottery—and decrepit" and of "the star of stars" "Prince Albert who is very, very handsome". A letter written by Walter to her when she was in London in the spring of 1838, the year of the Bedchamber plot, shows the grounding of political education.

> We are all going on very well without you, and Papa and I have such nice chats about Sir R. Peel and the little Queen. Papa has quite made up his mind since he had read our friend the Duke's speech that the Queen did right and blames "the Right Hon. Baronet" for making the ladies of so much

* Mr. Quekett's sons were no less remarkable. The eldest became a clergyman famous for his social work in London, and the subject of two of Dickens's articles in "Household Words". The second was an eminent botanist and one of the first people to use a microscope for studying plants. The third and most famous, John Quekett, was a histologist, the conservator of the Hunterian Museum and a Fellow of the Royal Society. The fourth was the Secretary of Stuckey's Bank.

consequences since they could only use the ladies' privilege of
railing against everybody and everything.

There is a charming priggishness in these letters, of a boy
dwelling and talking only with a serious man.

> The water has got up into the Moor which occasions great
> commotions in the school for fear it will be too wet to have a
> bonfire and let off fireworks. T. Paul surmises they have to let
> the water in because the boys shall not have a bonfire; but the
> fact wants confirmation, he having, as I can learn, no authority
> for it but his own thoughts.

IV

In August, 1839, at the age of thirteen, Walter was sent to
Bristol College. It was a natural and a fortunate choice. Bristol
at that time was no longer the fabulously rich city that it had
been in the great days of the West India trade, but it was still
the natural metropolis of Somerset and Gloucestershire. And
its commercial decline had coincided with its rise as an intellectual centre, with whose leaders the Bagehots were personally
connected. The father of Edith Bagehot's first husband, Dr.
John Prior Estlin, had been the co-pastor of the famous Lewins
Mead Unitarian church at Bristol and the friend of Southey
and Coleridge. He and his successor, Lant Carpenter, who
had tutored both James and Harriet Martineau, had become
the center of a group of Unitarians who had freed themselves
from the narrower aspects of dissent, who were Liberal in
politics, and interested not only in poetry and the arts but in
medicine and science.

Bristol Grammar School, now a most distinguished school,
was then a worthless institution, and in 1829 a group of
Unitarian ministers and doctors decided to start a school of
their own that would extend and consolidate the work of the
private academies which many of them conducted in their
own houses. The emphasis was on scientific subjects, and the
teaching of the Church of England was optional. It had a very
gifted and distinguished body of teachers. The elder John

Addington Symonds lectured on medicine, and Dr. James Cowles Prichard (who was Edith Bagehot's brother-in-law), a pioneer of ethnology, taught the history of civilization. In addition it had a resident mathematical professor. The advanced boy could go to the lectures of Dr. William Carpenter (the son of Lant Carpenter) who was already a well-known, and later a very famous, physiologist, on natural philosophy, chemistry and zoology. Probably no school outside Scotland, except Arnold's Rugby, offered such an advanced course of studies or taught them as well.

Unfortunately, Bristol College did not have the success it deserved. It started in the summer of 1831, and that autumn the Bristol riots in which the Cathedral was damaged and the Bishop's house burnt, brought the full wrath of the Established Church down upon non-conformity in general, and in particular on a college which taught dangerous subjects like science and permitted the teaching of Anglican doctrine to be optional. It had thirty pupils, by no means all from dissenting families, mostly from Bristol, although some came from Cardiff by packet each term. But it was dogged by hostility, lack of money and the establishment of a rival Anglican school called Bishops College. In 1842, the year when Walter left, it closed down: shortly afterwards Bishops College expired, and it was not until the rebirth of Bristol Grammar School and the founding of Clifton College many years later, that Bristol provided a first class education. Walter's good fortune can be judged by the account in the *Autobiography* of John Addington Symonds of the dismal private academy to which his father was forced to send him in the early fifties.

Edith Bagehot thought Bristol College "a heretical school", and probably would secretly have preferred Harrow or Westminster. But she could hardly resist the desires of her husband, the influence of her brother-in-law nor Walter's argument that Bristol was only a day's journey from Langport. Walter spent three years at Bristol College, and few boys of his generation can have had such a thorough schooling. The four subjects which he chose to study were classics (which was

compulsory), Hebrew, German and mathematics. Thanks to
the diligence of Mr. Quekett and his father, he was the head
of his class by the end of his first term. By intense application
he became as proficient in mathematics as in classics. At fifteen,
in addition to Homer and Demosthenes, Juvenal and Cicero,
he was reading integral calculus and studying Newton's *Principia*.

But the demands of his schooling did not exhaust his
studies. It was an age that was hungering after exact information, and nowhere can the search have been so keen as among
the intelligent professional families of Bristol. His Sundays
and his leisure evenings were often spent at The Red Lodge,
the home of his mother's brother-in-law, Dr. James Prichard,
whose research in the origin of civilization had made him a
figure of European reputation.* "I dined at the Prichard's a
day or two ago. The Doctor had two friends there talking
about the Arrow-headed character and the monuments of
Pentapolis, and the way of manufacturing cloth in the South
Seas." It was Prichard who first fired Walter's imagination
with the idea of civilization as process, which bore fruit in
Physics and Politics. Walter even borrowed a skull off a friend
in order to be able to understand Dr. Prichard's conversation
on craniology.

His father sent him to the political reviews, and he read
the *Penny Magazine* and the *Saturday Magazine,* respectable
weeklies full of respectable information. In April, 1841 he
writes to his father:

> I have been a considerable part of this morning puzzling my
> brains with the *demonstration* of the Parallelogram of Forces,
> which you will recollect, we learned together rather experi-
> mentally in the work on Mechanics published by the Useful
> Knowledge Society.

* The Red Lodge has a curious history. After Dr. Prichard's death in 1848
it was bought for Mary Carpenter by Lady Byron who was well disposed
towards her because her brother had been tutor to Ada, the Byrons'
daughter.

In addition there were long works of information, a Pictorial History of Palestine, Mitford's History of Greece, books on China. He wrote essays on Newton and on Galileo, as to the probable effect of steam on the destiny of mankind, and on the comparative Advantages of the Study of Ancient and Modern Languages. At the end of his time he embarked on long esays on "Alexander's successors". For a serious boy with a taste for knowledge Bristol and Bristol college in the early forties were the right places.

His literary tastes were also beginning to form, though there is no hint of the lightness and irony of his mature judgments. He read Boswell's *Life of Johnson* and

> what struck me particularly was that amazing love of life, which he seems to have had; I am afraid I should rather have said fear of death . . . like many other great and good men, his practice was not always in accordance with his principles; but the temptation of his career were many and great, while he must demand our gratitude for having been among the very first to consecrate poetry to the reprehension of vice.

And a little later:

> I have finished Moore's *Life of Bryon*: it is useful to contemplate a great mind, struggling in the darkness of scepticism, and divested of the assurances of a future life which the Gospel conveys to our hearts.

Walter's attention to his studies arose partly from the natural ambition of a clever boy, but partly from two other causes. One was his intense devotion to his mother and father. He seems to have wanted to work harder and longer than his father could possibly have desired, for Thomas Bagehot was a serious man, not a slave driver. Walter's letters to him are still in existence and almost every one of them contains an assurance that he is working hard. A class breaks up and leaves him with some leisure. "I am afraid you will think this too much holiday for me, and if so I will give it up and work as usual." Dr. Carpenter is to give a series of lectures which must be superimposed upon his usual courses but "I suppose you

would like me to attend them". And there is an evident sense
of strain. "I must be up before six if it is possible to finish
my work." To his Mother: "My heart smites me to talk of
sleeping since I fell asleep in the most curious way last night
over my books, and slept ever so long." Sometimes he was
unnaturally conscientious: he refused to join a party of the
Osler's to see the railroad opened for fear he should lose marks:
he could scarcely permit himself to go and see Brunel's new
ship *The Great Western* lying in Bristol harbor.

In his letters home he was clearly attempting to make up
to his father for his lack of formal education. The exact accounts of the books he was reading, and the assumption of a
common world of scholarship and ideas between them, were
his own contribution to his father's schooling, and thereby a
repayment of the cost of his own—a bargain quite common
in Scotland in the old days when the shepherd or the bonnet
laird sent his son to university to learn for both of them.

Not only was he deeply devoted to his parents and almost
nervously anxious to please them, he also showed a fastidious
contempt for his schoolfellows. School was to him merely an
exile from home enforced by the necessity to acquire learning:
it had no existence of its own. He had, it is true, two great
friends among his contemporaries at Bristol College, Edward
Fry of the great Quaker family* and Killigrew Wait, the scion
of a famous Bristol merchant family who was later a Tory
member for Gloucester and one of the founders of Clifton
College. With Fry he used to dispute questions of metaphysics
and mechanics, and Wait was one of his rivals for the head of
the class. But the rest of the boys were "the mob", whose noise
interfered with his work, and whose genial barbarism offended
his sense of privacy.

> I was carreid out just now to play with some of the other
> boys. I wanted to do my mathematics and to mug China; but
> they took me out, and because I would not play when I got out
> there, tied me up to the railings and corked me as hard as they

---

* Later a well-known judge and the father of Roger, Isabel and Margery
Fry.

could with a ball which made me play whether or no. They very often beg me to come out, when they have not enough to make up their game; and it is hard to spoil their game; and if I do I get a kick every now and then; and sometimes a blow for every time I open my mouth. It is not at all a pleasant thing to be on bad terms with any of one's schoolfellows, much more with all.

It was more than a mere dislike of games.

> Last night I was . . . rather low spirited for I had been *made* to play a game of prisoner's base. So I went up to comfort myself and looked into Shelley which is my restorative; and met with some lines on political greatness with the beautiful conclusion.
>
> *What are numbers rent by force or custom,*
> *Man who man would be, must rule the empire of himself.*

In this there is something of the country-bred boy's dislike of confinement and organised games. Throughout his life corporate action, mass enthusiasm, left him cold. He once said that he was between sizes in politics, and from his schoolboy letters one can see why it was so. But although he dwelt apart from his companions, he felt no bitterness towards school. Ten years later in his essay on Oxford, there is a hint of affection, and perhaps of regret.

> All that "pastors and masters" can teach young people, is as nothing when compared with what young people can't help teaching one another. Man made the school: God the playground. He did not leave children dependent upon the dreams of parents or the pedantry of tutors. Before letters were invented, or books were, or governesses discovered, the neighbours' children, the outdoor life, the fist and the wrestling sinews, the old games—the oldest things in the world—the bare hill and the clear river—these were education. And now, though Xenophon and sums be come, these are and remain. Horses and marbles, the knot of boys beside the schoolboy fire, the hard blows given and the harder ones received—these educate mankind.

Walter left Bristol College at the end of the summer of 1842. His cousin, G. H. Sawtell, noticed that his outward manner had changed very much in the years he had been there. Shyness had left him and he had become a bold horseman and a lively conversationalist. The unsteady pothooks of the early letters from school had given place to a vigorous, slapdash handwriting, which could still transmit elementary mistakes such as "I am heads and years in my work". He had tapped some inner spring of self-confidence and the over anxious little boy, who at eleven had begged of his father "that you will not go down to the counting house after dinner this winter", had given place to a "lanky youth" in Edward Fry's description, "rather thin and long in the legs, with a countenance of remarkable vivacity and characterised by the large eyes which were always noticeable".

Chapter 2

LONDON

The marked peculiarity, and, so to say, the *flavour* of his
mind, was a sort of truthful scepticism which made him
anxious never to over-state his own assurance of anything.   *Mr. Clough's Poems*

I

THERE was no question of sending Walter to Oxford or
Cambridge. Although the boy had been brought up an
Anglican, his father's Unitarian views were too strong to
permit his son to attend a university which demanded belief
in the Thirty-Nine Articles. The Bagehots had no connections
with Oxford, and Thomas Bagehot had a strong merchant
pride in being a member of the middle classes, which in some
was merely inverted snobbery but in him was a piece with
his political and religious views. He despised the aristocratic
flavor of Oxford, which seemed to him synonymous with in-
competence, privilege, High Church doctrines and Tory
politics. He wanted his son educated in hard subjects, and not
in an atmosphere of scholastic torpor and religious doubt.

In his essay on Oxford, written in 1852 when he was twenty-
six, Walter transcribed what must have been his father's
views:

> We do not suppose that the admission of the Dissenters (to
> Oxford) would be practically any amazing change. Not an
> enormous number would go . . . They (the Nonconformists)
> do not design their sons in general for an intellectual life, for
> the learned professions, for business on a large scale or of a
> varied bind; they do not wish their sons to form aristocratic
> connections; but to be solicitors, attorneys, merchants, in a pa-
> tient and useful way. For this they think—and most likely
> they think rightly—that twenty years of life are quite an ade-
> quate preparation; they believe that more would in most cases
> interfere with the practised sagacity, the moderate habits, the

simple wants, the routine inclinations, which are essential to the
humbler sorts of practical occupation.

But Walter was clearly too able to be denied a university
education, and he was sent accordingly to University College,
London, in the autumn of 1842.

University College, which had then been in existence for
some fourteen years had been founded for the same reasons
and by the same sort of men as Bristol College, although its
fortunes were very different. Campbell the poet, Henry Brougham, Zachary Macaulay, Grote, Tooke the economist, with
the support of influential Catholics and Dissenters had envisaged a university which would escape the cramping effects
of narrow, religious orthodoxy, and enable the sons of Dissenters and Anglicans alike to study in the hard, disciplinary
sciences which the other universities had forgotten or had
never known how to teach: mathematics, physics, the law,
medicine and political economy. Although from its motto
"Sciens Potens Omnia" it was vulgarly known as "Brougham's
Patent Omnibus" it had, in the course of its short life, already
become more than an extension of the Useful Knowledge
Society and had acquired high and severe standards of its own.
If it made no attempt to pursue that comprehensive and inte-
grated path to knowledge after which Matthew Arnold
hankered, it did provide a number of first rate mental disci-
plines.

The organization of the college was strongly influenced by
that of Edinburgh, and to a lesser extent by the German and
American Universities. Its general department offered a wide
range of subjects, not all of which had to be taken; instruction
was given by means of lectures and not by tutors; the students
paid their fees, as in Scotland, direct to their professors; and
the democratic atmosphere was more akin to a Scots or an
American university than to Oxford or Cambridge.

Walter sat for a preliminary examination at the end of his
first term which involved three-hour papers in Latin, Greek,
Natural Philosophy, English and Mathematics. Thereafter
his courses included classics, logic and moral, natural and

political philosophy, and political economy which was just emerging as a separate science. His course seems to have embraced what in modern Oxford terms would be both Greats and Modern Greats. A youth with a slower mind or a lesser application would have gained only a smattering from each subject or else would have fallen under the weight of work, but for Bagehot it served to diversify the range of his knowledge and extend the power of his mind. As it was, ill health forced him to miss the autumn term of 1843 and recoup his strength by hunting his grey mare over the Somerset moors. In 1845 he had to postpone his Bachelor's examination and take four years instead of three at it.

He was fortunate in his teachers. The great figure of the College was the Professor of Mathematics and Philosophy, Augustus de Morgan with "one eye and a large white face" whom Bagehot and all his contemporaries praised as a teacher and from whom he learned his love of paradox as a method of illustration. The Classics were taught by two men who had been trained at Trinity College, Cambridge, Henry Malden and George Long. Bagehot liked Malden:

> I think the best of all: he gives us an immense quantity of information on all manner of subjects; and seems delighted if you go and ask him a question which I have done once or twice. He dresses in clothes which look as if moths had long been their familiar inhabitants.

George Long, the professor of Latin, had come to University College by way of the University of Virginia, and the editorship of the *Penny Cyclopaedia*. To Bagehot:

> he is a dry, withered looking man, who seems ready to go through any amount of labour. He is very clearheaded, though with rather a narrow disciplinarian mind, and is very suspicious and rather sceptical. He has a dry humour which used to make me cry with laughing.

For someone to whom reverence for authority did not come naturally, Bagehot had through all his life a profound respect for those who could teach. In middle life he wrote:

> There is no falser notion than Carlye's that the true University of the present day is a "great collection of books." No university can be perfect which does not set a young man face to face with great teachers. Mathematics in part may teach themselves, may be learnt at least by a person of great aptitude and at a great cost of toil from written treatises; but true literature is still largely a tradition, it does not go straight on like mathematics, and if a learner is to find it for himself in a big library, he will be grey headed before his work is nearly over.

In his review of Mill's *Political Economy* he constructed the same idea into an aphorism: "Instruction is to the mind what the telescope is to the eye."

University College had no residences at that time, and Bagehot was sent to lodge in the house of a dreary classical professor, Dr. John Hoppus, in a dreary street in Camden Town. London was still a city of moderate size, some two or three miles deep on either side of the river. To the north of Gower Street, where the college buildings long stood, were the great smoking buildings of Euston Station, and to the east of Camden Town were the slums of Somerstown. Beyond there were scattered fields and villages below the heights of Hampstead, but London proper still had the foul drains and foul air of the eighteenth century, to which the railway terminuses and the domestic chimneys added a pall of smoke and soot. Bagehot's first reaction to London was an intense homesickness for the clean air and quiet fields of Langport, which was alleviated—so deceiving is the apparently closeness of early Victorian boyhood and our own time—by being lent "a very excellent work, Dr. Clarke's *Demonstration of the being of a God*".

But within a fortnight of his arrival he had encountered a more serious problem than homesickness. One of his fellow boarders was carrying on some connection with a woman at a time when Dr. Hoppus supposed him to be either in the chapel or in college, and Bagehot gathered from his conversation that he was about to lead a second youth astray. He sat down after several sleepless nights and wrote his father:

Now certainly I feel that it cannot be my duty to allow this state of things to continue . . . yet the office of tale bearer is so invidious, and in general so contemptible that I confess I am exceedingly loath to undertake it . . . This certainly must be stopped and I possess no other means of doing so, but informing Dr. Hoppus *immediately*

This he proceeded to do with the results which he had expected. His companions were furious with him, and Dr. Hoppus with the boys, who were immediately dismissed from his house. It reveals at the same time moral courage, a strong sense of right and duty, together with something which could be either officiousness or an overdeveloped fastidiousness. "It is my first taste of the troubles of life," he wrote to his father. "Henceforth I shall perhaps never be wholly free from them."

Thereafter the life of the college caught him up in its momentum. Timothy Smith Osler, whose family had been kind to him in Bristol and were distant kin of the Bagehots, proposed him for the Debating Society, and overcame the resistance of those who, because of the affair at Dr. Hoppus' house, had thought him an impossible prig. He made friends with William Caldwell Roscoe, the grandson of the famous William Roscoe of Liverpool, the historian of Lorenzo de Medici and Leo X, the man whom Horace Walpole had considered "by far the best of our historians". William Roscoe was a young man of considerable promise who became a minor poet and essayist, and who might have become more than that had he not died in his middle thirties.

Both Roscoe and Osler were older than Bagehot, and his closest friend was an exact contemporary, Richard Holt Hutton. Hutton was the son of a Unitarian minister and had come to University College from its own school. He subsequently had a long and distinguished career as a journalist and critic, outliving Bagehot by twenty years; in the course of thirty-six years of joint Editorship he raised the *Spectator* from a good paper to the best and most influential weekly of its day. This was not only the first of Bagehot's enduring friendships, it was also the closest. Throughout their lives they were in con-

stant association, and Hutton's various memoirs of Bagehot
are the best estimates of his personal qualities. He was in some
ways a more plodding version of Bagehot: he was perhaps a
more versatile journalist; in everything else he shared the same
qualities as Bagehot but at a lower power. He had a more
phlegmatic mind and a more moralizing attitude. He was a
good but not a sparkling literary critic, a more serious metaphysician but a less original one, a distinguished but not an
illuminating political commentator, and his theological views
later came in conflict with Bagehot's interest in science. The
Victorian age fashioned Hutton in the perfect image of itself;
Bagehot eludes any such classification. Both wore beards and
eyeglasses, but Hutton's beard did not curl nor his eyeglass
flash as Bagehot's did. One of Hutton's best characteristics was
that he was fully aware of this, from the day when he was
struck "by the questions put by a lad with large dark eyes and
florid complexion to the late Professor de Morgan".

II

Some undergraduate friendships have been invested with
an especial radiance by the quality or destiny of their members.
Gladstone, Canning, Elgin and Cornewall Lewis at Christ
Church in the thirties, the circle around Auberon Herbert and
Raymond Asquith at Balliol in the nineties, or around
Keynes, Lytton Strachey and Bertrand Russell at Cambridge in
the early years of this century. But the group of young men
at University College in the forties had a rare quality for they
were the first to enter an inheritance which had been denied
to their fathers. The social organization of England which had
snubbed their parents for their lack of acres or persecuted
them for their beliefs was withering. The world of knowledge
was expanding and the horizon of the imagination had, thanks
to Wordsworth, been immeasurably widened. If material
prosperity had for the moment ceased to increase in England,
the check was only a ripple in a long ground swell. And at
University College men were intent upon the future, not as

at Oxford in re-fighting ancient battles which sensible men assumed had been settled by the beheading of Laud. The young Bagehot and the young Hutton could explore the metaphysical basis of their religious beliefs without being drawn to the fatiguing controversies which had exhausted Arthur Hugh Clough.

Moreover, England was still in the forties a sufficiently dangerous place to quicken the blood of a young man: the railway mania was at its height with a rumor of a fresh enterprise or collapse each week, the Chartists loomed as a menace far beyond their real strength, Ireland boiled and occasionally boiled over with discontent, and from across the Channel came echos of revolution. And London itself was an essay in knowledge. The four years in which Bagehot was an undergraduate encompassed the full onslaught of the Anti-Corn Law League and the slow and lingering death of Protection. The young men could not listen to debates in Parliament for both houses were occupying temporary quarters while Pugin's great building went up on the embankment at Westminster. But they could go to Covent Garden to hear W. T. Fox or Cobden, O'Connell or Henry Vincent, the Chartist. Bagehot went to hear Oswald Garrison, the great American opponent of slavery, who was a friend of the Estlins and Prichards, and meeting him thought him "a bold benevolent man, but not with much tact". "We scoured London," says Hutton, "together to hear any kind of oratory that had gained a reputation of its own, and compared all we heard with the declamation of Burke and the rhetoric of Macaulay, many of whose essays came out and were eagerly discussed by us while we were together at college." They organised a new College Debating Society which Bagehot harangued on the economics of absenteeism and the proper way to deal with seditious libel.

They make an attractive picture, these children of the second English Renaissance, with their eagerness and vitality, their high seriousness, their high spirits, as they hurried from lecture to meeting, or from Covent Garden to scale the heights of a Primrose Hill on which primroses still grew. They were all gifted, but Bagehot was clearly the leader. He had read far more history than his companions, and a lonely mastery of immense, dull three-volume histories had made him "more alive" says Hutton "to the urgency of circumstance, and far less disposed to indulge in abstract moral criticism from a modern point of view". But it was clearly his powers of conversation which fascinated his friends, what Smith Osler described as a "power of keeping animation without combat. All stimulus and yet no contest". The charm of a man's conversation is something which those who have not heard it cannot easily feel, but Bagehot and Hutton have themselves left a sketch of what it meant to them. In his essay on Oxford Bagehot wrote:

> In youth, the real plastic energy is not in tutors or lectures or in books "got up", but in Wordsworth and Shelley, in the books that all read because all like—in what all talk of because all are interested—in the argumentative walk or disputatious lounge—in the impact of young thought upon young thought, of fresh thought on fresh thought—of hot thought on hot thought—in mirth and refutation—in ridicule and laughter —for these are the free play of the natural mind, and cannot be got without a college.

And Hutton gives the locus to the idea,

> I am sure that Gower Street, and Oxford Street, and the New Road, and the dreary chain of squares from Euston to Bloomsbury, were the scenes of discussions as eager and as abstract as ever were the sedate cloisters or the flowery river-meadows of Cambridge or Oxford. Once, I remember, in the vehemence of our argument as to whether the so called logical principle of identity (A is A) were entitled to rank as "a law of thought" or only as a postulate of language, Bagehot and I wandered up and down Regent Street for something like two hours in the vain attempt to find Oxford Street.

III

This bright coin had a reverse side. The animation of Bagehot's mind and the warmth of his nature were still balanced against long periods of self-distrust and ill-health. Examinations seemed to induce such an acute anxiety as to make him ill. Both in 1843 when he had to compete for classical honors and in 1846 when he took his Bachelor's examination he was so wretched in the preceding week that only a last minute's access of resolution enabled him to complete. In most of his letters to his parents there is mention of headaches, eyestrain or giddiness. In a letter to Edward Fry he says, that although he himself had unbounded high spirits, his mother's family suffered from "hereditary consumption".

In November, 1846 despite his gloomiest forebodings he got first class honors in his final examination and became a Bachelor of Arts. It had long been assumed that he would read for the Bar: at Bristol College he had told Edward Fry that "Crabb Robinson had got on at the Bar by his chin, and that he (Bagehot) hoped to do the like by his own eyes," and for the Bar the first step was to become a Master of Arts which required a further two years study. Accordingly in February, 1847 he moved to lodgings in Great Coram Street and settled down to ride hard at the last of his academic fences.

In his letters to his parents he still retained the modesty which had been set before him when a child as one of the prime virtues in clever boys. Distrustful as he was of his own powers of endurance, his mind was beginning to shape itself. He knew that he did not want to be a man of pure learning, but what it was that he was fitted for he was less sure.

The following letter to his father, written in May, 1845 shows how his mind was moving:

My dearest Father,
    Many thanks for your two long letters, which I will begin to answer before I go out to Chapel this morning. I am very sorry that my letters lately have been carelessly written. The defect in my mind which is the proximate cause of it, is, I think, that I have very great difficulty in that "making a thing complete" which Mr. Long is constantly inculcating on us. I would much rather exert my mind realy very hard for a short

time, than attend for a long time to a great number of comparatively easy things. My mind is very apt to wander when the subject to which I have to attend is a collection of easy details. It is the same defect of mental constitution, I believe, which makes me such a wretched observer—observation requires, or rather implies a constant attention to a considerable number of minutiae, and this which is to many a rest is to me the most irksome labor. I will do what I can to amend my inaccuracy in writing but I hope you and my mother will instantly pull me up if I relapse as I very likely may be tempted to do by indolence and carelessness into my former negligent habits. . . .

I do not in the least undervalue that precise acquaintance with every detail, and every nicety in the classical writings which forms the pursuit of profound scholars. It is absolutely necessary that *some* persons should become well acquainted with them, and thoroughly investigate and discuss their difficulties. But my taste does not lead me in that direction, nor is my mind fitted especially well for such pursuits.

The subjects he was studying were metaphysics, political philosophy and political economy. But he was equally absorbed in poetry and religious speculation, reading or re-reading Shakespeare, Keats, Shelley and Wordsworth, Coleridge, Martineau and John Henry Newman. The draft of his essay on Shelley was written at this time, and his letters to Hutton, who was studying theology under the great Unitarian teacher James Martineau, show that Newman acted as a catalyst on the formation of his religious views as he did on that of all his generation.

His views on economic questions were steadily forming. Adam Smith he had read as an undergraduate; and he now read Ricardo and Tooke, as well as the pamphlet literature of the day, and a newly founded weekly periodical *The Economist.*

In 1847, the speculation in railway companies had induced the worst credit crisis since 1825, had ruined investors not only in railways but in the commodity trade, had caused a number of bank failures, and had created great alarm throughout the country. Peel's Bank Charter Act of 1844 had been an attempt to prevent recurrent financial crises by restricting the note issue of the joint stock and private banks to the areas outside London, and to strengthen the Bank of England at the heart of the monetary system by requiring that, above the figure of fourteen million pounds, its note issue must be covered by reserves of gold and silver. During the autumn of 1847 it became clear to the Government that if Peel's Act was not temporarily suspended the whole structure of credit might collapse, and accordingly on 25th October, 1847, the Chancellor of the Exchequer, Sir Charles Wood, authorized suspension of the Act enabling the Bank to enlarge the amount of its discounts and advances.

Within a few weeks the crisis was past but the action of the Government rekindled an argument among the economists which had raged during the debates on the Bank Charter Act itself. Bagehot entered the lists with his first published article —in the *Prospective Review*, which was then the leading Unitarian Journal, conducted under the guidance of James Martineau with the assistance of William Roscoe. Its starting point was a review of several articles on the currency questions by James Wilson, the editor of *The Economist*, a pamphlet by Col. Torrens defending the Bank Act and the latest volume of Tooke's *History of Prices*. Wilson was a moderate opponent of the Bank Act for he agreed with Peel's object in protecting the note issue but not with the methods he had chosen. Torrens was its most vociferous defender, and Tooke its bitterest opponent. Bagehot's manner is, as one would suppose from a young man of twenty-two who had just mastered the text books, dogmatic and cocksure, but it is also remarkably clear. He concluded—the scion of one of the largest private banks of issue in the country—that a monopoly of the currency issue in the hands of the state was essential because "the object aimed at is not to reduce the cost price but to render it fixed; because fluctuations in value are attended with derangement of internal commerce; . . . and because as a result of the whole, the principle of individual self interest cannot here be trusted to a security for the welfare of the community".

In 1848, John Stuart Mill's *Principles of Political Economy* was published. Bagehot, reviewing it for the *Prospective,* admitted privately to Roscoe that he found Mill "tough and dreary". It is a more modest piece of work than its predecessor, because, in the opening words of the review, "the admirable qualities of mind displayed in it, and the extensive research out of which it has sprung, make it necessary for the critic to practice a humility to which he perchance is but little accustomed". The main interest of it is that Bagehot as a future economist attacks Mill, not on his economic theories, with which he substantially agrees, but for want of moral end to his theories. He points out Mill's inconsistencies in his theory of profits, but gets dangerously near talking nonsense himself in attempting a fresh analysis of different types of capital. On Mill's theory of population Bagehot attempts his own analysis of the remedies of overpopulation and low wages and arrives at a solution which differs only from Mill's huge "dead lift" in being vaguer and more optimistic—the working classes must be induced to behave like the middle classes.

> If the working classes could be raised to a state in which saving was a preliminary to marriage, there would be an efficacious obstacle to their reckless and indefinite increase . . . If the working classes could be brought within the range of the motives which now act on the rest of the community we might confidently anticipate a great immediate improvement in their physical condition.

When he tackles the theory of wages he moves on to a different plane and his ideas have a ring of Thomas Arnold, and a stern sense of moral duty far removed from the *laissez-faire* principles in which he had been educated.

> But it seems to us obvious that capitalists ought not to bend down labourers to the lowest possible amount. They have no more right to be greedy and avaricious than any other class, and it is discreditable to the economists to teach that such conduct is not hurtful to the public and indefensible in itself.

And he gives to Mill's gray, abstract dislike of poverty a sense of urgency and a relation to its time in politics.

> The difficulty is that the rate of wages is low; and the great problem for European and especially for English Statesmen in the nineteenth century is, how shall that rate be raised, and how shall the lower orders be improved.
>
> Whatever be the evil or the good of democracy, in itself it is evident that the combination of democracy, and low wages will infallibly be bad . . . Such is the lesson which the annals of Europe in the year 1848 teach English statesmen. The only effectual security against the rule of an ignorant, miserable, and vicious democracy, is to take care that the democracy shall be educated, and comfortable and moral. Now is the time for scheming, deliberating and acting. To tell a mob how their condition may be improved is talking hydrostatics to the ocean. Science is of use now because she may be heard and understood. If she be not heard before the democracy come, when it is come her voice will be drowned in the uproar.

Much of the history of the next thirty years is contained in that paragraph.

IV

In the summer of 1848 Bagehot took his Master's degree and was awarded the University's Gold Medal for Moral and Intellectual Philosophy. As with earlier examinations he had worked himself to a pitch of nervous exhaustion and had to be supported on the arm of a friend in order to receive it. After recuperating throughout the autumn at Herd's Hill, he returned to London in November to read law.

He was now something of a figure in the affairs of University College. A residence for undergraduates—University Hall— had been established with Francis William Newman, the brother of John Henry Newman, as its head, and Bagehot was on the council.* At the Newman's he met Arthur Stanley, "a little man with grisly black hair, and piercing black eyes that

* Both he and his father contributed fifty pounds towards it. (University Hall Records: Dr. Williams' Library.)

look like a Jew's"; and he renewed the friendship at Oxford where he stayed with his cousin Constantine Prichard, the son of the great doctor, who was then a fellow of Balliol. He went to a reception and met Lord Broughman who "looked very old and horribly ugly".

Roscoe and Osler introduced him to the breakfast table of Henry Crabb Robinson, who, by reason of his age, his kindness and his life history, was a special enchantment to young men. He had been the friend of Goethe and Schiller, Coleridge, Wordsworth and Hazlitt, *The Times* correspondent in the Peninsula and an indefatigable diarist and observer in literary London for half a century. He thought Bagehot "a young man of talent" and after a party at University Hall of which he had been one of the founders, his diary has a note of "Bagehot who has all the external marks of genius".

Twenty years later, after "old Crabb" had died at the age of ninety-two, Bagehot described these breakfasts in a review of Robinson's *Diary*.

> There was little to gratify the unintellectual part of man at these breakfasts, and what there was was not easy to be got at. Your host, just as you were sitting down to breakfast, found he had forgotten to make the tea, then he could not find his keys, then he rang the bell to have them searched for; but long before the servant came he had gone off into "Schiller—Goethe", and could not the least remember what he wanted. The more astute of his guests used to breakfast before they came, and then there was much interest in seeing a steady literary man, who did not understand the region, in agony at having to hear three stories before he got his tea, once again between his milk and his sugar, another between his butter and his toast, and additional zest in making a stealthy inquiry that was sure to intercept the coming delicacies by bringing on Schiller and Goethe.

The astute guest, said Hutton, with some disapproval of his ingratitude, was Bagehot himself "who confessed to me this was always his own precaution before one of Crabb Robinson's breakfasts".

The most interesting of his friendships during these three years was with Arthur Hugh Clough who had, so Hutton thought, "a greater intellectual fascination for Walter Bagehot than any of his contemporaries". Clough was seven years older than Bagehot, and had passed through the grand intellectual and educational process of the day, Rugby, Balliol and a Fellowship at Oriel. In ten years of being pounded between the opposing ideas of Thomas Arnold on the one hand, and Newman and Ward on the other, he had come to loathe Oxford. In the spring of 1848 he had decided that since he could not accept the Thirty-Nine Articles, he could not remain at Oxford and had resigned his Fellowship at Oriel. After a spell of private tutoring and a close view of the fall of Louis Philippe in Paris, he had been offered the headship of University Hall which had become vacant in December, 1848 by the resignation of Francis Newman. Bagehot and Roscoe were determined to have him, despite the obvious antipathy between Clough and the other members of the Council. They had their way, and in March, 1849 Clough was appointed and took up his duties in October. The appointment was never a success. Clough was miserable in London, he was underpaid and anxious to be married, he hated routine, Crabb Robinson bored him and University Hall which was meant for thirty students never had more than eleven. He refused to undertake the moral education of his charges and he hated lecturing to large classes which went with his occupancy of the Chair of English. Bagehot, who felt himself responsible for having brought him to London, had constantly to intervene between Clough and the managing body which consisted of clergymen and non-conformist business men. In 1852 Clough resigned the Principalship under a certain amount of pressure and departed for America, and the Hall acquired a principal more of its own kind, W. B. Carpenter, the eminent physiologist whose lectures Bagehot had attended in Bristol.

It is hard to be sure just what influence Clough had on Bagehot but, according to Hutton, it was profound: he held that he could discern traces of Clough in all Bagehot's later writings. Certainly Bagehot retained a great sympathy for Clough and took pains to have him to stay in Somerset when he himself had become a resolved and successful man and Clough was plodding unhappily in the Education Office.

Bagehot's first reaction to Clough was one of mild disapproval. Clough had recently published *The Bothie of Tober-na-Vuolich*, his "long vacation pastoral", and Bagehot wrote to Hutton:

> Written ages ago.
> March 1st 1849

My dear Hutton,

I have begun two letters to you both of which are now mouldy and superannuated. Would you like to take the Chaplaincy of Univ. Hall? Clough has been appointed, but declines to read prayers. Therefore a chaplain has to be appointed, and Roscoe and I want to know whether you would dislike to take it for a year or two. Roscoe and I have a scheme of going to live there ourselves. I should certainly settle to do so but I do not know very well whether my mother would like it or not. But at any rate I should be living close, so that you would be living with your own friends instead of being stuck down in the country with a congregation that you hated, a prey to all manner of dyspeptic ideas. I do not know so well about the article salary, but you would certainly have rooms rent free and £100 a year, or perhaps more—what would you take it for? You would have to read prayers, say grace, and have a fixed time for explaining things to me in Dr. Morgan's classes, which Clough cannot undertake. You might coach men in Mathematics to obtain coin. I think myself independently of wanting to have you in London, that you would be better able to study theology, and get through difficulties in London than in any other place, and there does not seem to me much object in your taking a congregation for a couple of years or so. You could preach in Carter Lane quite as often as *I* should think good for your mind at your age. Clough is guaranteed £130 for the first two years, for which he is to attend to the discipline and business of the house, and answer men's difficulties in classics and every thing but mathematics.

Clough you would like very much, I think. He is a man of

strong, and clear though not very quick intellect: so that I feel
like a gnat buzzing about him. He has a great deal of imagination, and has written a good deal of poetry; a proportion of
which is good, though he unfortunately has been in the High-
lands and talks of barmaids and potato-girls and other opera-
tive females there in a very humiliating manner as it seems to
me though Roscoe defends it. You would, I think, agree with
me in thinking that his mind was defective in severity of
moral feeling and in the conception of law generally as applied
to morals. But he is evidently a man of great honesty and moral
courage with an immense deal of feeling. C. Prichard says his
mind was injured he thinks by an overstrained asceticism when
he first knew him at Oxford, and has never recovered from the
evil. Roscoe and myself put him into the Principalship. There
was a committee to see him composed of Bush, a chancery
barrister, Le Bretton, an amateur furniture broker, and
Tagart. They came back with no end of blunders and said
nothing could be got out of Clough, and he would bind himself to nothing: and Tagart disgusted Clough by delivering
fractions of bad sermons on general subjects. Everybody at the
meeting was ready to concur in breaking off the negotiation
with Clough, except Roscoe and myself.

By the way I should feel obliged if you would assault
Martineau or singe off his children's eyelashes, or hurt his
feelings somehow. He wrote me a very affected and disagree-
able letter about Clough, saying that the less could not comprehend the greater and that he could not therefore give an
opinion etc. etc., and it was all in rhythmical sentences like
the most labored parts of the "Endeavoures". Taste in letter
writing certainly is not his forte.

But it must soon have been apparent to Bagehot that Clough
was deficient not in moral feeling, but in moral certainty. To
a youth brought up as Bagehot had been brought up in a
sheltered intellectual atmosphere of strict piety and hard work,
a fellow of Oriel who talked about barmaids was a shock, but
a man who refused to commit himself to any solution of moral
problems was an even greater one. As Hutton says:

> Clough's chief fascination for Bagehot was, I think, that he
> had as a poet in some measure rediscovered, at all events

realised, as few ever realised before, the enormous difficulty of
finding truth—a difficulty which he somewhat paradoxically
held to be enhanced rather than diminished by the intensity of
the truest modern passion for it.

Or as Clough used to say to his friends:

> Was it ordained that twice two should make four, simply for
> the intent that boys and girls should be cut to the heart that
> they do not make five. Be content: when the veil is raised per-
> haps they will make five. Who knows?

After Clough had died in 1861, Bagehot reviewed his poems
in the *National Review* and attempted to assess his sad, unquiet nature. "He had a straining, inquisitive, critical mind;
he scrutinised every idea before he took it in: he did not allow
the moral forces of life to act as they should; he was not content to gain a belief by 'going on living'. He said:

> *Action will furnish belief;* but will
>   that belief be the true one?
> This is the point, you know!"

His mind was formed thus, says Bagehot, because by a
double misfortune a serious intellectual boy had been exposed
to both Arnold and Newman.

> Dr. Arnold was almost indisputably an admirable master for
> a common English boy—the small apple eating animal whom
> we know. He worked, he pounded, if the phrase may be used,
> into the boy a belief, or at any rate a floating, confused con-
> ception, that there are great subjects, that there are strange
> problems, that knowledge has an indefinite value, that life
> is a serious and solemn thing . . . The common English mind
> is too coarse, sluggish, and woolly to take such lessons too
> much to heart. It is improved by them in many ways, and is not
> harmed by them at all. But there are a few minds which are
> very likely to think too much of such things . . . Mr. Clough
> was one of those who will . . . He required quite another sort
> of teaching, to be told to take things easily: not to try and be
> wise overmuch; to be "something beside critical"; to go on
> living quietly and obviously, and see what truth would come

to him. Mr. Clough had in his latest years what may be noticed in other of Arnold's disciples—a fatigued way of looking at great subjects. It seemed as if he had been put into them before his time, and seen through them, heard all which could be said about them, had been bored by them, and had come to want something else.

Such a boy, coming up against a disputant of the power of Newman, had no hope of standing out against him. The only thing that could have saved Clough would have been apathy, and it was exactly the quality "that Arnold prided himself on removing". But, Bagehot continues, Newman could not construct a religious system which could carry along those who had "distinct perception of real truth", so that in the end Clough ceased to believe in Newman and was left to wander for ever upon the face of doubt.

It is obvious that Bagehot is writing not only about Clough, but about himself. The truth is that Clough and Bagehot were in many ways very alike. They came from the same family background. They were both descended from landed families by a cadet branch that had turned to business—the Cloughs unsuccessfully. They had both been prize scholars; they had both, according to Hutton, the same characteristics, high spirits and a *gamin* sense of ribaldry. Clough came into Bagehot's life at a time when the educational process had taken its full toll of him, in the manner which Bagehot has described. It is true that Bagehot had not had such a severe schooling and had not experienced anything like the hero worship which Clough had given to Arnold or which he had himself received at Rugby, but Bristol College had been more nearly comparable to Rugby than any other school in England. It is true also that Bagehot had never been directly under the influence of Newman or Ward, but he had read Newman with the closest attention and in his letters to Hutton had been plumbing the depths of his religious beliefs. It is probable that Bagehot saw in Clough, seven years older than he, the image of what he might become, how a delicately poised mind could shatter itself by too much indulgence in speculative thought. For it is more than coincidence that in 1852, at the end of three years of close contact with Clough, the serious young scholar, who two years before had been preoccupied with moral causes and effects, "decided to go on living, quietly and obviously and see what truth would come to him". Clough, it seems, knocked the earnestness out of Bagehot, and so by casting doubts about his moral purpose enabled him to become a critic and an observer.

Chapter 3

THE BARRICADES

A dreamy mind—a mind occupied intensely with its own
thoughts—will often have a peculiarly intense apprehension of anything which by the hard collision of the world
it has been forced to observe.   *Essay on Shelley*

I

WHATEVER influence Clough may have had in deciding
Bagehot that he did not want to be a clever young man
about London, it was not the only influence at work. He had
never been strongly attracted to the practice of law, and as an
undergraduate had wrestled, in letters to his father, with
doubts about whether special pleading was morally defensible.
Having settled down to learn it he liked it even less. He was
living alone in lodgings in Great Coram Street; Hutton, who
had the power of quietening his mind, was away from London
studying theology under James Martineau in Manchester; and
he was suffering from the intellectual exhaustion which has
afflicted every young man in his early twenties after a brilliant
and successful university career.

In those days the first steps at the Bar accentuated this feeling of let down. There were then no lectures, no general course
of study and no examinations. The able young man, with
laurels of academic success still fresh on his brow, was articled
to a conveyancer and was set to watch how the most complex, archaic and uninteresting aspects of legal work were
conducted: he became a fee paying clerk and no attempt was
made to ground him in the principles on which the business
was conducted. "A heap of papers is set before each pupil,
and according to such light as he possesses, and with perhaps
a little preliminary explanation, the pupil is set to prepare
the documents for which these papers were sent . . . He is told
to 'write wide', which means that the lines of the pupil's writ-

ing should always be at so great a distance from each other
that the preceptor should have ample room to strike them out
if he pleased, and write his own words in between them?"
"This unprofitable and disgusting year" (as a witness before the
Oxford University Commissioners of 1852 described it) "at
length over, the youth is doomed to go through a second year
of the like probation at the same cost and almost as unprofit-
ably, in the chamber of a special pleader or an equity drafts-
man." As a result the number of law students who decided to
become schoolmasters or clergymen was very high.

Bagehot had too much natural inquisitiveness about the
mechanics of life not to draw some interest out of learning
conveyancing and pleading. But the fact that he found he
could stomach the work did not help him to solve the dilemma
with which life now confronted him. If he remained in London and continued at the Bar, he would be confined for many
years to a tedious routine which would neither satisfy his
imaginative and speculative instincts nor give him sufficient
leisure to indulge in literature as a hobby. Moreover, his health
—the bugbear of the Victorians—was frail; his eyes tired easily,
he still had persistent headaches, and his chest was weak; these
troubles would be accentuated by work at the Bar. If on the
other hand, he did not go on with the Bar he had little alternative but to go back to Langport and enter Stuckey's Bank
under his father. He had no wish to go into the church, he did
not come of a military family, he had no acres to farm. He
would have fresh air and a horse to ride and time in which to
meditate, but the routine of the counting-house was a different matter from an interest in the broad sweep of politics and
political economy; and after a brilliant university career it
was difficult to feel enthusiastic about a position in a country
bank. Finally, he would be separated by distance and differing
interests from Roscoe, Hutton, Clough and the intellectual
world of London in which he was beginning to find his feet.

The problem was made all the harder to solve by the circumstances of his family life. His mother's lapses from sanity
were as frequent, and they weighed more heavily on Walter

than they had as a boy. Her brother, Vincent Stuckey, who had been able to divert her mind and ease its periods of tension, had died in 1845, and Walter was the only other person who could deal with her. His father despite his devotion had too stolid a mind to be able to relieve her fits of melancholy or to laugh her out of her delusions. When she insisted that she must write to the Duke of Wellington about the state of the world, it was Walter who must reprove and reason with her, and the reassurances of his affection which recur throughout his letters are clearly in answer to a morbid anxiety for his love. When his friends went on reading parties, or to study abroad, Walter returned to Herd's Hill. There were no long vacation pastorals for him, nor was he encouraged to bring his friends to stay. He had been to the Rhineland in 1844 with Mr. and Mrs. John Stuckey Reynolds, his aunt and uncle, and he had later been on a riding tour in Scotland with his foster brother, Watty; otherwise he had permitted himself none of the other pleasures of a Victorian youth, the reading parties in the Lakes, the slow pilgrimages through France or Ireland, the langorous afternoons of meditation in Florence or Rome. Hutton had chided him in a letter in 1845 with being too aloof from his friends and wrapped up in his family: Bagehot did not try to explain to him the reason for his withdrawal: Herd's Hill was a citadel which must be defended constantly and in silence. The consequence was a deep dejection which revealed itself in sad little scraps of poetry.*

From Walter's letters to his father between 1848 and 1851 it seems probable that Thomas Watson Bagehot would have liked his son to have succeeded at the law; he had an intense pride in Walter's achievements in London. But Edith Bagehot had no such interest in intellectual success. As early as the

---

* For instance:

> The heavy steps of sad repentance lie
>   Along the burning sands by passion spread,
> But they who shrink not from a wintry sky
>   High o'er the Alps of sinless sorrow tread
> The pilgrim bent Messiah's land to gain
> Must pass a desert or a mountain chain.

spring of 1845 she had hinted very plainly to him where her desires lay:

> I used to say too, dearest, that if you could not bear the necessary hard study now, you could not bear the hard study and work of the Bar hereafter, and I think Mr. Estlin seems to thing the same, and gives a hint about *business,* whither, as you know, my wishes have almost somewhat turned, though I would never for the world say so to slacken or contract what I do hope you will have, a thoroughly good education. But turn your attention a little to business when you are at home, try and understand Papa's cleverness in it, and if very or totally inferior at first do not be depressed . . . I have often told dearest Papa, it was a fault more of his habit than his intentions, that he had not, as a matter of course, made you better acquainted with its practical details and mysteries.

She had in her letters to Walter used many blandishments to draw him back to Langport pointing out the dangers of his becoming a "mawkish scholar". And he was sufficiently like her, in taste, in private amusements, in the speed and colour of his mind, to find it difficult to resist them—from love as much as from piety. But in 1851 when his period in chambers came to an end, he still fought the idea of settling at home for good. At the end of a letter written from Langport to Roscoe in March, 1851 he wrote:

> I shall be up this day week and have settled to go into equity. I couldn't live cheerfully down here, and though I regret immensely that I ever opened a law book, I must stick to London now, come what may, and I am sure of enough to live on, in any case.

But his resolution was not as firm as he made out. Throughout the summer of 1851, while the nation's attention was focussed upon Paxton's glittering palace in Hyde Park, Bagehot's malaise deepened. His family trouble pressed heavily upon him and the dilemma of his life seemed incapable of resolution. During the summer Roscoe, who had gone through much the same process and had just quit the Bar, persuaded him to go to France. In the autumn he crossed to Paris and had the great good fortune to find it on the verge of revolution.

II

A young man, fatigued by intellectual pursuits, could hardly have chosen a better moment to arrive in Paris than October, 1851. A brilliant season was beginning, whose gaiety and excitement was heightened by the certainty of a political explosion. The Prince-President and the Assembly had disagreed bitterly over constitutional revision in the summer and there were few people in Paris who imagined that Louis Napoleon would wait tamely until the elections of May, 1852 when he would be disqualified from standing for re-election. The business community was apprehensive, the army divided, and moving among legitimists, Orleanists, Republicans, Socialists, Democrats a young man who had seen the failure of political revolution in England in 1848 could draw his own conclusions on the relation between politics and national character.

Bagehot settled in lodgings with a bourgeois family named Bein in the rue de Vaugirard and stepped out to survey the scene. His conversational French was halting but he knew some intelligent people with whom his mother had made friends on a visit, Monsieur Meynieux (a "round man fit to bowl with") and his wife. He was swept into parties and balls where the badness of his waltzing caused him both amusement and a feeling of isolation:

> It's very amusing running small French girls against some fellow's elbow, it's like killing flies years ago. There is, however, the inconvenience that one does not like to ask the same girl twice, she might say she had not insured her life. But if you are careful to select a fresh subject for each experiment the pastime will succeed. I do not fancy it pleases the girls: he dances *tout seul* I heard one of them say with great indignation to her female friends, as if a fellow of my age could be expected to keep time with her or the music either, and it pleases me, it being a new, if not humane excitement, and is better than talking feeble philosophy in out of the way corners.

He was introduced to the salon of Madame Mohl (probably by Nassau Senior), who as Mary Clarke, the daughter of a Scots family domiciled in Paris, had comforted the last days of Madame Récamier. In 1815 she had been married for four years to Julius Mohl, a distinguished Oriental scholar from Württemberg, who had become a naturalised Frenchman for love of her. Her house in the rue du Bac was thirty years the meeting place of French poets and politicians and of intelligent English travellers. In the early fifties Ampère, the poet, the Duc de Broglie, Guizot, de Tocqueville, Mignet, Nassau Senior gathered there. Mary Mohl did not take kindly to the introduction of women, especially English ladies who, she complained, ruined conversation. But a lively and intelligent young English man, with large dark eyes and sufficient diffidence to allow the great men to talk without interruption, was most welcome, and Bagehot began a close friendship with both the Mohls which lasted all his life.

He had been in Paris two months when the *coup d'état*, long awaited and several times delayed, was executed. On the morning of Wednesday, December 3rd, the Parisians awoke to find the walls plastered with a proclamation which announced that the Assembly and the Council of State had been dissolved, that the Prince-President had assumed the constitutional authority in the name of the people, that universal suffrage had been restored and that Paris was in a state of siege. Two regiments occupied the meeting place of the Assembly, the offices of the anti-government press had troops in them, and the leading Monarchists and Republicans were either arrested or being arrested. Some members of the Assembly made a determined effort to meet and to demand a call to arms but were in turn arrested. The Democrats, the left wing of the opposition, who had nothing in common with Thiers and the Monarchists except a hatred of Napoleon, attempted to rouse the working men of Paris and barricades were erected. But armed resistance never had a chance. During the next few days the troops systematically hemmed in the insurgents and by the 5th Paris was reduced to obedience.

Throughout the three days, Bagehot had been roaming over Paris. On the Wednesday he climbed over the railings of the Palais Royal, and he used to boast that he was the only person who had breakfasted there that day. On the Thursday he had gone to the Boulevard St. Martin, the traditional centre of trouble, and had looked on while the barricades—"palings, iron-rails, etc. and three overturned omnibuses and two upset cabs"—were going up. "I scrambled over two," he wrote to his father on the 5th, "and got as far as I dared towards the centre. The silence was curious: on the frontier a raging though industrious multitude, within the kingdom no one, a woman hurrying home, an old man shrugging his shoulders, all as quiet as the grave. I did not stay long in the inside, as I feared *the troups* would come and I might be shot that Napoleon might rule the French or some Montagnard might be so kind as to do it just to keep his hand in . . . I tried hard to hire a window to see the capture of the fortress as well as its erection but this was not to be, for everybody said they meant to shut their windows and indeed it would not have been very safe to look out on them firing. I therefore retired, though not too quickly. It is a bad habit to run in a Revolution, somebody may think you are the "other side" and shoot at you, but if you go calmly and look English there is no particular danger . . . I am pleased to have had an opportunity of seeing it *once* but once is enough, as there is, I take it, a touch of sameness in this kind of sight . . . My notion is that the President will hold his own."

Public opinion in England was profoundly shocked by the *coup d'état,* and Palmerston was forced to resign for expressing his approval of it. Not only Liberals and Radicals, but the whole central body of educated opinion was disgusted by the mixture of craft and naked force by which it had been carried through. Many of the French leaders were in London and de Tocqueville's sad, vivid despatch to *The Times* of December 4th which described the arrest of the members of the Assembly helped to heighten public disapproval. But Bagehot had had no doubt from the moment he arrived in Paris that some such action was necessary and even desirable in the circumstances. He had seen at first hand the unworkable nature of the constitution, the fragmenting of the opposition to Louis Napoleon, and had learned from men like Julius Mohl how corrupting this state of uneasy stagnation was to the economic life of the country. On December 7th he wrote to his mother: "I wish for the President decidedly myself as against M. Thiers and his set in the Parliamentary World; even *I* can't believe in a government of barristers and newspaper editors."

He now sought to elaborate his views and explain to an English audience, which had never, even in 1830 or 1848, felt such insecurity, that the moral rectitude of political action is relevant to political circumstance. The "young men of University College", Osler, Hutton, Roscoe were at that time helping J. L. Sanford, the historian, with the editorship of the *Inquirer,* the leading literary and theological weekly of the Unitarians. The gentle and high-minded readers of the *Inquirer* were treated to a weekly letter from Paris throughout January and February, 1852 in which Bagehot deliberately set out to defend all that they considered most odious and to disprove, or to assume as disproved, most of their cherished political beliefs.

The first letter merely stated his thesis: the certainty of a political explosion when the election was held in May, 1852 and the dread of a successful revolution of the left had created a state of chaos and stagnation in France. Louis Napoleon had fulfilled the first duty of government, which is to protect industry and employment, by bringing this situation to an end. And trade had enormously revived in consequence. Whatever other defects "Brummagem Boney" (as Mary Mohl was the first to call him) might have, "he has one excellent advantage over other French statesmen—he has never been a professor, nor a journalist, nor a promising barrister, nor, by taste, a *littérateur.* He has not confused himself with history: he does not think in leading articles, in long speeches, or in agreeable essays. But he is capable of observing facts rightly, of reflecting on them simply, and acting on them discreetly".

In the second letter he saw that he advanced a wholly utilitarian justification for Napoleon's action and elaborated upon the danger to which France had been exposed. This is the first sign of the concern with the preservation of the social fabric, which, as with Burke, grew out of his strong attachment to his home, and which colored all his political observation. Napoleon himself was no worse than any other French contemporary politician, and was all the better leader for having spent his youth on the turf instead of in a library, and having thus learned "the instinctive habit of applied calculation, which is essential to a merchant and extremely useful to a statesman". Of the political deportations he coolly approved: if restoring order and confidence was the object, it were folly to permit the Socialists political freedom, while Thiers and Girardin were playing the same selfish game as Napoleon and had merely been beaten by a better player.

In the third and subsequent letters he set out to attack the characteristic fallacy of his compatriots and of his age—that English parliamentary institutions were morally superior to other forms of government and are the guarantee of liberty. The "essential quality for a free people whose liberty is to be progressive, permanent and on a large scale" is stupidity. The Romans had it and the English have it. Peel and Walpole are our great statesmen, and the quality descends to the quarter sessions chairman. "The best security for fixedness of opinion is, that people should be incapable of comprehending what is to be said on the other side."

With the French it is otherwise: they have had so many political failures since 1791 that there must be an underlying fault, "so many bankruptcies a little suggest an unfitness for the trade". Bagehot finds it in their "quickness", their receptivity to new ideas, which is accompanied by a passion for logical deduction, and creates "a morbid appetite for exhaustive and original theories". Even the Catholic Church in France has turned this passion for speculation to its own account, and offers itself as a refuge of coherent and developed thought to the mind worn out with secular speculation. If

you give supreme power to a legislative assembly, on the pattern of the House of Commons, in a nation of men in which
so many conflicting ideas are held with such dogmatism, regime
after regime will continue to end in a street row for there
is none of the steady adherence to a central line of development which enables the party system to work in England.
Hippolyte Taine, deeply impressed by the social cohesiveness
and stability of England, in his visits a decade later, made
much the same point about his own country.

> Thus it follows that all our political establishments, republic,
> empire or monarchy, are provisional, like great sets of painted
> scenery which, turn and turn about, fill a stage to vanish or re-
> appear as the occasion warrants. And we see these scenes
> demolished and erected with a shrug of indifference. We are
> inconvenienced by the noise and the dust and the unpleasant
> expressions of the bought and paid-for applauders; but we
> resign ourselves to this discomfort. For what can we do? Who-
> ever and whatever our official representatives may be, and by
> whatever means chance or election gives them to us, the public
> will is never firm and decidedly behind their actions.

The natural factiousness of the French is made worse,
says Bagehot, by the press. Its influence is enormous, and the
reputation of a journalist is gained, as de Girardin's was
gained, not by superior knowledge or judgment but by an
acid wit and "a more pointed sharp way of exposing blunders
intrinsically paltry, obvious to all educated men". But
journalism is the highroad to political success and "if the revolutions of 1848 have clearly brought out any fact, it is the utter
failure of newspaper statesmen". For this reason he was not
prepared to condemn the limitation imposed by Louis
Napoleon on the freedom of the French press.

No system or new constitution will work if it does not
ultimately rest on public approval. "You may put down newspapers, dissolve Parliaments, imprison agitators, almost stop
conversation, but you can't stop thought. You can't prevent
the silent, slow, creeping, stealthy progress of hatred and scorn,
and shame. You can't attenuate easily the stern justice of a re-

tarded retaliation." It was possible to use the army against a minority, but not against the nation and only time would show if the French would realy support Louis Napoleon.

The letters end with a demand that English liberal opinion instead of being merely critical, should consider how the French could achieve constitutional government. There is no flippancy in his conclusion.

> And mind, too, that the system to be sketched out must be fit to protect the hearths and homes of men. It is easy to compose politics if you do but neglect this one essential condition. Four years ago, Europe was in a ferment with the newest ideas, the best theories, the most elaborate, the most artistic Constitutions. There was the labour, and toil, and trouble of a million intellects, as good, taken on the whole, perhaps as the world is likely to see—of old statesmen, and literary gentlemen, and youthful enthusiasts, all over Europe, from the Baltic Sea to the Mediterranean, from the frontiers of Russia to the Atlantic Ocean . . . Well, what have we gained? A Parliament in Sardinia! Surely this is a lesson against proposing politics which won't work, convening assemblies that can't legislate, constructing executives that aren't able to keep the peace, founding Constitutions inaugurated with tears and eloquence, soon abandoned with tears and shame; beginning a course of fair auguries and liberal hopes, but one from whose real dangers and actual sufferings a frightened and terrified people, in the end, flee for a temporary, or may be a permanent, refuge under a military and absolute ruler.

The Letters were a remarkable product for a young man of twenty-five. The underlying postulates are derived from Burke, but their application is entirely Bagehot's own. They are by no means the last word on the *coup d'état;* for one thing, they were written too soon after it had happened, and Bagehot later revised his estimate of Napoleon when he saw that the Second Empire was as stultifying to the long term development of France as the Second Republic had been. "France, *as it is,* may be happier because of the Empire, but France *in the future* will be more ignorant because of the Emipre." Moreover, he had talked too exclusively to Parisian business men and shopkeepers and assumed that the bourgeoisie would remain the dominant interest in the state; he did not see, as de Tocqueville did, that Socialism was not merely a utopian fad but the question of the future.

III

Paris had a great effect upon his spirits. In a letter to Crabb Robinson written just after the revolution, in which he sought help in order to widen his knowledge of the French scene, there is a strain of high-spirited bumptiousness, very unlike his depressed letters of a few months earlier.

> My dear Sir,
> I have often heard you say that you do not disapprove of young men being overbearing, dogmatic, abusive (?) and irreverent. Now I am going to be *impertinent*. Of course, I concede that this by no means falls within the list of vices which you so kindly tolerate in a youth, but I submit to you that it is closely allied to them . . . I have broken loose from law for a month or two and am living here tranquilly observing the barricades and revolutions of this agreeable capital —And it has seemed to me to be *possible* that besides knowing and having known (as all the rising race reverently believe) the very *élite* of all mankind, you might perhaps have condescended to be acquainted with one or two persons so low down in Paris society as not to be offended with the introduction of a crude and unformed lawyer . . .
> I was here during the only day of hard fighting which we have had and shall be able to give lectures on the construction of a barricade if that noble branch of Political Economy ever became a source of income in England . . . A naïve French lady —a keen Bonapartist—observed to me "C'est une revolution qui a sauvé la France. Tous mes amis sont mis en prison". She was delighted at this agreeable mode of saving her country.

The Letters did not get a cordial reception. Hutton found them exasperating and said that Crabb Robinson, who could never remember names, described Bagehot as "that friend of yours—you know whom I mean, you rascal—who wrote those abominable, those most disgraceful letters on the *coup d'état* —I did not forgive him for years after", though he also scribbled on this particular letter "Bagehot: A bel esprit and very able man." When John Morley came to write his reminiscences fifty years later he still remembered them with disapproval. But they were among the favorite reading of that most un-Napoleonic figure, Woodrow Wilson.

Nor did they establish Bagehot's reputation. The circulation of the *Inquirer* was not large; the Unitarians who read them shuddered and did their best to forget them and they were not re-published till after his death. But they convinced him that he could write, that he was not as he had thought "a wretched observer", that he saw things which others did not see, and that he had an independent and original contribution to make to political thought. His self-confidence was restored and the dilemma which had seemed insoluble in the gloomy rooms in Great Coram Street now proved to be unreal. Writing could bridge the distance between Langport and London. It would not be necessary to endure the toil and boredom of the Bar in order to avoid stagnation and the loss of his friends. He could go into business under his father, and "go on living quietly and obviously, and see what truth would come to him".

He returned to London in the summer of 1852 and went to Langport to discuss his future with his father. At first he thought of trying to combine business with some work at the Bar, but the idea was obviously unworkable and on August 31st, 1852, he wrote to his father:

> I have been considering carefully the question which we almost decided upon when I was at home. I mean my abandoning the law at the present crisis—and in accordance with what we very nearly resolved upon when I was with you—I have decided to do so at this juncture—utterly and for ever.

Chapter 4

THE COUNTRY BANKER

We are the English of the present day. We have cows and
calves, corn and cotton: we hate the Russians; we know
where the Crimea is; we believe in Manchester the great.
A large expanse is around us; a fertile land of corn and
orchards, and pleasant hedgerows, and rising trees, and
noble prospects, and large black woods, and old church
towers. The din of great cities comes mellowed from afar
. . . We have before us a vast seat of interest, and toil,
and beauty, and power, and this our own. Here is our
home.   *Essay on Cowper*

I

IT was a fortunate moment for a young man to decide that
he should live quietly and see what truth would come to
him, for, to the extent that one can talk of a national mood,
it would seem that the country itself had taken much the
same decision. England at the beginning of the fifties was in
some sense like a man recovering from a long fever. As with
a convalescent it is difficult to say at which precise moment,
1846 or 1848 or 1851, the change from sickness to health occurred: or what was effect and what was cause. But within
two or three years, somewhere between 1848 and 1851, the high
temperature of political and religious argument, the super-
heated emotionalism of the Romantic era, the threat of a crack
in the whole structure of European civilisation, seemed to die
out together, leaving men less afraid—of change, of foreigners,
of the working class—than at any time since the French
Revolution.

By 1852 a man could look back over the great political debates, which had dominated public discussion for sixty years,
from a foothold of security. The Crown had been disentangled
from open party warfare and removed to a position, if not of
affection, at least of respect. The aristocracy had loosened,

though by no means lost, their grip on political power and were now beginning to consider bringing in the respectable working class to balance the power of the middle classes. Free Trade had triumphed in 1846 without ruining British agriculture, and a year later the first effective Factory Act had been passed to soften the workings of *laissez faire*. A competent police force was in the making, together with a coherent theory of local government, and the Public Health Bill of 1848 had established the principle that the state was concerned with more than administering justice and keeping up the roads. The Peelites and the Radicals had proved that it was possible to reform the worst features of social and economic organization without destroying the basis of society.

There was still a strong contrast between the wealth of the very rich and the poverty of the very poor, but the gap between the "two nations" was rapidly filling up. Between the great merchant, landed or mineral fortunes and the unskilled labourer there was now an expanding gradation of middle class, lower middle class and superior artisans; the spirit of jostling social competitiveness and of money worship, so characteristic of the age, which glares at the reader in Thackeray, was the symptom, not so much of a fluid society, as of one whose infinite subdivisions were becoming easier to identify and to over-leap. The "condition of the people question" was still an urgent one, but the emphasis was less on wages than on conditions of work: in the later forties the working class cost of living index had fallen to a lower point than at any time since 1785, and wages had not for the most part fallen in parallel. Prices started to rise again during the early fifties, but the worst of the "bleak age" was over. With the failure of Chartism had come a great decrease in strikes and violence; the spirit of hostility had not, as in France, merely gone underground; it had been dissipated by material improvement or had been turned into other channels, trades unions or societies for self-improvement.* The problem of Mill's "huge dead-lift"

*. . . "mid-Victorian England was *not* the frontier society it might so easily have been. The frontier areas were humanised and disciplined and civilised by the adaptation of old institutions and the development of

remained, but a sensible and humane man like Thomas Watson Bagehot who believed in the measures of reform which had taken place, might feel that it was now up to the working class, by thrift and self-discipline, to take the next steps in raising their own standards of life. Since this view was propagated in most newspapers and innumerable books and pamphlets, the working class, by and large, believed it also.

With the decline in political tension, some of the bitter flavor had also gone out of religious controversy. The re-introduction of the Catholic hierarchy in 1851 had shown the strength of anti-Catholic feeling but it was a measure of toleration. Even before Newman's conversion to Catholicism in 1845, the power of the Oxford Movement had been declining, but that was not the only change. The Church of England had been permeated with liberalism, and the old High Church Toryism had lost its grip upon the hierarchy. The Broad Churchmen were concerned more with the unity of Christian doctrine than the enforcement of dogma, and in 1853 the *Edinburgh Review* counted ten Broad Church bishops on the bench of twenty-eight and a substantial following for them among the parish clergy. Croker and the *Quarterly* were still alive, and in 1853 F. D. Maurice had to resign his chair at King's College for his views on eternal punishment, but opinion was moving with Maurice not with Principal Jelf. The church was making up its mind to conform to the spirit of an age which had tired of rhetoric and emotion, still deeply interested in religion but in a more empiric fashion. The great question of the compatability of science and religion was impending rather than actual. Although Lyell's *Principles of Geology*,

---

new; by the churches and chapels, the universities and schools, the professional organisations and trade-unions, the judiciary and the police, the mechanics' institutes and friendly societies and co-operative societies. The degree of success attained was not the same in every sphere and in every district. It was less in urban housing than in voluntary education; the high crime rate in some districts to-day is probably to be traced to the fact that their population grew beyond the speed of civilising and humanising influences. Nevertheless, the frontier was substantially tamed."

"The Age of Equipoise," by Professor W. L. Burn. *The Nineteenth Century and After,* October, 1949.

published in 1830 and frequently re-printed, had made belief in the literal infallibility of the Bible all but impossible, it was not until the end of the fifties that Darwin and Wallace provided a challenge which no reflective man could evade. At the beginning of the decade, exploration ran where it listeth; the ranks were not yet arrayed in battle.

One well established legacy of the Romantic age in every European country was a revived sense of national patriotism —and ultimately of national jingoism. But there were signs too that something new, a national culture, was emerging in England. Illiteracy was still very high but it was declining fast (it fell from 31 per cent of the male population and 45 per cent of the female in 1851 to 25 and 35 per cent respectively in 1861), and a large newspaper and periodical press was rising to satisfy the needs of the new readers. More important, the reading public had got the writers it wanted and deserved. Dickens was a national figure, and Tennyson and Macaulay, Thackeray and Carlyle, the Brontes and Mrs. Gaskell, even the young Matthew Arnold, made a common language whereby the family, the unit of Victorian culture, could communicate in delight or disagreement. As Mr. G. M. Young has written: "It was part of the felicity of the fifties to possess a literature which was at once topical, contemporary and classic; to meet the immortals in the streets, and to read them with added zest for the encounter." And behind them stood Scott and Words-worth, who had kindled in the hearts of an increasingly urban public an awareness of, if not a care for, natural beauty.

The clearest difference between the fifties and the preceding decades is recognised to be the decline both in dogmatism and in emotionalism. In politics and religion the clash of sect upon sect had given way to a broader feeling of tolerance and cheerfulness. But it was still an age of strong feeling and high contrasts. Newspapers hounded their enemies and their con-temporaries with spite and gusto. Dandyism was declining but the young men of St. James's Street dressed with an ex-travagance of flared coats and coloured waistcoats, while the

Quaker bankers of Lombard Street dressed with extravagant simplicity. Henry Adams *en route* from Boston to Bonn in 1858, noted with disapproval the coachmen and the hammer cloths, the color, the grime and the insolence. There were more railway accidents in England than any other European country; factories burned to the ground entombing all their apprentices; mine disasters were frequent; mad dogs and run-away horses were the common stock of nursery tales; and the vast crowds which flocked to public executions demonstrated that the spirit of an older, crueller England was a long time dying.

II

In this young moment of intellectual peace and physical energy, against this background of vigor, optimism and reck-lessness, Bagehot embarked upon his first career—as a banker. Banking itself had altered considerably during the twenty-six years of his life. Stuckey's had been a joint stock bank since the year of his birth, and country banking was now a profession quite distinct from other forms of trading (although the distinc-tion was less marked for the Bagehots because they retained their merchant and shipowning business as a separate con-cern). Vincent Stuckey had carried out a great expansion of the bank's business between 1826 and his death in 1845, and it had acquired the business of ten private banks in Somerset. In addition it had a London office under the name of Stuckey and Reynolds, which was managed by Bagehot's uncle, John Stuckey Reynolds, who had been Lord Liverpool's secretary and who had given up a promising career in the Treasury and the prospect of a seat in Parliament on hearing a sermon in Dublin, thirty years before, on the dangers of worldly advance-ment. Stuckey's with its fourteen branches could by no means compare with great banks of the North, the National Pro-vincial of Birmingham with over a hundred branches, or the Manchester and Liverpool with over thirty, but it was con-siderably larger than the average country bank.

The function of its business was still the same, to hold the savings of the farmers and country gentlemen of the agricultural areas which it served, and to lend them through the medium of London to the capital-hungry industrial North. The amount of lending and accommodation to their own clients must have been on a fairly small scale. The circulating bill was still the main medium of exchange, although the bank deposit and the check were beginning to come in. With the great increase in gold (the Californian and Australian discoveries took place a year or so before Bagehot took up banking) the gold sovereign was beginning to displace the note as a means of small payments, although Stuckey's at the time of its absorption in 1907, had a larger note circulation than any bank except the Bank of England. There were many farmers and traders in the West of England who would accept only a Stuckey note.*

To work in the head office of a country bank was probably the soundest and most thorough way in which a young man could learn banking, but it was not the most enlivening. It lacked the romance of foreign lending like Rothschild's or Lazard's or the fine balancing of judgment required in a great house like Overend, Gurney. The inquiries into a farmer's credit or a shopkeeper's fitness for a loan were pallid pursuits to one who had seen the barricades go up in Paris. Although the Stuckeys and the Bagehots predominated in the business, it was a joint stock concern and there was no question of making Walter Bagehot a partner until he had learned the routine. His father, who had become Vice-Chairman on the death of Vincent Stuckey, was a stickler for correct office procedure, and both in the dark little general office at the Bank and in the merchant business at the Bridge, Bagehot had to learn the laborious intricacies of Victorian accounting.

He had never been able to add and at twenty-six, and even

---

* "A Somersetshire farmer is never satisfied as long as he has a Bank of England note in his pocket, or until he has changed it for one of Stuckey & Co., which he holds with confidence till the day of his death." James Wilson, Financial Secretary to the Treasury to Sir George Cornewall Lewis, the Chancellor, January, 1858.

at fifty, he still made howlers in spelling. In January, 1853 he wrote to Wait: "Here I am in my father's country house trying, (and failing) to do sums, and being rowed ninety-nine times a day for some horrid sin against the conventions of mercantile existence." And in the same month to Hutton who had for the time being succeeded Clough at University Hall:

> I have devoted my time for the last four months nearly exclusively to the art of book keeping by double entry, the theory of which is agreeable and pretty, but the practice perhaps as horrible as anything ever was. I maintain too in vain that sums are matters of opinion, but the people in command here do not comprehend the nature of contingent matter and try to prove that figures tend to one result more than another, which I find myself to be false as they always come different. . . . You see my friend Louis Napoleon is Emperor. I think there is no doubt his foreign policy will be mainly aggressive and this country must look sharp or he'll be upon us. I don't mean now or tomorrow but soon.

For a few months after his return, Bagehot found pleasure in his intellectual idleness. He collected a pack of harriers which he shared with Vincent Wood, Vincent Stuckey's grandson and heir, and together they pursued the long-legged Somerset hares over that treacherous countryside. (Fox hunting was then unknown in that part of the world, except for an occasional visit of "Mr. Luttrell's" from Dunster.) Throughout his life riding to hounds was his favorite recreation, the best physical outlet for a highly strung nature. Today hunting has become the preserve of "horsey" people, but a hundred years ago it was a natural part of country life. In one of his letters he says, "There is *no* time for quiet reflection like the intervals of a hunt."

His health came back and there was a nostalgic charm in living once more with his family. But he soon found that he must do something with his mind; banking and shipping absorbed only a fraction of its activity, for as he wrote later, "Banking is a watchful but not a laborious trade. A banker, even in a large business, can feel pretty sure that all his transactions are sound, and yet have much spare mind." Traveling in the slow and bumpy train between Taunton, Bristol or Liverpool, and in the long dull evenings at Herd's Hill, he must have some occupation. Yet it was difficult to find the *point d'affixe*. Political economy was too near his daily pursuits: his slight vein of poetry had petered out; political commentary meant a return to London: the great philosophical and religious questions did not for the moment interest him for, as he wrote to Killigrew Wait, "My friends say I am sceptical: I say I am only lazy in believing." His mind turned, responding to the revived vigor of his body and his emotions, to the great English classics, and from a wide array of talents the first he drew upon was literary criticism.*

It is difficult to write critical essays unless there is some demand for them. Hutton, who had married Mary Roscoe, the sister of their mutual friend, had taken her to the West Indies in search of a cure for his own weak lungs and there she had died of fever. On his return he had become involved, largely through Bagehot's intervention, in editing *The Prospective Review,* a quarterly which was intended to be the platform of a liberal non-denominational theology and for which Bagehot had written his reviews of Mill and of the currency controversy five years earlier. Hutton was only too pleased to have a literary contributor. In 1852 Bagehot had published in it his essay on Oxford which was prompted by the report of the Select Committee, and in the same year *Hartley Coleridge,* a figure who had intrigued him for some time. In the following year, he wrote for it one essay, *Shakespeare—The Man,* and in 1854 *Bishop Butler.*

Bagehot had taken an interest in the editorial problems of the *Prospective.* In January, 1854 he had advised against having an article on Comte. "Comte is *dead.* Might not Jevons do an article on reform if we cobbled his style. He is interested in it and would be cheap." But by the end of

---

* "You see," he wrote to a friend, "I have hunting, banking, ships, publishers, an article, and a Christmas to do, all at once, and it is my opinion they will all get muddled. A muddle will print, however, though it won't add up—*which is the real advantage of literature.*"

the year the *Prospective* was losing its best contributors and lacked the funds to get new ones. James Martineau, who had backed it, contemplated merging with it the *Westminster Review* but no agreement could be reached over the terms and it was decided to re-finance the *Prospective* and change its title. The money was put up mainly by a friend of Martineau's, S. D. Darbishire, partly by Lady Byron, and partly by Bagehot, who also enlisted the support of Crabb Robinson. Martineau and a fellow divine were to direct policy, while Hutton was to be made editor. In the complicated negotiations that followed Bagehot played the central part. It was he who persuaded the others to have no truck with *The Westminster Review* of which George Eliot was then assistant editor, and for which W. R. Greg, Francis Newman, W. E. Forster and Herbert Spencer then wrote. Its somewhat arid radicalism stirred an intense antipathy in Bagehot. "You may kill the Westminster and drive it to tears and agonies—by starting an opponent, but if you allow it to hold up its head as the only organ in which liberal religious opinions can be expressed, it will live and thrive—and propagate poison for a thousand years," he wrote to Crabb Robinson. It was he who found a printer and who persuaded Martineau to exclude Greg (who later became his brother-in-law and, with George Eliot, one of his closest friends) whose *Creed of Christendom* had made a considerable impact on serious liberal opinion. Lady Byron was the most difficult of the paper's various "angels" because she would not part with any money until she had seen the first issue.

At twenty-eight he took himself seriously both as a man of the world and as a journalist. When Crabb Robinson hinted that he was misrepresenting the position to the others he replied majestically, "I consider myself a man of business and should not indulge in such a scheme unless I thought the business aspect fair and reasonable." "You are to remember," he told Robinson who was fifty years his senior, "that as far as social connections go, reviews—especially news reviews—are not written by the high literary noblesse—but by accomplished paupers—barristers, ministers, and outcasts who are not so well known to people of high standing as the people of low—I think we may hope for a few good pens of name, but we must beat Grub St. for clever padding."

Hutton offered to share his chair with Bagehot, who declined the formal appointment but nevertheless interfered with vigor in most of Hutton's editorial decisions. After a good deal of argument it was called the *National Review;* and it was launched as a quarterly with 200 pages at four shillings. Its purpose was to cover "an open field" in Martineau's words "of unrepresented feeling and opinion between the heavy Whiggism and decorous Church-latitude of the *Edinburgh* on the one hand and the atheistic tendency and refugee politics of the *Westminster* on the other." It aimed to have a sale of 500 in its first years and to become solvent at a sale of 1,250.

The *National Review* lasted for ten years. Hutton was then only learning, and Martineau's diffuse theological articles, even when buttressed by Bagehot's literary ones, could not hold as large an audience as the radical *Westminster,* a paper which as Bagehot hinted to Hutton was far better edited. A serious periodical cannot flourish today without a definite view on politics: a serious journal could not then flourish without taking a definite position on religion. This was impossible for the *National* because Martineau and Tayler were serious Unitarians, while Hutton was becoming attracted to the Anglicism of Maurice and Kingsley. Nevertheless it achieved a circulation of 1,500, of which a high proportion was in the United States. It was the outbreak of the Civil War which, by cutting off its American sale, led it into financial difficulties. In 1862 Hutton resigned the Editorship in growing dislike of Unitarianism, and Bagehot after trying another editor brought it to an end two years later. But the foundation of the *National* was of great importance to Bagehot because he had both a financial and an editorial interest in it, and the fact that he was the mainstay of its literary side made him write at a time when his mind was fruitful but not energetic.

In it appeared all of what are called his *Literary Studies* and more than half the *Biographical Studies.*

It is difficult to overestimate the importance of the nineteenth century monthlies and quarterlies. Nothing like them exists today, and with modern reading tastes and modern production costs it is improbable that their like will ever be seen again. They were expensive (between four and six shillings on an average); some of them paid their contributors handsomely and some did not. They made no concessions to the frailty of their readers. Bagehot's articles in the *National* run to between twelve and twenty thousand words each, and Carlyle's articles in the *Foreign Review* are even longer. In column after column of smudgy unleaded 6 or 8 point type the contributor was allowed to develop his argument. Without the reviews and the reading public which supported them (though none had large circulations by modern standards), the ample, rounded, Victorian essay would have been impossible. Moreover most of them closely guarded the anonymity of their contributors, so that a young and unknown writer, if he could find a friendly editor, could gain a niche in the world of letters. If Bagehot had had, from the start, to condense his ideas and pare his style to the length of the weeklies, the *Saturday Review, The Economist* or the *Spectator,* for which he later wrote, many of his finest essays, needing considerable free water to develop their theme, would never have been written.

III

Hutton unwittingly did his friend a disservice when, republishing his articles and essays after his death, he divided them into *Literary Studies* and *Biographical Studies.* He would have done better to have retained the title, unhandy though it was, of *Estimates of some Englishmen and Scotchmen* which Bagehot himself used when he published them in 1858.* For the division has tended to perpetuate a distinction

---

* When, however, they were hardly noticed. Bagehot's literary reputation dates from Hutton's editions of 1878.

between Bagehot as a literary critic and as a political essayist. In fact, his interests were never divided into compartments in this fashion. He was drawn as if by some magnetic force to the study of mind and character, of poets, politicians, philosophers, business men. His literary studies are about writers much more than about writing.

But though he became, in time, one of the best informed and shrewdest judges of political character, he remained inhibited both by temperament and circumstance from any kind of scientific literary scholarship. Fiction and poetry remained his love, solace and recreation throughout his life, but he only wrote about them during eleven years of his youth. It is because he wrote as a gifted observer from outside the world of scholarship that his essays on poets and men of letters have remained so fresh and so widely read. It is because he wrote them in youth, and mostly at home, where he could not fertilize his ideas as he could have in a university or in London, that he threw off some slap dash theories which have enabled more scholarly critics to throw doubt upon his judgment.

Poetry, "a deep thing, a teaching thing, the most surely and wisely elevating of human things", was his early passion, though in later years he became much more absorbed in the novel. His betrothal present to his wife was a copy of Shelley and of Wordsworth, and in his courtship his love was expressed through reading poetry aloud. But his essays in poetic criticism are less penetrating and durable than those on prose writers, just as he was never able to write poetry himself, though he was a pioneer of a new kind of prose.

His first essay, written just after he returned to Langport, was a study of a man for whom he felt a strange affection, Hartley Coleridge, Samuel Taylor's unfortunate and unsuccessful eldest son—the sheltered fond child unable to come to grips with manhood. Though no other critic has been prepared to give Hartley Coleridge's "gentle and minute genius" the attention that Bagehot did, it is a remarkable study of an imaginative boyhood, the more so for having been written at twenty-five, an age when few people see boyhood clearly. By comparison with his writing of a few years later, the style is still hobbled by too many parentheses and small pomposities but in it he set out his own aiming mark.

"The knack of style is to write like a human being. Some think they must be wise, some elaborate, some concise; Tacitus wrote like a pair of stays; some startle as Thomas Carlyle, or a comet, inscribing with his tail. But legibility is given to those who neglect these notions, and are willing to be themselves, to write their own thoughts in their own words, in the simplest words, in the words wherein they were thought."*

From a minor figure he passed straight on to the greatest. In *Shakespeare—The Man* (1853), he showed his qualities of sympathy and imaginative reconstruction to their best effect. It is absurd, he says, to say that we know nothing about Shakespeare as the experts aver, that "others abide our question, thou art free". "People do not keep a tame steam engine to write their books: and if those books were really written by a man he must have been a man who could write them. . . . The difficulty is a defect of the critics. A person who knows nothing of an author he has read, will not know much of an author he has seen." First of all, he pointed out "Shakespeare's works could only be produced by a first rate imagination working on a first rate experience." The one without the other is valueless for "to a great experience one thing is essential, an experiencing nature", and he points to Guizot, whose recently published study of Shakespeare he was reviewing, as an example, a man who had been a Prime Minister and lived through several revolutions but whose writing was none the richer for the experience. "Nothing puzzles him, nothing comes amiss to him, and he is not in the least wiser for anything."

"The reason why so few good books are written," he says,

* There is a clear echo of Hazlitt in these sentences. Thus "To write a genuine, familiar or truly English style, is to write as any one would speak in common conversation who had a thorough command and choice of words, or who could discourse with ease, force, and perspicuity, setting aside all pedantic and oratorical flashes." *On Familiar Style*, 1821.

"is that so few people who can write books know anything."
Anyone can produce stock characters, but only a man with a
gift for observation, a Scott or Shakespeare can create original
characters. Consequently, one can deduce from Shakespeare's
imagery something of what he has seen. The passage, for
instance, in *Venus and Adonis* that describes a hare running
through a flock of sheep to put the hounds off the scent, could
only have been written by a man who had been hunting.
Milton goes out from his study to have a look at Nature and
makes a formal old-fashioned garden of it, but "there are no
straight lines in Nature or Shakespeare". Where Milton takes
a beautiful object "and accumulates upon it all the learned
imagery of a thousand years; Shakespeare glances at it and
says something of his own". Here again the young writer is
fashioning his own sights.

He used his deductive method to make some rather dogmatic replies to the dogmatic scholarship of the time; that
Shakespeare knew little of the middle classes, that he was
drawing on imagination rather than knowledge in his delineation of women, that it was absurd to say that he was unlearned
for he had obviously read all the readable literature as opposed to the dull books of his day. Bagehot read a lot of his
own thoughts, his love of people, color and movement, his
dislike of pedantry, into Shakespeare, and there is no passage
more characteristic of his own feelings than that in which he
attempts an answer to the question which preoccupied early
Victorian writers, whether Shakespeare was motivated in his
plays by a desire to carry a religious message. Of course he
wanted to fill the Globe Theatre, says Bagehot, but "if the
underlying and almighty essence of the world be good, then it
is likely that the writer who most deeply approached to that
essence will be himself good. There is a religion of week days
as well as of Sundays, of 'cakes and ale' as well as pews and
altar cloths. This England lay before Shakespeare as it lies
before us all, with its green fields, and its long hedgerows, and
its many trees, and its great towns, and its endless hamlets,
and its motley society, and its long history and its bold ex-

ploits, and its gathering power, and he saw that they were good. To him perhaps more than to anyone else, has been given to see that they were a great unity, a great religious object."

His next choice, *William Cowper*, (1855), was an ideal one, for into it he was able to put all his own sensitive observation of the problem of a disordered mind, and the defences of placidity and routine that must be built to buttress it. It is a long essay and deals only sketchily with Cowper as a poet, to whom nature is "simply a background" while to Wordsworth it "is a religion", and of whose translation of Homer "the condemnation remains, that Homer is not dull and Cowper is".

But his description of Olney, of Cowper's relations with Mrs. Unwin, of the disturbing impact of the Reverend Newton (the kind of hearty divine whom Bagehot disliked) are the more vivid because Olney and Langport had many points in common. Accounting for Cowper's popularity he writes: "Everything is so comfortable: the tea urn hisses so plainly, the toast is so warm, the breakfast so neat, the food so edible, that one turns away in excitable moments, a little angrily from anything so quiet, tame and sober. Have we not always hated this life. What can be worse than regular meals, clock-moving servants, . . . a slow parson, a heavy assortment of near relations, a placid house flowing with milk and sugar . . . Aspiring and excitable youth stoutly maintains it can endure anything much better than 'the gross fog Bœotion'—the torpid in-door, tea-tabular felicity. Still a great deal of tea is really consumed in the English nation. A settled and practical people are distinctly in favour of heavy relaxations, placid prolixities, slow comforts." This passage is the closest he came to a direct protest against his own fate.

In the next two years he wrote his two least successful studies of poets, *Shelley* and *Béranger*. It is not that his Shelley (1856) lacks interest, or did not break new ground. Rather Shelley did not provide him with suitable material to display his characteristic virtues as an essayist. There is not, or there was not then, sufficient information about Shelley's life, the color, quality and ordinary details of it, to build up a picture of the man and relate it to his writings, as he was able to do with Cowper, Milton and Gibbon. Matthew Arnold praised this essay warmly, but by later notions neither Arnold nor Bagehot gave Shelley his due.

Moreover, Shelley defies the efforts to evolve a psychological theory of types on which Bagehot's mind was at work all his life, the differentiation between the human and the abstract, the classical and the romantic, the imaginative and the fanciful, the pure, the ornate and the grotesque. He rightly calls Shelley's poetry imaginative rather than fanciful from the size and boldness of the conceptions on which it is based. But in defining him as a classical rather than a romantic poet because of his unity and purity of idea and expression in distinction to the sensuousness of Keats ("We can hear that the poetry of Keats is a rich composite, voluptuous harmony; that of Shelley a clear single ring of penetrating melody") he laid himself open to the charge of arbitrary selection and to having a great deal of Shelley and Keats quoted against him.

In *Béranger* (1857) he attempted an appraisal of what he calls "the poetry of society", of the tradition of Horace. It is full of delightful flashes. "Childishly deceivable by charlatans on every other subject—imposed on by pedantry, by new and unfounded science, by ancient and unfounded reputation, a prey to pomposity, overrun by recondite fools ignorant of all else—society knows itself. The world knows a man of the world." "Some have said, that one reason why physical science made so little progress in ancient times was that people were in doubt about more interesting things; men must have, it has been alleged, a settled creed as the human life and human hopes, before they will attend to shells and snails and pressure." "The poetry of society will tend to the most romantic part of society, away from aunts and uncles and antiquaries and wigs to younger and pleasanter elements." "There is no melancholy like the melancholy of the Epicurean."

What mars his Béranger is a display of complacent English

superiority towards French society and letters; since Mary
Mohl had shown him Paris from the inside he should have
known better. He depicts Béranger's *vers de société* as typify-
ing the frivolous superficiality of French life, while at the same
time he criticises him for his departure from the pure Horatian
traditions in holding and expressing radical political views.
For all his love and knowledge of France he never really appreciated the inner dilemma of French society, nor looked at
it through any eyes but English.

Milton (1859) on the other hand was a subject ideally suited
to Bagehot's technique and temperament. Distrustful as he
was of the wider implications of the Puritan mind and conscience—"it is from a tired and varied and troubled moral
life that the deepest and truest idea of God arises"—he was
drawn to Milton as the best type of the ascetic Christian. "In
this case, the extent to which the character of the man, as we
find it delineated, approached to the moral abstraction which
we sketch from theory, is remarkable." With Milton "we seem
to have left the little world of ordinary writers".

Admiring Milton's moral tenacity, he points out his lack
of ordinary sympathy and humor. "Catastrophies," writes
Bagehot, "require a comic element: we may read solemn descriptions of great events in history—say of Lord Strafford's
trial, and of his marvellous speech, and his appeal to his Saint
in heaven; but we comprehend the whole transaction much
better when we learn from Mr. Baillie the eyewitness, that
people ate nuts and apples, and talked, and laughed, and
betted on the great question of acquittal and condemnation.
It seems to be a law of the imagination, at least in most men,
that it will not bear concentration. It is essentially a glancing
faculty." Shakespeare's imagination on the other hand "always
seems to be floating between the contrast of things: and if his
mind has a resting place that it liked, it was the ordinary view
of extraordinary events". This is now an accepted truth in the
descriptive arts: a hundred years ago it was a fresh one, as
anyone who tries to reconstruct the atmosphere of contemporary events through mid-Victorian newspapers finds out.

Bagehot writes about Milton's marital troubles, the more sympathetically since he had just got married himself. "The poet in search of an imaginary phantom has never been successful with women: and the ascetic moralist is even less interesting. A character combined of the two—and this to some extent was Milton's—is singularly likely to meet with painful failure: with a failure the more painful that it could never anticipate or explain it. Possibly he was absorbed in an austere self-conscious excellence; it may never have occurred to him that a lady might prefer the trivial detail of daily happiness."

But in describing the curious theology in *Paradise Lost,* he is at his best. One of Milton's "fatal errors" is that "he has made God *argue* . . . Even Pope was shocked at the notion of Providence talking like a 'school divine'. And there is the still worse error, that if you once attach all reasoning to Him, subsequent logicians may discover that He does not reason very well." "Another way in which Milton has strengthened our interest in Satan is the number and insipidity of the good angels . . . They appear to be excellent administrators with very little to do: a kind of grand chamberlain with wings . . . When an angel possessed of mind is contrasted only with angels possessed of wings, we sympathise with the former." And in a later essay he wrote of *Paradise Lost* "it professes to justify the ways of God to man, to account for sin and death, and it tells you the whole thing originated in a political event: in a court squabble as to a particular act of patronage and to due or undue promotion of an eldest son. Satan may have been wrong, but on Milton's theory he had an arguable case at least. There was something arbitrary in the promotion, there were little symptons of a job: in *Paradise Lost* it is always clear that the devils are the weaker, it is never clear that the angels are the better. Milton's sympathy and imagination slip back to the Puritan rebels whom he loved, and deserted the courtly angels whom he could not love, although he praised them."

Five years later in 1864, Bagehot, in the last of his major essays on literary figures before politics and economics engrossed him, made his most ambitious attempt at the definition of poetry. *Wordsworth, Tennyson and Browning or Pure, Ornate and Grotesque Art in English Poetry.* He begins with the suggestion that literature needs an analogous adjective—"literatesque"—to painting's "picturesque" which means—or meant a century ago before it became debased—subject matter that perfectly suits the form of art. Poetry as opposed to mere verse is a very specialised form of expression. "It should be memorable, and emphatic, intense and *soon over.*" Though he rejects Matthew Arnold's belief that poetry could only delineate great actions, he accepts the view that it can cover only a limited range of actions and ideas.

"Pure" poetry is that which has fastened on the most perfectly "literatesque" subject, which deals in types that are universal, in ideas that express the Platonic forms. "Ornate" poetry, dealing with a more prosaic subject, must clothe it in richer language and imagery. He denies that the distinction is synonymous with "classical" and "romantic" poetry, but clearly he would accept it as a rough division. To Bagehot *Paradise Lost* and Wordsworth's Sonnets are the finest examples of the pure form. Though he had earlier made fun of the plot of *Paradise Lost,* he suggests that Belial's speech, cautious and craven, is "one among several *typical* characters which will ever have their place in great councils, which will ever be heard at important decisions, which are part of the cautious and inalienable whole of the statesmanlike world". Certainly re-reading the description of the council in Hell with Bagehot's phrase in mind, the arguments for a bold and weak foreign policy advanced sound uncannily like the deliberations of the Soviet Praesidium, the President's National Security Council or of a British Cabinet meeting.

As the best example of ornate poetry he puts forward Tennyson's *Enoch Arden,* which had recently been published. To show what improbable material Tennyson had provided himself with, Bagehot boils the story down to a sentence: "A sailor who sells fish, breaks his leg, gets dismal, gives up selling fish, goes to sea, is wrecked on a desert island, stays there some years, on his return finds his wife married to a miller, speaks to a landlady on the subject, and dies." Tennyson can only bring this irrelevant and untypical story within the realm of poetry by "a splendid accumulation of impossible accessories". This is the use of romantic poetry, to bring alive the world of illusion, the untypical world, the unpleasant rather than the purely tragic.

His third classification—the grotesque—the universal type at odds, in embryo, or in combat, he centers around Browning. It is the least successful of the three for his comments reveal his one literary blind spot, his consistent equation of experiments on the boundaries of poetry with lapses of taste.

The whole essay is an extremely adventurous piece of criticism, though he is highly selective in the choice of his quotations from all three poets to prove his theory. It was, as Saintsbury pointed out, "one of the earliest to estate and recognise Tennyson—the earliest perhaps of importance to estate and recognise Browning—among the leaders of mid-nineteenth century poetry".

As a critic of poetry Bagehot suffered perhaps from loving it too much. He had been reared like all his contemporaries under the far-reaching shadow of Wordsworth, whose verse nourished and suited his own intense feeling for landscape, for "the bare hill and the clear river". As the shade withdrew, he viewed with distaste the more catchy, popular notion of poetry that was developing. "We live," he concluded, "in the realm of the half-educated. The number of readers grows daily, but the quality of readers does not improve rapidly. The middle class is scattered, heedless: it is well-meaning but aimless; wishing to be wise but ignorant how to be wise. The aristocracy of England never was a literary aristocracy, never even in the days of its full power, its unquestioned predominance, did it guide—did it even seriously try to guide—the taste of England. Without guidance young men and tired men, are thrown among a mass of books: they have to choose which they like: many of them would much like to improve their culture, to chasten their taste, if they knew how. But left to themselves they take, not pure art, but showy art." It sounds an arid conclusion for a young man to reach, but it is a perceptive analysis of what was actually happening.

This same awareness of the need to bridge the gap between the small, highly educated minority which the traditional educational system still produced, and the big half-educated, energetic middle class that was arising, the necessity to evolve a mass culture, he emphasised in *The First Edinburgh Reviewers* (1855). "Even if we had a profound and far seeing statesman, his deep ideas and long ranging vision would be useless to us unless we could impart a confidence in them to the mass of influential persons, to the unelected commons, to the unchosen Council, who assist at the deliberations of the nation." It is an idea to which he is constantly returning, this fear that the demands of the growing middle class—particularly the rise of the semi-educated woman reader—would produce a literature that was unheroic, sentimental and formless.

Hence his interest in serious journalism, the new means of communication, and the first of the great periodicals—*The Edinburgh*. But his essay is less remarkable for its character sketches of the three men, Horner, Jeffrey and Sydney Smith who founded it (he left out Brougham because he was writing on him separately) as of the man they rose up to do battle with, Lord Eldon, the Lord Chancellor who opposed any form of parliamentary or legal reform. "As for Lord Eldon, it is the most difficult thing in the world to believe that there ever was such a man," the man who, from "geniune, hearty, craven fear", effectively blocked even the mildest reforms for a quarter of a century. It also contains the famous passage, contrasting the facile mind of Jeffrey with that of his arch enemy, Wordsworth.

> The world has given judgement. Both Mr. Wordsworth and Lord Jeffrey have received their reward. The one had his own generation; the laughter of men, the applause of drawing rooms, the concurrence of the crowd; the other a succeeding age, the fond enthusiasms of secret students, the lonely rapture of lonely minds . . . Nature ingeniously prepared a shrill artificial voice, which spoke in season and out of season,

enough and more than enough, what will ever be the idea of the cities of the plain concerning those who live among the mountains; of the frivolous concerning the grave; of the gregarious concerning the recluse . . . the notice of the world of those whom it will not reckon among the righteous—it said "This won't do"! And so in all times will the lovers of polished Liberalism speak concerning the intense and lonely prophet.

Reflections on Jeffrey and Sydney Smith naturally involved Bagehot in a study of the Whig mind which in turn led him to Macaulay. The two final volumes of the History of England from the Accession of James the Second were published in 1855: he reviewed them for the *National* of January, 1856 in an essay which combined genuine admiration for Macaulay, the organiser of history, for his technique, for his style, for his way of making dull facts and figures come alive, with a strong distaste for Macaulay the cool Whig, impervious to the deep undertones of Cavalier and Puritan feeling alike. Macaulay's character, as Bagehot conceived it, was the opposite of what he admired, or wished his own to be: aloof, "an orator should never talk like an observatory"; unimpressionable, "you could never tell from his style what he had seen or had not seen"; obsessed with the opinion of posterity, "the way to secure its favour is to give vivid essential pictures of the life before you . . . he (Macaulay) regards existing men as painful pre-requisites of great-grandchildren".

For the same issue he wrote his essay on *Gibbon* which, like his Cowper, is more a study of the man—the kind of retreating incompetent figure of whom he was fond—than of his work. As Professor Irvine has written, Bagehot "tears away the pages of a formidable volume and shows you the living author behind it". He gives a gently ironic description of Gibbon's timid and prosaic character, "his wise preference for permanent money", the schoolboy sense of wonder with which he approached ancient history. Of his career in the militia, "the English have discovered pacific war. . . . A 'constitutional militia' is a beautiful example of the mild efficacy of civilization which can convert even the 'great manslaying profession' (as Carlyle calls it) into a quiet and dining association". Of his conversion to Rome: "the English have ever believed that the Papist is a kind of *creature*: and every sound mind would prefer a beloved child to produce a tail, a hide of hair, and a taste for nuts, in comparison with transubstantiation, wax candles and a belief in the glories of Mary". He sets Gibbon's style within the framework of the audience he wrote for. "In literature the period may be defined as that in which authors had ceased to write for students, and had not yet begun to write for women." And he has an excellent capsule sentence to describe it. "All through this long period Gibbon's history goes with steady consistent pace; like a Roman legion through troubled country—*haeret pede pes*; up hill and down hill, through marsh and thicket, through Goth or Parthian—the firm, defined array passes forward—a type of order, and an emblem of civilization. Whatever may be the defects of Gibbon's history, none can deny him a proud precision and a style in marching order."

The studies of Dickens and Scott which he wrote more or less simultaneously in 1858, the year of his marriage, are his closest attempt at real literary criticism rather than at character studies of writers.

The Waverley Novels should, I think, be reckoned the finest of his literary studies, and one of the most judicious in the whole vast literature of adulation and distaste that surrounds Scott's writings. He had been brought up on a heady diet of Sir Walter in the days before the reaction, led by Carlyle, had set in against him. Moreover, Scott personified his ideal of himself, the active laird, whose novels "read as if they had been written on horseback", yet with a sensitive appreciation of the elemental in men and women, in contrast to the urban figures of Dickens and Thackeray. Scott in his eyes had the Shakespearian qualifications of an "experiencing nature".

"As in the imagination of Shakespeare, so in Scott, the principal form and object were the structure—that is a hard word —the undulation and diversified composition of human society; the picture of this stood in the centre, and everything else was accessory and secondary to it."

Scott, above all writers, filled his prescription that "Toryism is enjoyment". But he was not a slavish admirer of the novels. He was as hard as Scott's severest critics on his heroines, and pointed out that he had no power of abstraction nor of delineating intellect as opposed to character. He lacks the "consecrating power" says Bagehot: he is too content with his cheerful matter of fact world.

Dickens he approached more warily. He had started his essay on Scott, by propounding two classes of fiction, the ubiquitous and the sentimental, that which "aims at describing the whole of human life in all its spheres, in all its aspects", and that which is dominated by plot. He had no hesitation in putting Dickens in the first category, but he propounded yet another dichotomy—perhaps his most successful—regular and irregular genius. The first has an instinctive sense of symmetry, and proportion. Plato among philosophers, Chaucer among descriptive writers, are his two principal candidates. The second is patchy, the undergrowth often hiding the trees, a particular faculty more highly developed than any other. Dickens is an irregular genius, and the failures are more marked for the ubiquity of his themes. "His pictures are graphic snaps . . . He is utterly deficient in the faculty of reasoning . . . He is often troubled with the idea that he must reflect, and his reflections are perhaps the worst reading in the world."

This is acute criticism though Bagehot spoilt it by occasional pomposities:

"His abstract understanding is so far inferior to his picturesque imagination as to give even his best works the sense of jar and incompleteness, and to deprive them altogether of the crystalline finish which is characteristic of the clear and cultured understanding."

But he admired Dickens, for his special excellences: "He describes London like a special correspondent for posterity." He disapproved of his sentimental radicalism, but admired him for having widened the frontiers of taste, of the subjects and situations that could be written of and described, while Thackeray merely sailed close to the wind.

He expressed an even more stringent view of the distinction between the printable and the unprintable in *Sterne and Thackeray*, the last of his major literary character studies. He was a devoted reader of *Tristram Shandy*, for he was one of the first of his generation to appreciate the writers of the eighteenth century, but he felt real concern at its indecency. This view was of a piece with his feeling about the restrictions that were closing in on literature with the rise of a large reading public. "A young ladies literature must be a limited and truncated literature." Like French memoires, it "may very easily do harm; if generally read among the young of the middle class, it would be sure to do harm". In a mind otherwise so symmetrical, this curious strain persists.

The subsequent estimates of Bagehot as a literary critic have ranged across a wide spectrum. Maynard Keynes, admiring his psychological insight into the minds of economists and businessmen, had no opinion of the literary essays. On the other hand Sir Herbert Read, a better judge than Keynes, wrote of Bagehot's literary criticism as "almost the best of its time, and only the speculative figure of Matthew Arnold prevents us from pronouncing it quite the best". Bagehot's American biographer, Professor William Irvine, concentrated his study around the literary essays, while Saintsbury dismissed them in a few lines.

"Bagehot" wrote Oliver Elton "has been cried up as a critic for excellences at which he did not aim, and has also been cried down as an amateur. He is an amateur, but it is a pity there are not more like him. He must be judged from his own point of departure. He does not begin with theory, or philosophy, or learning; nor again does he begin with form; in fact, he often never gets to form at all, being beguiled on the way by the study of character." This is a fair answer to Saintsbury. "The evils of dissipation of energy have been lamented by the grave and precise in allages; and some have held that they are specially discoverable in the most modern times. It is very probable that Criticism may charge to this account the comparatively faint and scanty service done her by one who displayed so much faculty for that service as Walter Bagehot."

He was an amateur and a careless one at that (as his exasperated American editor, Forrest Morgan, soon found when trying to check his quotations, many of which appear to have been set down from memory alone, many of them wrong). But this was his strength, for it enabled him to bring fresh experience to bear upon familiar themes. No study of the writings of Scott or of Macaulay, to name only two examples, can neglect Bagehot's judgments of the writer. Though his literary essays contain some of the best phrases and aphorisms in the language, what debars him from being accepted as a critic on a level with Arnold, or a student of writers on a level with Stephen, are two characteristics which gave him a certain timidity. One was a preoccupation with the effect on the audience as much as with the purpose of the writer, a concern with the tastes of the ordinary and with ease of communication, which was as much a defect in his literary studies as it was a great virtue in his political and economic writing. The fun which he could extract from grave authors and great subjects was the beneficent aspect of the years of mid-Victorian confidence. But wonderful reading as they are, Bagehot's literary essays make one see the point of Matthew Arnold's protest in *Essays in Criticism* against the critical standards of the late fifties and early sixties.

The other arose from his personal life—a fear of probing too deep beneath the surface, an instinctive aversion from the tragic in literature and life. He had seen a great deal of private tragedy, he had with difficulty steeled himself to live in and accept the real world, and he had put a barrier of what was at first bravado and only later confidence between himself and dark thoughts. The consequence was a certain jocosity which was admirably fitted to leaven subjects like economics, but which denied him the full range of emotions that a great and comprehensive student of literature must have. This, I think, he knew very well, for he was one of those rare men who keep few secrets from themselves.

Chapter 5

THE SIMPLE TRUTH

He early received from fortune the inestimable permission to be himself.   *Essay on William Pitt*

I

BY the beginning of 1857, Bagehot had been living in Langport for nearly five years. He was thirty; "tall and thin",
said his sister-in-law,

> with rather high, narrow, square shoulders; his hands were long
> and delicate and the movements of his fingers very character-
> istic. He held his fingers quite straight from the bone knuckles
> and would often stroke his mouth or rub his forehead when he
> was thinking or talking . . . He had a very fine skin, very
> white near where the hair started, and a high colour—what
> might be called a hectic colour—concentrated on the cheek
> bones, as you often see it in the West Country. Such a colour
> is associated with soft winds and a moist air, cider growing
> orchards, and very green, wet grass. His eyelids were thin, and
> of singularly delicate texture, and the white of the eyeballs was
> a blue white. He would pace a room when talking, and, as the
> ideas framed themselves in words, he would throw his head
> back as some animals do when sniffing the air. The way he
> moved, his voice, everything about him was individual.

He was now an established figure in the hierarchy of
Stuckey's and the secretary of its Committee of Management.
His health had returned and, by quiet living and an enjoyment of what was to hand, he had avoided the intellectual
exhaustion which had left Clough stranded. His literary essays
had formed his style and the previous year he had written
the first, and in many ways the best, of his biographical
sketches, *The Character of Sir Robert Peel*. He now had a
modest reputation as a man of letters and when he wrote arti-

cles for the newly established *Saturday Review* he was accorded
the privilege of big type.

What he clearly needed was a wider field of activity on
which an "experiencing nature" might graze. Langport might
be his source of strength and refreshment, but it compre-
hended too small a part of life. The local county society was
not stimulating; the country neighbors found young Mr.
Bagehot alarming for his wit and cynicism despite his dash
in the hunting field; he found them dull. "He used to say,"
records Hutton, "that he wished he could think balls *wicked,*
being so stupid as they were, and all the little blue and pink
girls, so like each other—a sentiment," Hutton, who was more
at home with women, added drily, "partly due, perhaps, to
his extreme shortness of sight." His mother was urging him
to get married but no girl had captured his imagination. Moreover, though he might defend the heedless, enjoying Cavalier
temperament, there was too strong a strain of intellectual ambition in his nature to permit him to abandon himself to the
life of a country gentleman.

But the cords that bound him to Langport were as strong
as ever and still deterred him from taking himself off to enjoy
a literary life in London. To ignore, as an only child, the love
of a devoted father and a frail endearing mother, needed a
burning sense of purpose which he did not possess. Life at
Herd's Hill cannot have been easy for him. A few years earlier
he had written to his friend, Killigrew Wait.

> My mother who many years ago was subject to attacks of
> delirium, has of late fallen into a good deal of habitual de-
> lusion and aberration, which, I fear, will end in ultimately
> disqualifying her for society. Indeed except with her oldest
> friends who are quite used to her it has done so already.

It was an accidental chain of events which saved Bagehot
from being merely a country banker with a taste for literary
criticism and carried him into a world where his restless and
active mind could find real employment.

A year before, in 1856, Hutton had been offered the editorship of the remarkable and successful weekly, *The Economist,* but the idea did not appeal to him. He was in a troubled frame of mind, jarred by his wife's death, making up his mind to marry again (two years later he married his first wife's cousin, another grand-daughter of William Roscoe), and afflicted by a common malady of the time—conversion from Unitarianism to the Church of England. Bagehot had urged him to take the job. "Offers of this kind are not to be picked up in the street every day. As for holidays, it is one of the lessons of life to be independent of them." Hutton had refused to make up his mind until he had made a pilgrimage to his wife's grave in the Barbados, and in the meanwhile the offer was in abeyance.

Bagehot had never had any dealings with *The Economist.* He had read it as a student and presumably the bank had subscribed to it, for, though it was a young publication, it commanded respect. He had written some economic articles for the *Saturday Review* and writing for *The Economist* with its more specialised interest and wider influence appealed to him. (Disraeli classified the former as the organ of the educated classes, the latter as the spokesman of the middle classes.) By 1857 he had arrived at two conclusions that he wanted to air in print: one, the importance of extending the newly recognised principle of limited liability to banks and banking as well as to industry and commerce; the other, that the effect of the amount of gold and currency in circulation upon the level of prices had been overestimated and needed re-examining.

He had never met James Wilson, the owner and founder of *The Economist* who was now also Financial Secretary to the Treasury in Palmerston's government, (though he had criticised Wilson's views on the Bank Act nine years before) but they had a connecting link of acquaintances. One of Wilson's closest friends, who was at that time managing the paper on his behalf, was William Rathbone Greg. Greg was a paternalistic mill owner whose *Creed of Christendom,* published six years before, had cast doubt on the authenticity of

the gospels and had earned him some reputation in the new
hinterland between atheism and belief that biblical criticism
was opening up. Greg was a friend of Martineau and Bagehot
and had been involved with both of them in the founding of
the *National*. A letter from Martineau took Bagehot to Greg
and on the latter's recommendation he was asked to come and
stay the night of January 24th, 1857, at Claverton, James Wilson's house outside Bath, where he lived with his wife and six
daughters, in order to discuss his ideas on banking.

II

James Wilson was a genial, able and conscientious Scotsman
who had worked his way up to an influential position among
the Liberal *haute bourgeoisie* of the fifties. He had been born
at Hawick in Roxburghshire where his father owned woollen
mills, the fourth son in a family of fifteen children. His father
had become a Quaker and had sent him to the Friends' school
at Ackworth in Yorkshire. There he had shown an intellectual
bent but his father had frowned on his becoming a lawyer
and had set him up in a hat business in London with his elder
brother. At twenty-seven he married Elizabeth Preston of New-
castle, a dashing pretty girl whose father, the younger son of
a landed family, had run away to sea in his youth. The Wilsons settled down in Dulwich to a prosperous merchant's life,
and twelve years after going into business he had expanded
twelvefold his original capital of two thousand pounds. But
in the panic of 1837 he lost everything he possessed in a speculation in indigo and had to start again from nothing. He was
a resolute and cheerful man and took great pride in the fact
that he had paid off all his debts and had subsequently completely re-established himself without any outside assistance.

The rebuilding of his fortunes and the support of a growing family of daughters did not exclude an interest in political
and economic ideas. While a young man he had become a
friend of Cobden and Francis Place, and in 1839 he published
the first of many articles and pamphlets "The Influence of the

Corn Laws". Wilson did not play a leading role in the Anti-
Corn Law League nor emerge as a public figure in the debates
of the forties that led eventually to Repeal. For one thing he
was much too staid to approve of some of the League's
methods. But he did more than almost anyone else to supply
the League with the ammunition for one of its most telling
arguments, by showing that protection injured landowners and
farmers as well as industralists and traders by keeping the
general level of prosperity artificially low. Long afterwards
Cobden acknowledged his debt to Wilson for having helped
to steer the controversy away from one of class interest, of
industry versus agriculture, bourgeoisie versus aristocracy.
Even the Duke of Wellington, who had no love for business
men in politics, was converted in a personal interview by
Wilson's arguments in favor of the repeal of the Navigation
Laws.

Wilson's interest in economic questions during the forties
ranged wider than the free trade issue. He was a moderate
exponent of *laissez faire* and disliked the arid dogmatism of
the Manchester School. He had strong views on public finance
and about the way in which Peel and the young Gladstone
were setting out to produce order out of the financial chaos
they had inherited from the Melbourne era. In 1842 Albany
Fonblanque, Leigh Hunt's powerful successor as Editor of
The Examiner, turned down one of his articles on the grounds
that it was too long, as well as his offer to write a free economic
article in each issue. Wilson with his own fortunes still in the
balance decided to start a weekly paper of his own.

Cobden was actively discouraging. "Newspapers have been
graves to fortunes. Have you made up your mind to a great
and continued pecuniary loss?" But Bright and Charles Villiers
and that intelligent nobleman Lord Radnor, who had been the
friend of Cobbett and many enterprising radicals, lent him
money. Mrs. Wilson and the children were packed off to
Boulogne, the haven of Victorians trying to economise, so that
the house in Dulwich could be let.*

---

* No great privation by modern standards. Mrs. Barrington, the youngest
daughter, remembered that "All servants were dismissed except Susan, our

On 2nd September, 1843, appeared the first number of *The Economist* or the Political, Commercial, Agricultural and Free Trade Journal, the most enduringly successful and influential weekly paper of the past century. In the words of its present Editor, Wilson:

> drew a winning ticket in the lottery of journalism. He founded a paper whose contents were to be based upon, though not bounded by, a systematic weekly survey of economic data at the very beginning of a century in which the economic aspect of social, political and international relations was to be the dominant theme.

But for Wilson it was an act of faith and courage.

The Economist was an almost immediate success and within a few years Wilson had consolidated his financial recovery. In 1847 he entered the House of Commons as Liberal member for Westbury (through Lord Radnor's influence) and within six months had been given junior office by Lord John Russell. He had a prodigious memory which made him a good debater and even Disraeli, who opposed his views, described him as "a great accession to the House". In 1852 he became Gladstone's Financial Secretary to the Treasury in the Aberdeen government and remained there until the fall of the Whig-Liberal coalition five years later. F.S.T. was, then as now, an influential position and it became a highly important one when the government split over the management of the Crimean war, and Palmerston, who knew little about economic or financial policy, succeeded Aberdeen. The scholarly but torpid Sir George Cornewall Lewis, who came after Gladstone at the Treasury, relied greatly upon Wilson's judgment in financing the first war in forty years, and when the sudden panic of 1857 occurred, Wilson played the leading part in negotiations between the Treasury and the Bank of England. To the clerks in the Treasury, whose sleepy ways and untidy office procedure he reformed, he was a second Huskisson. Cornewall Lewis, who loathed administration, once said to

---

nurse, Emilie, my mother's maid, and a man and a housekeeper to look after my father in London". Mrs. Russell Barrington, *The Servant of All* (London: Longmans, 1927), Vol. I, p. 62.

him after listening to Wilson's exposition of some needed reform, "No, I can't do it. The fact is, Wilson, you are an animal
and I am only a vegetable." It was to discuss the Government's policy towards the impending crisis that he invited
the young West Country banker, who was so well spoken of
but whose name he was unsure how to pronounce (was it
Bagot, or Badget, or Bagge-hot?), to dine and spend the night
at Claverton.*

III

As Bagehot's dogcart turned up the precipitous drive to
Claverton from the Frome road, a murmuration of Wilson
daughters turned from a walk through the woods to listen
with disfavor to the sound of approaching wheels. Another
boring man to divert Papa's attention with more interminable
talk about economics, or worse about the nature of biblical
evidence, or the situation in India. But within twenty-four
hours their world had been turned upside down.

At breakfast the next morning the young man electrified
the three smaller sisters who had not been allowed to sit up
the night before, Sophie, Zenobia and Emily, by turning his
great eyes upon them as their German Fräulein left the room
and saying, "Your governess is like an egg." They collapsed
into enchanted giggles. In the tolerant but solemn Wilson
household, there had never before been a son or brother to
share iconoclasms with. However, it was among the three
grown up daughters, Eliza, Julia and Matilda, that Walter's
arrival had caused the greatest havoc, and upon Eliza, the
eldest, that his eye had rested. He was attracted to her

* The pronunciation of Bagehot's name has been a source of argument,
particularly since there are only a few people now living who bear it as a
surname. There is, however, no question that he and all his friends pro-
nounced his name Baggeott with the accent on the first syllable. If there
was any doubt, it was disposed of by Mr. R. B. Kerr, who wrote to the
Sunday Times (London) in October, 1939 giving as his explicit authority
for this pronunciation Professor Shield Nicholson of Edinburgh who was a
student of economics when Bagehot was alive and well known. There were,
however, some local Somerset variations of its pronunciation just as there
are of many more familiar names.

from the moment he took her into dinnei on the first night.

A very proper Victorian courtship began. When the family migrated back to London for the session Bagehot was asked to dine regularly at Hertford Street. Wilson found him a good listener on economic questions; Greg aired his literary theories upon him; Walter kept his eye on Eliza. He became the indispensable young man at the Wilsons' dinner parties. George Ticknor, the Boston *littérateur*, described dining with the Wilsons that year.

> He (Wilson) never reads a book; he gets all his knowledge from documents and conversation, as Greg tells me, that is at first-hand. He talks uncommonly well on all subjects; strongly and with a kind of original force that you rarely witness. He has a young wife and three nice grown up daughters, who with Greg, a barrister whose name I did not get (Bagehot)— one other person and myself, filled up a very luxurious table as far as eating and drinking are concerned. And who do you think that other person was? nobody less than Mme. Mohl; who talked as fast and amusingly as ever, full of good natured kindness, with a little subacid as usual to give it good flavour. The young ladies Greg accounts as among the most intelligent of his acquaintance, and they talk French as few English girls can, for de Tocqueville came in after dinner and we all changed language at once, except the Master who evidently has but one tongue in his head, and needs but one, considering the strong use he makes of it.

There were expeditions to Kew to meet the great naturalist, Mr. Hooker (of Bentham and Hooker), a visit to Millbank to see the *Great Eastern,* and another to visit the *Agamemnon* with the huge Atlantic cable coiled within her womb.

When Parliament rose for the summer and the Wilsons migrated back to Claverton, Bagehot was invited to stay. He was intrigued by the family as well as by Eliza, with the scale and vitality of life in a large household after the *ménage à trois* in Langport. On fine days there were picnics on the Wiltshire downs with Walter escorting Eliza's donkey, for she was thought not strong enough to walk, and giving it surreptitious kicks to get her away from her sisters. When her hair came down on an expedition to Orchardleigh, he knew he was in love. "On wet days there would be games of battledore in the picture gallery, Walter's characteristic eyeglass floating about in the air on its black string as he ran hither and thither after the elusive shuttlecock," wrote Emily, the youngest. "On every visit he seemed more and more to become one of us; yet the crisis so eagerly awaited by us of the schoolroom, tarried."

The stately progress of Eliza and Walter towards engagement emerges from the laconic entries in her diary.

Sept. 27th. Sat in the conservatory where Mr. Bagehot told me his mother was mad.

Oct. 3rd. I took Mr. Bagehot to see the view and lost the donkey.

Oct. 8th. Mr. Bagehot read us Morte d'Arthur and Ulysses in billiard room, seated on stove. He is going to publish his essays.

Oct. 25th. I sat in the conservatory with Mr. Bagehot who told me the plot of Lady Georgina Fullerton's novels.

Oct. 28th. Walked with Mr. Bagehot before the house. Beautiful moon. Fall of Delhi.

And at last—

Oct. 31st. Papa received a letter from Mr. Bagehot with an enclosure for me and invited him to come here.

Nov. 2nd. Mr. Bagehot came at 2.30. He gave Papa a letter detailing his affairs and Papa sent him out riding with me, Julia and Mr. Greg. Papa and Mr. Bagehot had a long talk before dinner, and settled that he would speak to me next morning. Papa quite ill. Mr. Bagehot and I played at Beggar my Neighbour, and he gained a queen's head from me.

Nov. 4th. Mamma held a consultation with Mr. Bagehot in the library before breakfast, and then he got me in there under the pretext of looking for a book, and proposed to me.

Nov. 5th.   Talked over my proposed marriage with mamma
            and went to bed at 9, but did not sleep till 3.
Nov. 7th.   Mr. Bagehot came at 10 for my answer. I was in
            the dining room and engaged myself to him then
            and there.

They were no sooner engaged than separated, for at that
moment came the full onslaught of the financial panic of 1857
which had spread during the year from America to England
as a result of the glut of wheat and the inability of many
American businesses to meet their financial commitments in
Britain. Bagehot dashed off to hold the fort at Stuckey's. Wilson labored long hours at the Treasury, and a few days later
the Government, largely on his initiative, suspended Peel's
Bank Act to enable the Bank of England to support the
foundering Scottish and North Country houses. Eliza and Julia
were packed off to Edinburgh where a Dr. Beveridge was
thought to possess miraculous powers of massaging away eye
strain and headaches, and throughout the first winter of their
betrothal Walter and Eliza could communicate only by letter.
    Eliza Wilson was just twenty-five, six years younger than
Walter. She was a pale, handsome girl with a wide forehead
and large, calm eyes.* Julia, who later married W. R. Greg,
was considered the dashing and amusing member of the family; Eliza the sensitive and graceful one. She was extremely
well read, and from her diary she seems to have read almost
every novel of the last half of the nineteenth century within
a few weeks of its being published. Her greatly admired Gre-
cian profile and fine eyes came, so her family thought, from
the high-spirited Prestons rather than the homely Wilsons. She
was considered to be very delicate, and throughout her married

* And, if Chichester Fortescue is to be believed, red hair. He dined at
Claverton three days before they were engaged and surveyed the ebullient
family with aristocratic languor. "October 24th, Claverton Manor. Thought
it worth while to accept his (Wilson's) invitation, a man to get knowledge
from and useful to be on good terms with. A number of red haired
daughters, intelligent and unaffected. A Mr. Bagehot here, partner in a
great bank of these parts, writes for National Review, etc." Osbert Hewett
(ed.), *And Mr. Fortescue. A selection from the diaries from 1851-1862 of
Chichester Fortescue, Lord Carlingford K.P.* (London: John Murray, 1958)

life, her diaries were full of references to headaches, days in bed, and her inability to meet people. Yet she out-lived her husband by forty-four years, dying in 1921 at the age of eighty-nine.

Delicate or not, the first exchange of letters between Walter and herself showed that she had in many ways the stronger and calmer of the two natures.

"I think I should warn you," he wrote from Herd's Hills to Edinburgh on December 1st, 1857, "that in practical things I have a rather anxious disposition. I am cheerful but not sanguine. I can make the best of anything but I have difficulty in believing that the future will be very good. The most successful men of action rather over-estimate their chances of success in action. I cannot do this at all. I have always to work on the cold bare possibility. My energy is fair and my spirits are very good, but this difficulty of intellect I have always had . . . If you *will* soothe me in this it will be almost too great happiness, though you are a little anxious naturally too, still we will have headaches in life together, and that will be to me *immense*. Talking of headaches I cannot be reconciled to your staying in Edinburgh. I am rather learned in head complaints from my own experience. My impression is that they are one half of the mind, and that cheerful easy excitement is better for them than anything else, and you are quite out of the way of that."

To this Eliza replied:

I am very glad I elicited the little self-analysis in your last letter, for I had not felt before the distinctive characteristic of one part of our minds. I am not anxious in the sense that you are; anxious is not the word for what I am. I have languid spirits and am distrustful of self, but I am decidedly sanguine. I always expect things to turn out well, they think at home too much so . . . I believe my nature is very womanly, I mean that I love to lean on a stronger nature, though I may appear to be somewhat independent on the surface. I *can* stand alone if I must, but it makes my heart heavy to have to do it.

In his mood of hilarity and anticipation he poured all his spirit into his four months of correspondence with Eliza:

> I don't believe much in your being ill. I think you are jaded and have not been made enough of and want more rubbish talked to you. . . . My spirits always make me cheerful in a superficial way, but they do not satisfy, and somehow life even before I was engaged was sweeter and gentler, and the jars and jangles of action lost their influence, and literature had a new value since you liked my writing and everything had a gloss upon it. . . . No one can tell the effort it was to me to tell you I loved you—why I do not know, but it made me gasp for breath, and now it is absolute pleasure for me to tell it to you, and bore you with it in every form, and I should like to write I LOVE YOU in big letters across the page by ways of emphasis. I know you will think me very childish and be shaken in your early notion that I am an intellectual but I cannot help it . . . I go about murmuring, 'I have made that dignified girl *committ* herself, I have, I have' and then I vault over the sofa with exultation.
>
> I am afraid I plague you with my wild and wearing feelings. . . . Pretty women with beautiful expressions naturally cause great excitement. Long awkward currency people do not. A man's imagination is—at least mine is—a seizure. Certain expressions of countenance take hold of my mind and whirl it about. I fancy your feelings are gentle and continuous.

If Eliza's replies are a true guide to her character, he was right. Throughout his letters runs this continuous need for reassurance of her love. "I am nervous at times about your overrating me intellectually, but I get over it. I do not mind being thought too well of." Writing from Langport in January, 1858,

> I shall always be very rude, and treat you ill, and have a very small house, but that is nothing . . . By a miraculous advantage, I think your judgment is in my favour and you are sure to act on your own judgment. The only question is whether I can *delude* your judgement for a sufficient time . . . What can Miss Greg mean by calling you fast. I suspect Mr. Greg has been praising you and she finds it necessary to find

some fault. However, she looks as if she were capable of great prejudices. These narrow, natural people are.

His stringent comments on strangers, especially women, often use the same images in words that Edward Lear was using in line.

There are signs of awakening ambition. Greg and Wilson had praised his article on Money in *The Economist,*

> "*Four* columns of leader type. Everything was postponed to it, an article of Mr. Wilson's! ! !, one of Hutton's, no end of your sisters' literature" (the Wilson girls, especially Julia, wrote the literary notes in *The Economist* for many years). "Your father seemed to like it and Greg said, 'Better than any of your literary things, Bagehot', which is paying a compliment and spoiling it rather. I feel I should like to have more of a reputation about these subjects because you would like it. Of course, I should always have liked it but reputation is not my strongest temptation . . . I am afraid I covet 'power', influence over people's wills, faculties and conduct more than I can quite defend."

And when the collection of his early essays of *Estimates of some Englishmen and Scotchmen* was published, he wrote of the reviews:

> I am afraid I am callous, possibly proud, and do not care for mere general reputation . . . First rate fame, the fame of great productive artists, is a matter of ultimate certainty, but no other fame is. Posterity cannot take up little people, there are so many of them. *Reputation* must be acquired at the moment, and the circumstances of the moment are matters of accident.

Ambition with a keen desire to propitiate the gods of hubris.

But this slight defensiveness did not prevent him from sending on to Eliza with obvious pride a letter which Hutton had recently had from Matthew Arnold, now Professor of Poetry at Oxford, praising his essay on Shelley as of "the very first quality, showing not talent only, but a concern for the *simple truth* which is rare in English literature as it is in English politics and English religion". And when Eliza responded with her delight, he answered with a phrase which showed the direction which the new circumstances of his life, happiness, health and modest literary success, were giving to his conception of his own value.

> I am reading his (Arnold's) new tragedy which is clever, but too much "high art" and not addressed enough to the feelings and minds of ordinary people. I used to tell Clough he believed legibility to be a defect and I am sure the high art criticism and practice tend steadily in that direction. Possibly my essay being a trifle dull was the reason Mr. Arnold liked it.

The work in question, Arnold's *Merope,* was one of his least successful, but Bagehot's criticism of it is of a piece with his growing interest in the communication of ideas as much as ideas themselves, which in the end limited his value as literary critic and enhanced it as a political critic. Throughout his letters to Eliza before they were married (the only complete exchange of correspondence which Mrs. Barrington's hand has spared) there runs a current of awareness that he lacked the talent for abstraction and the highest ranges of criticism, that he could not subscribe to Arnold's desideratum in a critic as "disinterestedness". If he was to have a reputation, he must make up in acuteness of eye and ear what he lacked in voice.

Their notes flowed back and forth at intervals of a few days —it took no longer to send a letter from Somerset to Edinburgh than it does today—and their warmth increased with each exchange. Like all Victorian correspondence they contained an immense to do about practical arrangements, about trousseaux, bridesmaids, where to live, when to meet trains— railways had speeded up the tempo of life and the telephone had not yet come to simplify it. Walter interfered with vigor in all the wedding arrangements:

> I quite approve of your sisters having a dance after our wedding. They will be anxious to push you out as they cannot commence till you are gone, and I shall bear you away with the greater felicity. Don't you think you should go away from

the Church? You will never get up the hill without the donkey, which might look odd at the head of the bridesmaids . . .

By the interest and talk that are spent on your trousseau, you seem to be likely to have apparel now which will be enough till the end of your life. I approve of this as I shall *save* by it. Let me advise enduring materials (canvas, I am assured, wears well), at any rate, if that is not ladylike, which I am too ignorant to be sure of, something which will stand the wear and tear of life. It would be pitiable to be found in old age with only gossamer gowns (what is gossamer?) I must go to bed now as it is past one in the morning and I have to hunt.

There was no meanness in him but a great deal of frugality. (He never smoked, because he felt that he could not afford both cigars and books. In his youth at least, he was a tee-totaller.) One of the advantages of living in the West Country, he pointed out to Eliza, was that "You can do anything *there,* as a *gentleman* can wear very cheap clothes."

In the spring of 1858 Eliza returned from her medicinal banishment in Edinburgh. With the fall of Palmerston's government in February of that year, James Wilson's unremitting labor at the Treasury had come to an end and the whole family gathered at Claverton, with Walter as the *gamin* foil to the genteel routine of the six sisters. Games of cup and ball with all eyes concentrated in suspense on him to see whether he could screw his monocle into his short-sighted eye long enough to balance the thing, alternated with furious horsemanship, games of cards, and readings from Shelley and Jane Austen. The tendency of the mid-Victorians to mask love behind the language of camaraderie, to divert desire into a sort of teasing sister and brother relationship generally strikes a false note for their descendants. But in this one instance, the ecstatic portrait that both Bagehot and the Wilson sisters have painted of their communal affection had a foundation in reality. After his myopic gaucherie with other women, "the horrid little pink and blue girls", Bagehot's delight at being drawn into the Wilson family and away from the loneliness of a loyal only son, out of the provincial book-keeping at Stuckey's and into real life, induced a buoyancy in him which those, like Hutton, who had known him throughout his depressed and difficult twenties, found enchanting. To James Wilson, whose Tweedale passion for achievement had been fulfilled by almost every reward save a successor, this bright-eyed, febrile young man from the West Country, who took him seriously, who shared his political views, who listened to his advice, and, above all, who could write, as Greg and Hutton could not, was the perfect son-in-law, even though the idea of losing one of his six daughters made him take to his bed. They went off on expeditions by themselves and sat up talking half the night.* Though Eliza's five sisters all married, all stayed devoted to Walter and to his memory throughout long lifetimes—the last of them dying only some twenty years ago.

Eliza and Walter were married at Claverton on 21st April, 1858, with a friendly M.P. to propose the bride's health and a Hanoverian band to provide music for a *fête champêtre* in the evening. For a honeymoon they wandered around Devonshire partly by poste chaise, partly by train—the watershed between two eras of transport. Though Bagehot was now to work more and more in London with Wilson, he had dug in his toes against living in a London suburb; he had been horrified after meeting Fitzjames Stephen at dinner in Wimbledon to discover that he had to trek all the way to Bayswater that

* "What do you think your father and myself did the moment you were gone," Bagehot wrote to Eliza in Edinburgh, "We went to see the antiquities of Halicarnassus. They are a set of odd legs, arms and bodies of great statues just arrived, and alleviating our feelings very much. It happened in this way. We drove past the British Museum on our way home, and Mr. Wilson asked if I had seen the new reading room, and as I had not, he forthwith took me to see it. We were ushered in to old Panizzi ('the great librarian'), who was doing nothing in a fine armchair, and he proposed we should see the venerable fragments just arrived from Greece. I am not sure we appreciated them. I have an unfortunate prejudice in favour of statues in *one* piece, at least in not more than *six* pieces, and these are broken very small indeed, and it is a controversy whose arm belongs to whose body—but I believe real lovers of art admire these perplexities. On the whole, however, we spent our time cheerfully, and in consequence the Chancellor of the Exchequer and a heap of Scots bankers were kept half an hour waiting." *Love Letters.*

night. Moreover he still had heavy obligations to the bank and to his own family. So after much argument they compromised by settling at Clevedon, the watering place of Bristol, where Arthur Hallam had been buried and where "the Danube to the Severn gave, the darkened heart that beats no more". In that pleasant town where,

> *Twice a day the Severn fills;*
> *The salt sea water passes by,*
> *And hushes half the babbling Wye,*
> *And makes a silence in the hills.*

they rented a house called "The Arches" from Sir Arthur Elton, the contemporary member of that talented family which owned and had developed Clevedon.* From there he could straddle his interests at Langport, Bristol and London, for the age of the railway commuter had begun. Bagehot began it characteristically by plunging straight down through the pinewoods which surrounded the house to catch or miss his train by seconds while his more sedate neighbors got up earlier and went round by the road.

IV

For the first two years this pleasant triangular life continued. Eliza was taken to Langport to do her "sitting up"—the ancient custom of exposing a bride to the scrutiny of the bridegroom's relatives and acquaintances at an endless At Home, which still survived in the West Country and was considered there almost as important as the service in church—and then they settled down by themselves. Walter was to all intents and purposes in full charge of the Bristol branch of Stuckey's bank, which was one of its largest, and for a while

---

* His father, Sir Charles Elton, was a friend of Wordsworth and Coleridge and a good poet himself. His sister, Mrs. Brookfield, was supposed to have been the original of Amelia Sedley. His son Sir Edmund, the eighth baronet, was a famous potter and the rival of William de Morgan.

he was too busy for serious writing. Business took him regularly to Langport, as much to keep an eye on his mother as on finance, for, in Mrs. Barrington's good phrase, "he never let her wander out alone into the desert of her aberrations" and her brilliant, racy conversation when her mind was clear gave a fillip to his own. She appears to have taken to Eliza and her only obvious eccentricity for a while was to insist on chanting the Psalms to the butler as he cleared breakfast away in order to ensure that he got some bible reading each day. Eliza bowed to her father-in-law's Unitarian principles, though Mrs. Bagehot never had, and went to Mr. Bagehot's Sunday service in the drawing room. Froude and Kinglake were near neighbors to Clevedon, and Hutton and Clough came to stay, while Bagehot lived in a storm of writing, reading aloud, hunting, playing billiards and catching trains.

But London exerted a stronger and stronger pull. The Wilsons had a house in Upper Belgrave Street (his father-in-law must by now have been tolerably rich, for he returned home one day having bought two Wilsons and a Turner), and the Bagehots began to migrate there regularly. It was then that Bagehot began to meet the political and literary figures whom he had hitherto judged only from a distance, in particular Matthew Arnold and Thackeray (who was a neighbor and close friend of Wilson's), Gladstone and Granville.

It was a good moment to have arrived upon the political scene, for complete confusion reigned. The long entracte in party politics, which had begun with the fall of Peel, was dissolving into chaos, for neither Derby nor Palmerston could rule the nation effectively and neither would give way to those who thought they could. British politics have never come closer to the British idea of what French politics are like, and as Disraeli wrote: "The House of Commons is broken into sections which, although they have no unity or purpose, can always combine to overthrow the Queen's Government however formed." Palmerston, the leader of the opposition, was closer to Derby, the Prime Minister, on most questions except foreign policy, than to Bright and the Liberals. Russell, grown

more Whiggish than ever in his old age, was on bad terms with
Palmerston, and the Whig-Liberal business men like James
Wilson who knew the temper of Manchester and the City felt
discouraged by their growing exclusion from the higher councils of the party. With Gladstone absent in the Ionian islands,
the Peelites remained uncertain of their ultimate political
allegiance.

Bright and the Liberals hammered away at the necessity for
a further instalment of parliamentary reform, and by the
beginning of 1859 Disraeli, Derby's Chancellor of the Exchequer, had become convinced that the only way the government could regain any political momentum would be to
introduce a new reform bill of its own. There was fairly general
agreement that the borough franchise—the ten pounds householder defined by the 1832 Act—was now too exclusive, and
that a formula was desirable which included at least some of
the working class. At the one end of the scale Bright was for
enfranchising all ratepayers. At the other, the Derbyites feared
that any tinkering with the franchise would lead inevitably to
the breakdown of all limitations and to the invasion of manhood or household suffrage and that dreaded force, "American
democracy".

Consequently, Bagehot's article "Parliamentary Reform", in
the *National* of January, 1859 was opportunely timed and
attracted considerable attention. He was no democrat in the
contemporary meaning of the word, no believer in abstract
political rights; the American democratic suffrage produced,
he believed, merely a vulgar and uninformed legislature. "The
true principle is, that every person has a right to *so much
political power as he can exercise without impeding any other
person who would more fitly exercise such power.*" (His italics.)
What was needed was not the overthrow of the rule of the
educated classes but to make that rule more sensitive. The
1832 Act had been a success but the landed interest was still
over represented, and the growing urban and industrial communities carried too little weight. It was true, he pointed out,
that the contemporary House of Commons coincided fairly

closely with educated and intelligent opinion. But that was not sufficient. For the House had two functions: the *ruling* function which it discharged well enough, and the older *expressive* function. "In every free country it is of the utmost importance—and, in the long run, a pressing necessity—that all opinions extensively entertained, all sentiments widely diffused should be *stated* publicly before the nation . . . The diffused multitude of moderate men, whose opinions, taken in the aggregate, form public opinion, are just as likely to be tyrannical towards what they do not realise, inapprehensive of what is not argued out, thoughtless of what is not brought before them, as any other class can be . . . A free government is the most stubbornly stupid of all governments to whatever is *unheard* by its deciding classes."

This threw him back on the dilemma which haunted liberal and moderate men in the fifties and sixties, before Disraeli's "leap in the dark" took the problem out of their hands; how to enable the voice of the working class to be heard more effectively without admitting it to a share of government, by devising a franchise which would include a large working class element without accepting "the rule of mere numbers". A great deal of thought was being devoted to special franchises, to the six pounds, to the five pounds householder, to plural constituencies and so on, and Mill, simultaneously with Bagehot, produced his own remedy, a universal franchise with additional votes for the middle and upper classes on a scale determined by their educational qualification. Bagehot opposed all forms of "fancy franchise", just as he later opposed Mill's advocacy of "Mr. Hare's scheme" for proportional representation. His remedy was a straightforward and arbitrary one: to maintain the influence of the educated classes by retaining the existing ten pounds qualification in general, but to make the working class influence felt by enfranchising all ratepayers in the larger towns that had a high industrial population.

Bagehot's proposals brought him into the center of Liberal politics. Gladstone, who had just returned from Greece and was short of ideas for the coming debate on the Tory bill, was delighted, and the beginning of Bagehot's long friendship with him dated from that spring. On this particular question Bagehot's views were at that time more advanced than Gladstone's, for though both wished to see the educated classes keep their political predominance, Bagehot wished to see the remaining closed boroughs abolished while Gladstone defended them as "nurseries of statesmen", a view which Bagehot in his essay "The History of the Unreformed Parliament" (1860) showed was historical nonsense. Thackeray was an enthusiast for Bagehot's idea and described it as "wonderfully clever". Robert Lowe, who became Gladstone's first Chancellor of the Exchequer in 1868, expressed to him fears that lowering the franchise in some place would "serve as a lever for it obtaining it all", doubts which eventually led him to organise the Whig revolt against the second Reform Bill from the Cave of Adullam.*

When the Conservative's Reform Bill, which included Bagehot's central idea for redistributing seats to the growing towns but also proposed a number of "fancy franchises" for the upper working class, came before the House in March, 1859 Palmerston and Russell quite cynically joined forces to defeat it and the government. At the ensuing general election James Wilson was returned for Devonport and became Vice-President of the Board of Trade in Palmerston's second and last government.

But the pattern of Bagehot's life was transformed when, two months later, Wilson was asked to go out to India for five years, to the new post of Finance Member of the Viceroy's council to grapple with the economic chaos that had resulted from the Indian Mutiny. In October, 1859 he sailed with his wife and some of the children to do for Britain's economic administration of India what Macaulay had done for its law and education twenty years before. But within a year he was dead.

* Catherine Gladstone with the characteristic scattiness of the Glynnes and the Lytteltons always referred to Lowe's followers as "The Dolomites". Georgina Battiscombe, *Mrs. Gladstone* (London: Constable, 1956), p. 138.

V

Bagehot had a great affection for his father-in-law, a great respect for the way in which he made himself a central figure in English public life. When he died of dysentery and the effects of the Calcutta heat at the age of only fifty-five, he wrote a long biographical sketch of James Wilson which he issued as a special supplement to *The Economist.*

> Mr. Wilson's predominating power was what may be called a business imagination. He had a great power of conceiving transactions. Political economy was to him the science of buying and selling, and of the ordinary bargains of men he had a very steady and distinct conception. In explaining such subjects he did not begin, as political economists have wittily been said to do, with "Suppose a man upon an island" but "What they do in the city is this" . . . The *practical* value of the science of political economy (the observation is an old one as to *all* sciences) lies in its "middle principles". The extreme abstractions from which such intermediate maxims are scientifically deduced lie at some distance from ordinary experience, and are not easily made intelligible to most persons . . . The business-like method and vigorous simplicity of Mr. Wilson's arguments converted very many ordinary men of business, who would have distrusted any theoretical and abstruse disquisition, and would not have appreciated any elaborate refinements.

Bagehot's portrait of Wilson, its outlines necessarily softened by affection and by the circumstances in which it was written, was the fourth in a chain of biographical studies which he wrote at odd intervals from 1856 onwards. The objects of his study, Peel and Pitt, Brougham and Bolingbroke, Guizot and Gladstone, were a diverse and seemingly haphazard choice, but they all attracted him for the same reason—that they were men of mind and brain who had been called either by circumstances or ambition to apply them in the service of politics. The man of action pure and simple did not interest him (he had none of Carlyle's preoccupation with the hero) nor did the man of ideas or principle who had never been forced to submit them to the test of responsible action: he was scornful of Fox, and never attempted more than passing judgments on Burke. It was mind in action, the pressure of political circumstance upon political principle, that fascinated him.

Moreover, his studies in political biography had a more urgent purpose than his literary essays: the latter were recreation: the former were one aspect of his search for the kind of man, the type of political character, which could rule both wisely and effectively in modern England. A permanent succession of Chathams was both unthinkable and undesirable: but the direction of modern Britain could not be left to chance, to a Spencer Perceval, a Goderich or even a John Russell. What were the qualities required for ruling this strong yet sluggish country with its complex administration and its growing complexity of interests?

The first of his biographical studies, on Sir Robert Peel, which he wrote in 1856 when he was just thirty, is the most interesting of them all, not so much for its appraisal of Peel himself, as of the standards by which a Prime Minister must be judged.

"A constitutional statesman" he begins "is in general a man of common opinions and uncommon abilities." Just as the most successful newspaper is that which pitches its arguments only a fraction ahead of the minds of its readers, "so the most influential of constitutional statesmen is the one who most felicitously expresses the creed of the moment, who administers it, embodies it in law and institutions, who give it the highest life it is capable of". It is a sad but unescapable fact that, except at a time of crisis, a politician must sacrifice originality if he wishes to retain influence. Look at Peel, he says:

> No man has come so near our definition of a constitutional statesman—the power of a first-rate man and the creed of a second-rate man. From a certain peculiarity of intellect and fortune, he was never in advance of his time. Of almost all the great measures with which his name is associated, he attained great eminence as an opponent before he attained even greater

eminence as their advocate . . . As long as these questions
(Currency reform, Catholic Emancipation and the Corn Laws)
remained the property of first class intellects, as long as they
were confined to philanthropists or speculators, as long as they
were only advocated by austere, intangible Whigs, Sir Robert
Peel was against them. So soon as these same measures, by the
progress of time, the striving of understanding, the conversion
of receptive minds, became the property of second class intellects, Sir Robert Peel became possessed of them also. He was
converted at the conversion of the average man.

He was a great administrator, says Bagehot, and a great
debater, in the sense which constitutional government requires, not a profound orator but a man who can make the
most reasoned case for a policy—"a specious orator".

If we picture in our minds a nature at once active and facile,
easily acquiring its opinions from without, not easily devising
them from within, a large placid adaptive intellect, devoid of
irritable intense originality, prone to forget the ideas of yesterday, inclined to accept the ideas of today—if we imagine a
man so formed cast early into absorbing, exhausting industry
of detail, with work enough to fill up a life, with action of
itself enough to render speculation almost impossible—placed
too in a position unsuited to abstract thought, of which the
conventions and rules require that a man should feign other
men's thoughts, should impugn his own opinion—we shall
begin to imagine a conscientious man destitute of conviction
on the occupations of his life—to comprehend the character of
Sir Robert Peel.

It is a cold judgment, as cold as Peel's personality, reminis-
cent, like many of Bagehot's political judgments, of a schoolboy impaling moth specimens. He says nothing of the lonely
agony through which Peel passed in applying his "large adaptive intellect"; or of the odium he faced so gallantly, of his
blanched face, when on the announcement of Repeal his own
back benchers bayed him with all the cruelty of their kind;
or of the hush of sorrow that spread among the common
people when he lay dying. But as an analysis of the source of

his power, and that of many of his successors, it has rarely been bettered.

For his next subject he took the very opposite of Peel, *Henry Brougham* (1857), the professional man of opposition. It is less revealing, for Brougham's career had been spent so much in the open that there was little to reveal, and it is really an analysis of the qualities necessary for a successful agitator—"an eager principle of disinterested action", quickness, versatility, strong nerves, and a certain prickly quality. "If he were a horse, nobody would buy him: with that eye, no one could answer for his temper."* In one of his best sallies he describes why Brougham, despite his tireless speech-making, both in opposition in the House and elsewhere, was never a great orator. Oratory requires an exercise of the imagination which in turn requires a capacity to stay still. "He who runs may *read,* but it does not seem likely he will think."

Bagehot quotes the opening lines of Tennyson's *Godiva* to show how a poet could transmute a miserable train connection into a work of art:

> *I waited for the train at Coventry;*
> *I hung with grooms and porters on the bridge*
> *To watch the three tall spires; and there I shaped*
> *The City's legend into this.*

But

> Lord Brougham would not have waited so. He would have rushed up into the town; he would have suggested an improvement, talked the science of the bridge, explained its history to the natives. The quiet race would think twenty people had been there. And, of course, in some ways this is admirable; such life and force are rare; even the "grooms and porters" would not be insensible to such an aggressive intelligence—so much *knocking* mind. But, in the meantime, no lightly touched picture of an old story would have arisen in his mind.

* He had an unprincipled habit of using his own *bon mots* again in quotations attributed to an anonymous source. In his obituary of Brougham in 1868, he quotes this phrase with "someone is reported to have said" after it.

Bagehot had an excellent way of going off at a tangent to make his point.

The finest of his biographical studies, the most balanced and yet vivid, is that on *William Pitt* (1861). In it he shows a rare gift for narrative, for arranging facts and events to make them tell their own story. Compared to Lord Stanhope's *Life,* of which this essay was ostensibly a review, it has a fine sense both of pace and of sympathy. After a long neglect the mid-Victorians were beginning to look back upon the eighteenth century with appreciation, just as the last of its children, Palmerston, Crabb Robinson, Dr. Routh, were disappearing from the scene. For him, Pitt "had in the most complete perfection the faculties of a great administrator" and "added to it the commanding temperament, though not the creative intellect of a great dictator".

> The first qualification of the highest administrator, is that he should think of something he need not think of—of something which is not the pressing difficulty of the hour. For inferior men no rule could be so dangerous. Ambitious mediocrity is dangerous mediocrity: ordinary men find what they must do amply enough for them to do: the exacting difficulty of the hour, which will not be stayed, which must be met, absorbs their whole time and all their energies. But the ideal administrator has time, has mind—for that is the difficulty—for something more: he can do what he must, and he will do what he wishes. This is Mr. Pitt's peculiarity among the great English statesmen of the eighteenth century . . . It is the distinctive characteristic of Pitt that, having a great opportunity, having power such as no parliamentary statesman has ever had, having in his mind a fresh stock of youthful thought such as no similar statesman has ever possessed—he applied *that* power steadily and perseveringly to embody that thought.

And he compares him to Burke whose vision was far wider.

> But in the mind of Burke ideas were a supernatural burden, a superincumbent inspiration. He saw a great truth and he saw nothing else.

Bolingbroke as a Statesman (1863) is a study of the causes of political failure. Bagehot was not interested in the author of the *Patriot King*, dawdling "on at the coffee houses far into George II's time, a monument of extinct profligacy, and a spectacle and wonder to a graver generation", but in the intriguing, brilliant politician of the three last years of Queen Ann.

> We see in Bolingbroke's case that a life of brilliant license is really compatible with a life of brilliant statesmanship; that license itself may even be thought to quicken the imagination for oratorical effects . . . but on the other hand, that these secondary aids and occasional advantages are purchased by the total sacrifice of primary necessity; . . . that he will not observe how few and plain are the alternatives of common business, and how little even genius can enlarge them.

It is a grave beginning to a racy account of the involved politics of the early eighteenth century, in which even Bagehot himself gets somewhat lost. But through it all one of Bagehot's central themes repeats itself—the contrast between the prosaic material out of which a political reputation is made and the brilliant and erratic men whom politics attracts.

Throughout the rest of his life Bagehot wrote short biographical sketches, some in the form of obituaries, but it was only at the end that he returned to the full length essay in his studies of Adam Smith and Lord Althorp. The latter, written in 1877, is largely taken up with his sombre reflections on the political dangers of extending the franchise, but includes a delightful description of Althorp himself, the cheerful, imperturbable rustic nobleman who was Chancellor and leader of the House of Commons in the Whig Cabinet that passed the great Reform Bill, and who, as soon as the government fell, went off to oil his fowling pieces which had rusted in office.

> He embodies all the characteristic virtues which enable Englishmen to effect well and easily great changes in politics; their essential fairness, their "large roundabout common sense",

their courage, and their disposition to give up something rather than to take the uttermost farthing. But on the other hand also behind all the characteristic English defects: their want of intellectual and guiding principle, their even completer want of the culture that would give that principle, their absorption in the present difficulty, and their hand-to-mouth readiness to take what solves it without thinking of other consequences. And I am afraid the moral of these times is that these English qualities as a whole—merits and defects together—are better suited to an early age of politics than to a later.

In the mood of doubt about the political equilibrium of England which grew on him in his later years, even his favorite kind of open air, commonsense man of experience failed to satisfy him, just as the ambitious intellectual had failed him earlier.

"Every generation," he wrote in a criticism of Matthew Arnold's views on education, "is unjust to the preceding generation: it respects its distant ancestors, but thinks its fathers were 'quite wrong'." But most of Bagehot's judgments about the figures of his own immediate past either in the longer studies or in *The Economist's* obituaries and leaders have withstood the revision of those to whom they are in fact ancestors. It is not only the aphorisms: of Cobden that he was a "sensitive agitator"; of Swift that he "was a detective in a dean's wig"; of Adam Smith that he possessed "intolerant commonsense"; or of Palmerston's ordinariness, which made him intelligible, "he was not a common man but a common man might have been cut out of him". Or of Sidney Smith who

was a "molar". He did not run a long sharp argument into the interior of a question; he did not, in the common phrase, go deeply into it; but he kept it steadily under the contact of a strong, capable, jaw-like understanding—pressing its surface, effacing its intricacies, grinding it down.

His finished sketches hold fast as much by their accuracy as by their vividness: when John Lawrence, one of the most energetic but limited Viceroys, was made a peer, he wrote in *The Economist* that he took to the work of governing Asiatics in the same spirit and using the same powers as a self-made engineer or contractor, a Brindley or Brassey, employs in some great material undertaking. Throughout his life till he became Viceroy he was always engaged in reducing something or somebody to order, compelling men and things to work in the groove in which they could be of most use to the common weal as he judged the common weal to be. Now the obstacle was a mountain to be bored, and then a swamp to be filled up; here was a province choked with nobles to be tamed; there was a great city to be rescued from anarchy; now there were mountaineers to be bridled, and again there were mutineers to be pulverised; but whatever it was the work was always done . . . There was a great foresight in the Viceroy and great incisiveness of vision, but he wanted the aristrocratic quality—a certain largeness of field, and the quality of the highest genius for government, that of evolving new power . . . He quits India without having rendered it less necessary to use white troops to watch dark troops, or more possible to allow the native army to use breech loading rifles . . . He is a Nasmyth hammer which can chip an egg or flatten an iron bar, but only within its groove.

Or more succinctly of Macaulay as a politician,

he was admirable in his treatment of a well understood crisis, involving old, dear, and well discussed principles, on which conflict ran high. But he had not that quick and ready appreciation of transient symptoms—that half instinctive, half empirical tact, which is needed in the constitution of a party leader or a great statesman.

He never found his ideal statesman to lead the new age of mass societies, but in the search he illumined the portraits of many lesser figures.

Chapter 6

DASH AND DOUBT

"There is as much variety of pluck in writing across a
sheet as in riding across a country."
The First Edinburgh Reviewers

JAMES WILSON'S death at Calcutta in August, 1860 turned
Bagehot into a professional journalist. He was Wilson's
executor and the only reliable son-in-law he possessed at
that time. All the family problems descended on his head at
once. Mrs. Wilson and the girls had to be brought back from
India and settled down; Wilson's estate had to be looked after;
and above all *The Economist* had to be directed. Wilson had
left him in general charge of it when he went to India with
Hutton as Editor, but Hutton had none of Bagehot's training
in finance and was ill at ease on the paper.* A year later, in
1861, he left it to revitalise the moribund *Spectator* which became in the end his life's work. Bagehot gave up writing for the
Saturday Review and inserted into his essay on Gladstone a
parting shot at its stodgy and remote conservatism. Four years
later he wound up the insolvent *National Review* after failing
to find a satisfactory editor, and henceforth all his energy as a
journalist was concentrated on *The Economist.*

He gave up his directorship of the Bristol Branch of
Stuckey's in exchange for a less onerous one in the London
branch, and he and Eliza migrated from Clevedon with its

---

* "My friend Bagehot has undertaken a sort of general supervision of *The
Economist* and Hutton remains Editor under him. Will you kindly allow
Bagehot to call upon you occassionally?" Wilson to Sir G. C. Lewis: October
19th, 1859.

Walter Bagehot is generally described as the Second Editor of *The
Economist* in succession to Wilson. This is essentially correct for though
Greg put the paper together for Wilson during the latter's spells in office,
and though Hutton bore the nominal title of Editor, from 1858 to 1861,
the full responsibility for both policy and management never left Wilson's
hands during his life time and then passed direct to Bagehot.

pines and sea winds to the Wilsons' house in the former snipe
bog of Upper Belgrave Street. The change was not of his
making nor greatly to his liking. He was not ambitious in any
conventional social sense. He loved good conversation especially at breakfast, but ordinary London life, which the Wilson
sisters enjoyed, bored and intimidated him. "At London din-
ners you talk nothing: between two pillars of crinoline, you eat
and are resigned." He wrote to one of his sisters-in-law: "It
is inconceivable to me to like to see many people and even to
speak to them. Every new person you know is an intellectual
burden, because you may see them again, and must be able
to recognise and willing to converse with them." His eyes
were also beginning to give him trouble in another direction,
and Eliza was writing of their search "for a quick boy to come
and write his dictation in the evening". Of his own inclination,
he would probably have preferred to continue his free-lance
career with its mixture of interests, with the perpetual wrestle
with Bradshaw that it involved, but also with the chance of a
day's shooting or hunting as well.

But his duty to the Wilson family was paramount and
Wilson's principal legacy must be his prime concern. James
Wilson had become not only his father-in-law but an intimate
friend as well, and he had confided every detail of his affairs
to Bagehot when he went to India. He had kept *The Economist* closely informed about his views on India, about his insistence on imposing direct taxation on the British model to
repair the enormous post-Mutiny deficit, and on the sharp,
victorious clash with Sir Charles Trevelyan, (grandfather of
the historian) the Governor of Madras, which it had produced.*

Bagehot was so loyal to his family obligations that when he
was privately sounded by the government on his willingness to
succeed Wilson as Finance Member for India, he unhesitat-

* A month before his death he sent Bagehot a letter of stern parental
reproof for having jeopardised the anonymity of *The Economist's* Indian
correspondent, who was on Wilson's staff, by printing his initials after his
dispatch, thus laying Wilson open to the charge that he was using *The
Economist* to further his own policies.

ingly refused. It was a heady offer, for the post carried enormous power in India and would have led on to a public career at home. He was only thirty-three and still unknown outside a small circle of politicians and writers. It would have set him in the center of the public eye, which, at that stage of his life at least, he would probably have disliked and would have landed him in the midst of a sea of administrative troubles which he was probably too delicate to grapple with. He would have worked in harmony with Canning though not perhaps with John Lawrence, and how well his ironic mind and gentle sarcasm would have been received in the Anglo-Indian world of "The Competition Wallah" may be doubted. In any case he appears hardly to have given the offer a second thought.

The position of political influence in London which he developed for himself throughout the sixties arose as much from his personality as his office, for *The Economist* was still a relatively small and specialized paper. During his Editorship it is doubtful if its circulation reached much more than 3,000 a week, one-twentieth of its present size (though it is a tribute to its international outlook and influence that it had then almost the same proportion of foreign to domestic circulation as it has today). It is difficult to tell at this distance precisely what kind of people read it. Certainly Ministers read the political and economic articles then as they do today, and it was widely read in the European governments. To the City, the bankers, the Stock Exchange, the traders, it was indispensable, not only for its judgments and general information but for its statistics. In industry it was read much less than today, in the universities hardly at all. The great expansion of its influence and circulation has taken place chiefly in the last quarter century—in the Editorships of Walter Layton and Geoffrey Crowther—through the remorseless demonstration of events that there is an interlocking relationship between economics and politics, and from the rekindling of Bagehot's style and original approach to both.

Bagehot himself had few illusions about its general influence. In a memorandum, written for the benefit of the family in 1873, he insisted that it was primarily a specialized paper. "The politics of the paper must be viewed mainly with reference to the tastes of men of business. It is among them and among them only that *The Economist* will ever circulate." Bagehot's phrase "man of business" embraces a rather wider category, however, than the modern word "businessman." Though it primarily meant those engaged in trade and finance, he often used it to cover all those seriously interested in "affairs" in the literal sense, in getting things done, as opposed either to dabblers or to academic theorists. Similarly an "economist" and by definition a reader of *The Economist* did not mean a man trained in a recognized branch of academic science like a physicist, but one whose philosophical method in any field, the money market, sanitation or whether Bacon wrote Shakespeare, was to test theory against facts and calculations.

Not only in the size of its circulation but in the size of its staff it was a very different paper from today. Instead of the scores of grave and industrious young male and female B.A.'s (Oxon.) and B.Scs. Econ. (Lon.) who now impart to its large offices off St. James's Street the air of an alternative government, it was produced by Bagehot himself with the help of a part-time statistican and a few clerks. Herbert Spencer had been James Wilson's assistant from 1846 to 1853 in return for one hundred pounds a year, a room on the premises at 340 Strand (where the Gaiety Theatre later stood) and a right to the paper's free theatre tickets. He wrote *Social Statics* from there in the intervals of what he considered to be very light duties. W. R. Greg, from whose observations and correspondence it is clear that he felt that he ought to have had the Editorship after Wilson's death, had lent a hand as an old family friend during Wilson's periods in office (though Wilson supervised the paper and fed it information from the Treasury to a much greater extent than would be considered proper nowadays). Nassau Senior had also written leaders on foreign policy for Wilson but gave up shortly after his death.* For the first eight years of Bagehot's editorship, as long as his health permitted, he kept the reins firmly in his own hands, and wrote the two main articles and much else beside.

Periodical journalism was in those days a much more specialized craft than today, except in the Quarterlies which accepted what were really short books from statesmen and professors. The journalist-don, the retired ambassador and "the expert" had not made their appearance in Fleet Street, and Bagehot throughout his lifetime, and Hutton at *The Spectator* till the end of the century, accepted few outside contributions. But one secret of *The Economist's* success was that Wilson had created and Bagehot maintained a network of reliable provincial, European and American correspondents who kept it supplied with accurate commercial and general news. As he remarked in the *English Constitution* "the great commercial houses in England are the most natural and most effectual conveyors of intelligence from other countries to Europe" and the fact that *The Economist* was on good terms with the City gave it a great advantage in news-gathering. As the late Sir John Clapham pointed out, *The Economist* has been neglected, just as *The Times* has been overworked, as a general guide to the tenor of opinion in mid-Victorian England. Wilson, Nassau Senior, Greg and Bagehot had access to very good sources of political information, both at home

* In his review of Senior's *Journals,* Bagehot painted a clear cruel minia-
ture of the journalist bore. "As years went on, it used to be said that the
value of his journal was impaired, because persons of eminence prepared
for their interviews, and corrected (as he was kind enough to let them)
their sayings into what they would wish to have said rather than what
they did really say. The conversations thus became minor manifestoes, not
unguarded utterances, and lost their greatest interest.

"And independently of having to ask as a habit questions too direct to
be pleasant, most people would rather go to the galleys than be bound
to put down at the end of a party what was said in the course of it. The
pang of the coming task would poison most men's pleasures. And Mr.
Senior often looked as if it spoiled his pleasure. His face had a care down
it, as if he were keeping up the recollection of what *had* been said, rather
than enjoying what was *being* said." (*Fortnightly Review,* August, 1871.)
There are several well-known contemporary British and American journalists who might shudder at this sketch.

and abroad, and though they evaluated it from a Liberal stand-point, their treatment of news was much more dispassionate than that of, say, *The Times* under Delane.

Bagehot's position of Manager and Editor of the paper was a strange one, for the proprietors to whom he was responsible were his own wife and his five sisters-in-law. As one of the trustees of Wilson's estate, he could acquire no interest in it, and he was paid a salary of four hundred pounds a year, space rates for his contributions and half the profits above two thousand pounds a year. The paper, after a prosperous start, went through the financial doldrums in the late sixties (when the money market "was so motionless, that there was nothing to tell the public about it"), and the average reward of the immense energies which Bagehot put into the paper was, by his own reckoning, seven hundred and eighty pounds a year.

But the fact that both he and Wilson had sources of inde-pendent income and did not have to milk it for a large profit, was one of the foundation stones of *The Economist's* tradi-tion of independence, not only politically, but—what was harder to maintain—in commenting on finance and business. London was full of commercial and financial sheets, prepared to puff an issue or a company for a price. Early in the paper's history Wilson had published a warning to speculators that *The Economist* would give them no advice.

> "In all discussions in *The Economist*," wrote Bagehot to his sisters-in-law in 1873, 'it must be remembered that the main part of its reputation (and therefore its income) depends on its supposed *honesty*. I have been told that it was 'the only finan-cial journal in Europe which had not a shop behind it', and this is a reason why its management must never be left to a salaried Editor. Such a person will in speculative times be very likely to establish a 'shop' which might easily at such moments be made very much more profitable than the Editorship of the paper. But the effect would be the ruin of the paper."

The fact that *The Economist* clearly has not, and has never had, a "shop" behind it, and that its honesty has become, over three generations, not a supposition but an unquestioned assumption of the world, shows how strong was the tradition of independence that he fostered. His line of successors, from Inglis Palgrave and Daniel Lathbury to Donald Tyerman and Roland Bird, have long falsified his fears about the integrity of a salaried editor.

It was one aspect of the very close understanding that existed between Wilson and Bagehot that the latter built upon but did not alter the structure of the paper. When the emphasis on Anti-Corn Law propaganda was reduced as Repeal became an eventual certainty in 1844, Wilson had revised the prospectus. This set as his goal a paper that would discuss political and general as well as economic questions, coupled with accurate commercial reporting, and allied to a strong statistical section which would enable economic views to be tested weekly against fact. Being written for the pioneers of the new Renaissance, books and theater reviews were naturally included, together with a great deal of miscellaneous information and comment on the law, parliament, the Court and social events. It was this balancing of general comment and economic fact which accounted for its rapid success and the immediate praise it won from men like Frederic Bastiat, the great French economist, who wrote in 1845: "There never was a periodical work in which all the questions of political economy were treated with so much depth and impartiality."

Though Bagehot humanized and enlivened the political content, he did not try to convert *The Economist* into an ordinary review nor broaden the general aspect of the paper at the expense of its central core of economic fact. He expanded the statistics and added a Banking Supplement, a Budget Supplement, an annual Commercial History and an index of wholesale prices. He retained the services of William Newmarch who was the manager of Glyn Mills and the best statistician of his day, and then took in Robert Giffen who later became a famous practitioner of that dry art. Hasty and inaccurate as he was in the minutiae of ordinary writing— misquoting authorities, mis-spelling names, like a brilliant schoolboy with a good essay to finish but longing for the fresh air—Bagehot's unique "quantitative" sense and what Giffen called "his knowledge and feeling of the 'how much' in dealing with the complex workings of economic tendencies", made him pay close attention to figures. Much as he hated the detail, for close columns of figures were agony to his bad eyesight, he had a flair for statistics, for seeing whether a particular table told a story, or for detecting a hidden flaw in the basis of an arithmetically accurate calculation.

> . . . one of the difficulties he had to contend with in life, was a repugnance to minute detail, including an aversion to manipulate figures, all but amounting to inability to "add up". The petty detail which most people find easy enough was beyond measure irksome to him; and the irksomeness was aggravated, when I knew him, by weak eyesight. But columns of figures are not statistics, though they are the raw material of statisticians; and this Bagehot fully proved by his remarkable appreciation of the numerical element in economic problems, all the while he had these technical difficulties in his way. In this quality he was second to no statistician I have ever met, and infinitely superior to most. Though it is a less material point, I should like to add, for the sake of bringing out the true meaning and value of statistics, that irksome as the detail of figures was to him, and naturally also the detail of constructing statistical tables, he was a singularly good judge and critic of such tables and the results they brought out. He knew what tables could be made to say, and the value of simplicity in their construction. He had an intense dislike for that vice of almost all amateur statisticians, and not a few experts, the attempt to put too much into their tables.*

II

But facts, however ably and accurately presented, do not make the reputation of a paper. What Bagehot brought to *The Economist* as well as style and humanity, was an open mind, a certain tentativeness about conclusions. Wilson had lived too striving a life, doing battle for his business, for his

* Sir Robert Giffen, "Bagehot as an Economist", *The Fortnightly*, April, 1880.

class and for his principles, not only against Tories but against his Whig colleagues, to have much tolerance for ideas other than his own. Bagehot by contrast was a subtler blend of the twin strains in the English political heredity, of Cavalier and Puritan, Anglican and Dissenter, Conservative and Liberal— of Edith Stuckey and Thomas Bagehot for that matter. The bent of his life and his conscience, his interest in science and in business, the bank, London, Bristol, made him a Liberal. But unlike Hutton or Greg or Wilson, he had lived much of his life in the deep countryside, in an old and pleasure-loving society, and he had a keen instinct for the irrational forces which bound England together. When his friends and colleagues could feel a strong sense of middle class, urban solidarity, and damn dukes and squires and rectors and business men for their obscurities and resistance to change, he could not. The squires and the business men might well have a sounder ear for public opinion, a closer instinctive affinity for the real aspirations of the country than the intellectual Liberals.

Knowing that he was, as he said, "between sizes in politics", he did not try to reconcile his own inner conflict by exorcising one part of his own nature. He remained to the end of his life a conservative Liberal, a member of what he called the Left Center which "will neither drive so slow as to miss the train, or so fast as to meet with an accident", which "wants to introduce tested innovations when the average man begins to comprehend them, and not before; and to introduce them in a shape in which he comprehends them, and not in any other I hope". It was the job of the Liberal to propound the new ideas, of the Conservative to resist them until, and no longer, they had been thoroughly understood and assimilated.

This ability to feel the force of both sides of the argument could have made him an indecisive editor, or have reduced *The Economist* to a dull impartiality. But here a fortunate conjunction of the times, the paper, and his own interests came to his aid. After the fifties, "the age of equipoise", in Professor W. L. Burn's phrase, the country was stirring with

new ideas and tensions. The paper had built up a reputation
for its factual treatment of the questions of the day. He himself enjoyed the exploration of the sociological and political
landscape rather than advocating a particular policy or principle.

Hutton said that:

> Bagehot's great characteristic as a writer, whether on eco-
> nomic or literary subjects, was a very curious combination of
> *dash and doubt;* great vivacity in describing the superficial im-
> pressions produced on him by every subject-matter with which
> he was dealing, and great caution in yielding his mind to that
> superficial impression.

He knew he was not a radical; he did not believe in an
equalitarian society. He believed rather in what he called "the
system of *removable inequalities,* where many people are inferior to and worse off than others, but in which each may
in theory, hope to be on a level with the highest below the
throne, and in which each may reasonably, and without
sanguine impracticability, hope to gain one step in social
elevation" despite the snobbery which such a system necessarily
induced. He was too deeply aware of the tangled and matted
roots of English society to have faith in any one nostrum.
What he demanded was a grand and continuous inquest on
the right avenues and methods of social advance.

The Whig-Liberal government which came to power at almost the same time as he came to *The Economist,* had plenty
of political strength but it lacked anything like an agreed
legislative program. "The age of Repeal," he wrote in 1861
at the end of his first year in control of the paper, "has nearly
closed: the age of legislative construction has to begin." But
what legislation? Political reform: land reform: church reform?
What did the new power of the trades union imply, what did
the new limited liability companies portend? What was to
happen to education? The following spring he expressed, not
only this sense of questioning but the growing concern with
the future of the British community in a world of other

rapidly expanding communities which distinguished the Liberalism of the sixties and seventies from that of the earlier
years.

> . . . Before the next step can be taken safely in political reform,
> it is indistinctly felt that a considerable study of the structure
> of English society will be desirable and needful,—that the vari-
> ous classes now widely separated from each other, and living
> under very distinct conditions of life, will have to learn to
> understand better each others' peculiar talents, merits, and
> defects. The lull in home-politics is the more remarkable when
> the interest of England is increasing so rapidly in the genuine
> political movements of foreign nations. Abroad we see nation
> after nation entering on just that stage of our career which we
> have left behind us, and we watch them with a far more eager
> interest than England has ever before felt in the internal
> politics of other nations. But the stage which we have passed,
> and on which Italy and Germany are entering, is the entrance
> of the large middle class into the political organisation of
> the nation. The importance of this step we know. We know
> that in some sense it may be said to date the real origin of all
> distinctly national feeling, for the full development of which,
> neither monarchies nor aristocracies are at all adequate. But
> for the second step which we hesitate to make,—which it is
> quite possible even that some of our slower neighbours may yet
> make before us, for many of them have not neglected social
> problems for political so long as England,—we are not yet
> prepared; and the public mind instinctively turns to what are
> apparently duller questions,—education, the relation of labour
> to capital, the position of women, the reformation of criminals,
> the care of the *dangerous* classes, the homes of the poor,—in
> short, to the *social* relations of the different elements in English
> society, as the only sufficient preliminaries for the final dis-
> tribution of political power among the various English classes.

So throughout the early years of his Editorship—certainly
from 1860 until 1867—he conducted the paper as a sort of
one man Royal Commission, especially on social problems, asking questions as much as attempting an answer. In the process,
he quietly softened much of the hard middle class dogmatism
that he had inherited. Wilson, for instance, had viewed the

Factory Acts with distrust as an encroachment on individual liberty: Bagehot, driving fast enough to catch his train, wrote of them in 1864 that no one who knew how they had worked in the industrial areas "had any doubt *now*" of their wisdom.*

But politicians were much more subject to Clough's "ruinous force of the will" than editors. When party rivalry, after the death of Palmerston, made it certain that one party or the other would plump for a new Reform Bill, long before the social problems which Bagehot had postulated had been even properly considered, he came out in strong opposition to a general extension of a franchise, and during 1866 wrote fifteen articles on the subject in *The Economist*. He called Disraeli's Bill of 1867, which extended household suffrage to a working class which he thought wholly unready for it, "a proposition so mischievous and monstrous". He sided openly with Carnarvon and Cranborne, who at the last moment resigned from Disraeli's cabinet. "The Reform Question," he wrote at the height of the crisis "approaches one of those stages so common in real business when, after a prolonged and half-understood discussion, the board of directors, or the meeting of shareholders, out of weariness and necessity, accept some solution which satisfies all immediate needs, but which leaves the higher necessities of the case unsatisfied, and throws over the future a great shade".

The range of his political friendships expanded steadily. Gladstone had taken to him when Wilson had first introduced them, and in November, 1859 five months after he had returned to the Treasury, he was writing confidentially, though cautiously, to Bagehot at *The Economist* about his financial policy. Bagehot considered him "by far the greatest Chancellor of the Exchequer of this generation, one of the greatest of any generation", but was as puzzled as many others as to what sort

---

* Compare this economical *obiter dicta* with Gladstone in the same year, "It is an interference of which it may be said that the Legislature is now almost unanimous with respect to the necessity which existed for undertaking it, and with respect to the beneficent effect it has produced both in mitigating human suffering, and in attaching important classes of the community to Parliament and the Government."

of national leader he would make, and in the spring of 1860 he contributed a long article on him to *The National*. It is a study that repays the historian's attention for it was written thirty-eight years before Gladstone's death and yet when he had been in public life for nearly thirty years, at the half way mark in his transition from Toryism to Liberalism, when no one, least of all his colleagues, knew what to make of him.

> Mr. Gladstone is a problem . . . Who can tell whether he will be the greatest orator of a great administration; whether he will rule the House of Commons; whether he will be, as his gifts at first sight mark him out to be, our greatest statesman? or whether, below the gangway, he will utter unintelligible discourses; will aid in destroying many ministries and share in none; will pour forth during many hopeless years a bitter, a splendid, and a vituperative eloquence?

He conceded his great power as an orator:

> He has the *didactic* impulse . . . He is sure, if they (his audience) only knew what he knows, they would feel as he feels, and believe as he believes . . . he had the *contentious* impulse . . . He can bear a good deal about the politics of Europe; but let a man question the fees on vatting, or the change in the game certificate, or the stamp on bills of lading—what melodious thunders of loquacious wrath!

He is zealful, he is industrious, he is scholarly though with a schoolman's taste for hair splitting. But—and Bagehot goes on to show how Gladstone's oratory carried him as well as his audience away. He points out his lack of intellectual consistency and his maddening habit of producing the loftiest principles to justify some small administrative point. "It must be pleasant to have an argumentative acuteness which is quite sure to extricate you, at least in appearance, from any intellectual scrape. But it is a dangerous weapon to use, and particularly dangerous to a very conscientious man." And he concludes with three warnings to Gladstone: first that "he must learn his creed *of* his time" not "impose his creed *on* his time". Second, that he could not follow the path of Peel and be content with repealing old abuses. "We have now reached the term of the destructive period . . . the questions which remain are questions of construction." Bagehot under-rated the constructiveness of Gladstone's colleagues, Lowe, Forster and Cardwell (as he later somewhat overstressed the powers of Prime Ministers in general). And finally, that he must not spend too much in opposition as he had done in the immediate past. "It is *necessary* that England should comprehend Mr. Gladstone. If the country have not a true conception of a great statesman, his popularity will be capricious, his power irregular, and his usefulness insecure."

Gladstone himself took this lecture in good part and long afterwards wrote to Eliza, "I remember feeling, and I still feel, how true the article on myself is in the parts least favourable to my vanity." Bagehot became a regular member of the Gladstones' breakfast parties at Carlton House Terrace, and many years later their daughter Helen could remember the quick, bearded figure who told her that "he knew what a nut felt like when it was going to be cracked, as he once got his head caught between a cart and a lamp post".

He never solved the problem of Gladstone's character, his sensitivity and indifference, his courage and his inconsistency. No one indeed except that Supreme Being, with whom Gladstone communicated in terms of almost bilateral equality, ever will. But Bagehot dwelt at his elbow during his most fruitful years, his Chancellorship and his first term as Prime Minister, and he approached him with a sense of respect which was noticeably absent from his dealings with other great men.

Eleven years later, in 1871, he saw—not wholly with approval—that Gladstone had not only found his place as a leader but that he was devising an entirely new basis of political leadership. Commenting on a speech to his constituents at Greenwich (where he spoke bareheaded for nearly two hours in the rain and converted an hostile audience, mostly of laid-off dockyard workers, into an enthusiastic one), Bagehot saw that

"it marks the coming of the time when it will be one of the
most important qualifications of a Prime Minister to exert a
direct control over the masses." "Mr. Gladstone has illustrated
most remarkably his reserve power outside Parliament . . .
Parliament may not like it" (Bagehot did not either) "—may
think it even a dangerous power,—may echo the grumblings
of three years ago over Mr. Gladstone's stumping tour in
Lancashire; but Parliament will recognise and respect it as a
new store of political force . . ."

He once said to Mountstuart Grant Duff that "the most remarkable thing about Gladstone is his quantity", the mere
size of his political credit and debit ledgers.

His instinctive sympathy for the Peelites, for the men of
liberal instincts with an ear for common sense and an eye for
effective government, drew him also to Sidney Herbert, who
died worn out with work at fifty-one, the same age as Bagehot
himself, within two years of the latter's arrival at *The Economist*. "He was an unstained and undamaged man," he wrote.
"Power in his estimation was too sacred a trust to be either
neglected or abused . . . He was above everything a man to
confide in." He seems to have been almost as grieved by Herbert's death as by that of their mutual friend, Clough.

A close friendship, which he inherited from Wilson, was
with one of the oddest political figures of the day. Sir George
Cornewell Lewis had been Gladstone's successor at the Exchequer in Palmerston's first government and therefore Wilson's nominal superior, and when Bagehot had just arrived
in London he was grappling rather indifferently with the War
Office. He had originally been a civil servant, well-known for
his anti-colonial views, who had gone into politics and risen
rapidly. He had for a brief period edited *The Edinburgh Review* and was the author of an immense dull book on Roman
History. He must have been one of the stodgiest of men, with
a dry subacid humor. Here is Bagehot's engraving of him:

Few more curious sights were, not long since, to be seen in
London than that of Sir G. C. Lewis at the War Office. What
is now a melancholy recollection was, when we used to see it,

an odd mixture of amusing anomalies. The accidental and bit-by-bit way in which all minor business is managed in England has drifted our public offices into scattered, strange, and miscellaneous places. It has drifted the War Minister into the large drawing room of an old mansion, which is splendid enough to receive fashionable people, and large enough to receive a hundred people. In this great and gorgeous apartment sat, a few months since, (1863) a homely scholar in spectacles whose face bore traces of sedentary labour, and whose figure was bent into the student-stoop. Such a plain man looked odd enough in such a splendid place. But it was much more odd to think that that man in that place supremely regulated the War Department of England. The place should have been a pacific drawing-room, and the man was a pacific student. He looked like a conveyancer over deeds, like a scholar among treatises, like a jurist making a code; he looked like the last man to preside over martial pomp and military expeditions.

Bagehot was devoted to Lewis and regarded him as unique; for his lack of hustle which, when war with America seemed impending, enabled him "at three o'clock on a busy Parliamentary day, to discuss with the writer of these lines, for some twenty minutes, the comparative certainty, or rather *uncertainty*, of the physical and moral sciences"; for his "complication-proof" mind and simplicity of judgments; and for his ordinariness, his vegetable quality. Lewis was to Bagehot the apotheosis of the plain, dull Englishman who gets things done slowly, bringing a better judgment to affairs than the fiercer spirits who lack his sense of the possible. "He was the soundest judge of probability we have ever known . . . It is this judgment of probability that makes the man of business. The data of life accessible, their inference uncertain; a sound judgment on these data is the secret of success to him who possesses it, and the reason why others trust him." He had "the business imagination" like James Wilson. There was no trace of anti-intellectualism in Bagehot: indeed one reason for his devotion to Lewis was the scholarly aridity of his intellect. He compares a passage from Niebuhr's *History of Rome* with Lewis's treatment of the same subject. "It is beautiful to see the heavy and sluggish diligence with which Sir George Lewis reckons all his poetry back into mere prose." What fascinated Bagehot was the translation of ideas into political beliefs and beliefs into political action and in Lewis he felt he had isolated a perfect specimen.

Of the other Liberal statesmen of his day he retained a great affection for Cobden, the "sensitive agitator"; but he believed that, for all his radicalism, Bright was at heart really a conservative, for he wished only to enact the reforms with which he had become familiar in his youth and hated new ideas such as female suffrage. Of the younger leaders he was faintly contemptuous of Robert Lowe, Gladstone's Chancellor, perhaps because the latter defeated him for London University, and admiring of W. E. Forster, for having risen to the top by "solid sense and determined energy". Of Cardwell whom he respected, he wrote: "The faculty of disheartening adversaries by diffusing on occasion an oppression of businesslike dulness is invaluable to a Parliamentary statesman."

He came to London with a strong distrust of Disraeli, which matured into active dislike after the latter's espousal of the Reform Bill of 1867. He granted Disraeli's tactical genius and ascribed his success to the fact that beneath his theatrical show he had not only a very sensitive but also an unoriginal mind, which was able to accept other people's views and ideas gracefully. "His mind was made to receive impressions and interpret the tendencies of others . . . He has adopted the opinions of parties as he would a national costume." Bagehot saw well before the issue on the Second Reform Bill was finally settled in Parliament wherein Disraeli's calculation lay: "The most ignorant and uneducated classes of England are in the main, anti-Liberal, as in France, and it is upon this theory, as we believe, that Mr. Disraeli has been resting all along."

He could be fair to him as well, acknowledging that he had been a highly responsible leader of the Opposition especially during the American Civil War and the arbitration of the *Alabama* claims, when it would have been easy to make capital out of popular emotions. But he woefully under-estimated

Disraeli's future hold on the public imagination, when he denied him at the beginning of his second Ministry that extra-parliamentary position which Gladstone had won for himself. "Such vast power over Englishmen," he wrote in 1876, "as has been possessed by Lord Palmerston and Mr. Gladstone was out of the way altogether. Between Mr. Disraeli and common Englishmen there was too broad a gulf—too great a difference. He was simply unintelligible to them . . . the special influence of this great gladiator never passed the walls of the amphitheatre; he has ruled the country by ruling Parliament, but has never had any influence in Parliament reverberating from the nation itself." This was in the year that Queen Victoria was made Empress of India.

Bagehot's contempt for Disraeli did not arise from snobbery or anti-semitism—indeed he greatly admired him for the way in which he had risen in the world of politics by his own efforts. It was partly because he considered Disraeli a glib lightweight with no capacity for "business", for getting things done in Parliament and Whitehall—"it is like entering a light hack for a ploughing match"; and partly because he distrusted any intellectual theory of Conservatism as leading inevitably to extremes. "The true conservatism of Great Britain, the Conservatism for example of the City, and of most country gentlemen is of a very much more moderate and cautious kind than party Conservatives always allow—is a stab of feeling rather than a passion, a sense of content with what is rather than apprehension of what is to come."

But he had a close affinity for the more moderate, instinctive Conservatives. One of his closest Tory friends was a high-minded young contemporary, Lord Carnarvon, who had been Under-Secretary for the Colonies in Derby's government, and who, in Disraeli's two administrations, became the most effective and far-sighted Colonial Secretary of the whole nineteenth century. Bagehot had often defended the political flair and value of the "great houses" and their owners. Highclere was his first experience of one of them, and its catholicity both amused and alarmed him.

"I have been at Highclere, Lord Carnarvon's," he wrote in 1863, "who is one of my sort, and has run to mind, and wanted me to help to keep his house more decently reasonable, while the fast people were there. We had Lord and Lady Ashley, Lord Stanhope (Lady Carnarvon's brother), Lady Dorothy Neville—a pretty woman with an old husband, and several young men. The women wore wonderful dresses, and we played cards rather high, always in the evening and sometimes in the morning—at least some people played in the morning—I kept my character for wisdom and did not . . . Lady Carnarvon is very clever and literary—at least with *snaps* of Literature. They will be *people* for some years to come, for they are both clever, very ambitious and have a beautiful place near London to entertain in."

Carnarvon was indeed a person. As much as any one in Britain, he was responsible for the modern British Commonwealth, for it was his skill which piloted the British North America Act through Parliament in 1867 against time and against the old-fashioned radicals and the dissident leaders of the Maritime Provinces, who wanted the various colonies to go their own way. He tried and failed to create a united South Africa a quarter century before it happened. He was also the leader of the Tory peers who revolted against Disraeli's *volte face* on a Reform Bill in 1867, and Bagehot's close friendship with both Carnarvon and Gladstone is the reason why *The Economist* was one of the best informed papers on the twists and turns of that involved crisis.

III

A close friendship with some of the leading politicians of the day was rewarding enough. But Bagehot had spasms of that desire to move from the gallery to the floor of the House of Commons which from time to time comes over every political observer. "Members of the House," he wrote, "see the Parliamentary machine itself; literary people only judge of it, as it were, by plates and descriptions."

By the time he joined *The Economist* in 1859 he was convinced that if he was to wear a party label, he must call himself a Liberal. He was too convinced a Free Trader to accept membership of the Conservative party, too much a realist to be a Whig, too sceptical to be a Radical. In 1860, while he was still living at Clevedon, he had toyed with the idea of standing for London University. But family complications, work, money, Wilson's absence in India, his father's opposition held him from pressing his claim and the nomination passed elsewhere.* At the election of 1865, Wilson's old friend from the days of the League, Charles Villiers, who was Member for Wolverhampton for sixty-three years and at that point President of the Poor Law Board, asked Bagehot to stand for first Dudley and then Manchester. He went up to Manchester, with a letter from Gladstone, a masterpiece of that master's tepid and involved style.

> It would be a great presumption on my part, in expressing an opinion as to your qualification for Parliament, were I to connect that opinion with any particular constituency. But of the qualifications themselves neither I, nor, as I believe, any one who knows you can have any doubt whatever; and undoubtedly, they point, of themselves, to the class of our great commercial and manufacturing constituencies in an especial degree.

Bagehot had a bad reception for he was a poor public speaker, and gave up. "Manchester could not 'see it'," he wrote in a family letter. "I had a letter from Mr. Gladstone recommending me, but it was of no use. They said 'If he is so celebrated, why does not Finsbury elect him'." He returned to London and wrote a slightly embittered article pointing to the danger that urban constituencies would return only elderly members of the local plutocracy and deprive the House of young independent-minded politicians.

But the following summer came the opportunity to contest a

* Eliza to Wilson, April 2nd, 1860: "I do not know what Papa Bagehot will say for he is so *very* prudent, and has such a dread of Walter being a *poor* member of Parliament." She gave Bagehot's income as one thousand pounds a year, while an earlier entry in her diary shows that they had been living at the rate of one thousand four hundred pounds.

seat very much after his own heart, the little borough of Bridgwater in his own county. Two literary country neighbors, Alexander Kinglake, the historian of the Crimea and the sitting member, and A. E. Freeman, the historian of the Norman Conquest, were his chief supporters.* His family wondered how he could complicate his already overburdened life still further but his mother, who thought little of editors and much of the M.P.s, egged him on, and he cheerfully threw himself into electioneering. But Bridgwater was traditionally one of the most corrupt boroughs in England (Bub Dodington and Charles James Fox had represented it), the ballot had not yet been introduced, the hustings and the open vote still prevailed, and with them the rule of "Mr. Most". Since Bagehot refused to bribe the electors and made corruption his theme, he was beaten by seven votes in a total poll of 595, and the hope that he might gain the seat on petition did not mature. "I won't vote for gentlefolks unless they do something for I. Gentlefolks do not come to I unless they do something *of* I, and I won't do nothing for gentlefolks unless they do something for me." Bagehot reported this conversation that had occurred during his canvass to a commission enquiring a few years later into Bridgwater's corrupt practices—for which it was disfranchised.

There is no doubt that he minded his defeat, the more so since a Liberal was elected in a by-election there the following year. They were his own people and to be rejected by them cut at the roots of his theory of leadership. In a paper on irrational belief and the power of an idea to carry conviction which he read before the Metaphysical Society six years later, he used his own feelings to illustrate his point.

> But for years I had the deepest conviction that I should be "Member for Bridgwater"; and no amount of reasoning would get it out of my head. The borough is now disfranchised; but

* Two more peppery supporters it would be hard to find, for Freeman was one of the most quarrelsome of pedants, and an opponent of blood sports as well, while Kinglake perennially regretted that duelling had fallen out of use.

even still, if I allow my mind to dwell on the contest—if I think of the hours I was ahead in the morning, and the rush of votes at two o'clock by which I was defeated,—and even more, if I call up the image of the nomination day, with all the people's hands outstretched, and all their excited faces looking the more different on account of their identity in posture, the old feeling almost comes back upon me, and for a moment I believe that I shall be Member for Bridgwater.

The following year he tried once more, at Hutton's insistence, to get the Liberal nomination for London University, which was tantamount to winning the election. But he was beaten by Robert Lowe who was a better known public figure in London and who got the support of the Conservatives, partly because he had deserted the Liberals over the Reform Bill, but largely because Bagehot, with characteristic unwisdom, accused Disraeli, in his election address, of personal corruption. Once more, a year later, Freeman and Chichester Fortescue tried to persuade him to stand for Mid-Somerset, and even sent a telegram to Gladstone, which routed the great man out of church at Hawarden, asking him to use his influence with Bagehot. But Bagehot had had enough. In 1873 he was asked to stand for Liverpool, but he declined.

Bagehot had no illusion that it was his own rather overbearing air of intellectual superiority that made him unsuccessful with the electors.

A man who wants to represent others must be content to seem to be as they are, and it will be better for him if he is as they are. A man who tries to enter Parliament must be content to utter common thoughts, and to bind himself to the formularies of common creeds, or he will not succeed in his candidature. And to some minds there is no necessity more vexing or more intolerable.

On the whole he was fortunate in his failure, for either his work at *The Economist* or his books would have suffered. He was no orator, and his judgment often needed the winnowing of manuscript and galley proof to retain balance. Parliament, even with the touch of the Whip as light as it was in those days, would have strained his objectivity and destroyed his leisure. Sir Mountstuart Grant Duff, who was for many years a Liberal member and became a close friend of Bagehot's, was right in saying that "he was in his proper sphere as a deeply interested spectator and critic of public affairs".

IV

On foreign affairs his opinions were much less tentative than on domestic questions, for he fully endorsed Wilson's belief that Britain's interest in the world was trade not power. Abroad he identified himself more with the Liberals, was further to the left of the "extreme centre" (one of his successor's phrases) than at home. Throughout his editorship and for long afterwards *The Economist* opposed Britain's entanglement in Europe's quarrels. In 1861 he was resisting any idea of British intervention in the American Civil War, and in 1876 he was denouncing Disraeli's desire to intervene against Russia on behalf of Turkey:—"the rise of Germany has so completely protected Europe against Russia, that it does not at all matter whether she takes Turkey or not". In the intervening years of war and dispute over the unification of Italy, over Schleswig-Holstein, over the Austro-Prussian and the Franco-Prussian wars, Britain, he argued in each case, should remain detached, watchful, well armed, ready to mediate but not to intervene: her diplomacy should foster a concert of Europe of which Britain should be a leading member. The inconsistency between demanding that Britain's voice should be decisive in Europe while she remained militarily aloof from its struggles, neither he, his contemporaries nor his successors ever satisfactorily reconciled. Dying just before the Treaty of Berlin, he did not live to comment on Disraeli's apparent success in doing so.

Certainly his expression of the prevailing isolationism of the time was not due to ignorance about Europe. Nassau Senior was one of the best informed Englishmen of his day on Europe and Bagehot inherited his contacts. Senior had never

shared Bagehot's youthful acceptance of the utility of Louis
Napoleon to France and throughout the sixties Bagehot became increasingly distrustful of the "cardboard Caesar" for
his dabblings in the troubled waters of Europe and the new
world. *The Economist* denounced Napoleon's Mexican ad-
venture in terms so strong that it is believed that the British
government put private pressure on Bagehot to modify its
tone lest Anglo-French relations, which were then bad, became
irretrievably embittered.

But even after Sedan Bagehot retained a certain respect
for Napoleon, despite the denunciations of Mary Mohl who
hated him, the more so because her precious collection of
cats had been eaten during the siege of Paris. He refused to
accept the French myth that the defeat of 1870 was entirely
Napoleon's fault, and at his death called him "perhaps the
most reflective and *in*sighted, not far-sighted, of the modern
statesmen of France". Of Bismarck, on the other hand, he
had always an instinctive fear, not so much for his military
adventures, for he regarded the outcome of 1870 as beneficial
to Britain in transferring European supremacy from "France, a
nation that always hated us, to Germany, a nation that never
hated us", as for his economic nationalism. Even so, like many
good free traders of his day, he consistently underrated the
force of political nationalism, which he tended to regard as
"a sort of political measles to which great nations in the infancy
of their conscious unity and power are very liable".

The importance that was attached to his opinions on foreign
affairs can be judged from this postscript to a letter from
Lord Granville, the Foreign Secretary, to Bagehot in October,
1870.

> May I ask you in anything you say, which always comes with
> so much weight both from the high character of your paper
> and the great ability of the articles, not to write anything which
> will give thoughtful Germans reason to believe that they have
> just cause of complaint against us.

For a man so thoroughly civilian by taste and experience
Bagehot wrote with realism on the relation of defence to

foreign policy, presumably since his friendship with Lewis, Sidney Herbert and Cardwell forced him to examine the assumption of most Liberals and many bankers that defence expenditure could be pared to the bone after the Crimean War, just as his friendship with Carnarvon forced him to re-examine his instinctive prejudice against overseas possessions. The military problems of the sixties were in microcosm exactly those of today; the need to accept an unprecedentedly high expenditure on defence just after a great war, France being then the potential aggressor, together with a series of rapid technological "break throughs", then in ships as today in aircraft and missiles, which made weapons obsolete before they were produced. The ordinary taxpayer (and with the income tax accepted as likely to be a fixture, that figure had made his entry into the literature of protest) was bewildered and Bagehot expressed his feelings.

> First, the Admiralty took away some money with which it made wooden ships; and then it "discovered its error," and acknowledged that wooden sailing ships were useless; so it asked for additional money and made wooden *steam* ships with much *éclat*. And I for one was convinced it would be all right, and that England was now safe. But in less than a year the Admiralty discovered its error again, and pronounced all wooden ships, whether steam or sailing ships, to be useless; so it abstracted further money and constructed "iron-plated ships", the *Warrior* and that sort of thing, which cost almost fabulous sums apiece; and now "the Admiralty is discovering its error" again, or something like it, for it wants more money, and is making what I must call naval *nondescripts*—a sort of Merrimacs and Monitors—things more like an ugly insect than a ship.

Change ships to aircraft and you have the history not of 1860's but of the 1950's. His phrases "Do not unnecessarily invest a million sterling in the patent of Captain Monstrous, when it may be upset tomorrow by the better patent of Captain Fitzmonstrous", or "It would appear that science is very adequate to expend money, but very inadequate to defend a country" might be engraved above the portals of any modern Ministry of Defence.

What was the remedy for this state of expensive public confusion? Not Cobden's advocacy of unilateral disarmament or Disraeli's of subservience to France; clearly it was to produce far better intelligence estimates of the strength of our potential enemies, to know rather than guess what force could be deployed against us, and having done that, to take defence policy out of the shelter of the royal prerogative where it still dwelt, and make it the subject of proper parliamentary debate. Bagehot was really arguing for an annual Defence White Paper eighty-five years too soon. In the darkening atmosphere of the seventies he continued to insist that as defence became more important so general public knowledge and debate were essential. His views were of a piece both with his "quantitative sense" and of his belief that a liberal society required not only public assent but real comprehension of the ends of policy. He was convinced that the Germans would defeat the French army in 1870 and the weekly commentary on that campaign in *The Economist* shows a remarkable grasp of contemporary strategy.

Bagehot's isolationism was partly due to the fact that he saw more clearly than most of his contemporaries the opposite pulls exerted by the defence of a world empire and of a European motherland which was not merely its political but its economic heart. The only way the dilemma could be avoided was on the one hand to be very cautious about going into Europe, on the other to develop local self government and responsibility throughout the Empire. The defence of Montreal and Melbourne could never be as important as that of London, for they could be recovered if Britain remained inviolable, whereas if London fell the Empire would be conquered piecemeal and for ever. His views in the 1860's read strangely like a Chief of Staffs paper of the early 1940's, but despite his respect for Carnarvon he foresaw none of the latent possibility of transmuting Empire into Commonwealth.

"Nobody in this country wants, we suppose," he wrote in 1865, "to fight for Canada *qua* Canada, to suspend commerce and interrupt industry and mortgage the future, in order to retain a titular authority over a vast region whose inhabitants will not even give us a low tariff upon our produce."

But, in part, his opposition to the developing conception of Britain as a great Imperial and European power, arose from a personal belief that the English were dissipating abroad energies and abilities which should be directed towards improving their own society—an argument that has come full circle in three generations. Hutton, recalling private conversations which Bagehot never committed to print in their extreme form, says that

> he would have been glad to find a fair excuse for giving up India, for throwing the Colonies on their own resources, and for persuading the English people to accept deliberately the place of a fourth or fifth rate European power—which was not, in his estimation, a cynical or unpatriotic wish, but quite the reverse, for he thought that such a course would result in generally raising the calibre of the national mind, conscience, and taste.

To which Hutton added his dissent,

> I suspect that the real effect of suddenly stopping the various safety valves, by which the spare energy of our nation is diverted to the useful work of roughly civilising other lands, would be, not to stimulate the deliberative understanding of the English people, but to stunt its thinking as well as its acting powers.*

But the international question that dominated the editorial pages of *The Economist* during the first years of his Editorship —the question on which a strong and consistent view was both

---

* In *Lombard Street* there is a classic statement of the feelings of a Victorian anti-Imperialist. "Railway debenture stock is as good a security as a commercial bill, and many people, of whom I own I am one, think it safer than India stock: on the whole, a great railway is, I think, less liable to unforeseen accidents than the strange empire of India." *Works*, Vol. VI, pp. 129-30.

essential and influential—, was the American Civil War. Lincoln was elected President and war became virtually a certainty within a few months of Bagehot's assumption of full control of *The Economist*. His general views were fairly representative of intelligent Liberal opinion in London: he had no love of the North, of the "Yankee brag" and the high tariff New England and Pennsylvania industrialists. But he had a hatred of slavery, inherited from his father, and fewer illusions than some Englishmen about the aristocratic or English quality of the South, the "deeply ulcerated semblance of civilization" he called it. The South had a right to secede even in a bad cause, he argued, but he hoped devoutly that it would be allowed to go in peace, for war in a country the size of North America would be both horrible and inconclusive. For Lincoln he had at first nothing but contempt, his Emancipation Proclamation was "dishonest and foolish", the Union Administration had "fallen into the hands of the smallest, weakest, and meanest set of men who ever presided over a great nation at the critical epoch of its affairs" (1863), and as late as the autumn of 1864 he was quoting with warm approval an earlier saying of Cornewall Lewis that the North could never reimpose Union in the South and describing Lincoln as "that village lawyer".

But Bagehot kept his head better than many of his contemporaries. *The Economist* never went as far as most of the British press in laying the blame for the war on Lincoln, and he was clear from the start that Britain must in no circumstances intervene. He insisted on Britain's rights as a neutral, condemned the Union government when Mason and Slidell, the confederate commissioners, were taken off the *Trent,* and commended Lincoln when he released them. But he insisted that Britain must respect the Northern blockade even though the Lancashire mills ground to a halt for lack of cotton. For a paper so deeply involved in the fortunes of Lancashire (and in particular of the employers who did not share their work people's stand for the Union on the point of principle) it was a courageous line to take, though Hutton who had a different sort of constituency took an even stronger line in *The Spectator*. Better to face temporary ruin of Britain's large export trade to America and subsidize Lancashire from the Exchequer than risk war with the North, argued Bagehot, not only on material grounds but since future peace and prosperity depended on Anglo-American solidarity.

And in the end he revised his view of Lincoln. The Second Inaugural could not but move a man with so sensitive an ear for language and its meaning, and at his death he made amends,

> It is not merely that a great man has passed away, but he has disappeared at the very time when his special greatness seemed almost essential to the world . . . We do not know in history such an example of the growth of a ruler in wisdom as was exhibited by Mr. Lincoln. Power and responsibility visibly widened his mind and elevated his character. Difficulties, instead of irritating him as they do most men, only increased his reliance on patience; opposition, instead of ulcerating, only made him more tolerant and determined.

In all the vast literature that surrounds Lincoln's name, there are few juster tributes than those economical sentences, struck off in haste as soon as the news of his assassination reached England.

But it was one of the tragedies of Anglo-American comprehension in the nineteenth century that Bagehot never visited America. For, though he knew a great deal of the material facts about the country, he understood little of its spirit or the quality of its society, and the superficial picture of the American political system which he painted in the *English Constitution* did much to perpetuate the English fear of the instability of American governments and to reinforce English distaste for American democracy. He was never given an opportunity to visit the United States and appears never to have sought one. Though he was fully aware of the economic and industrial potentialities of the United States, there was no way he could have discerned the quality and promise of American life, for there was then little indigenous American literature to

hold up a mirror to the nation as there is today, and he seems
to have accepted the caricatures of Dickens and Mrs. Trollope
at their face value. De Tocqueville, his only serious authority,
had placed all his emphasis on the overwhelming force of
democracy in American politics and government. Bagehot
added Dickens and de Tocqueville together and found mob
government.

> "A low vulgarity," he wrote at the outset of the Civil War
> "indefinable but undeniable, has deeply displeased the culti-
> vated mind of Europe; and the American Union will fall, if
> it does fall, little regretted even by those whose race is akin,
> whose language is identical, whose weightiest opinions are on
> most subjects the same as theirs . . . They have existed during
> two generations as a democracy without ideals; and are likely
> to die now a democracy without champions."

Moreover, he completely misjudged the nature of American
life, mistaking political democracy for a dead level of social
mediocrity. As his first American editor, Forrest Morgan, wrote:

> All literature may be challenged to furnish anything equal in
> absurdity to the grave deliverance in *Physics and Politics* that
> "A Shelley in New England could hardly have lived, and a race
> of Shelleys would have been impossible". Shelley would have
> been no whit more out of key with the community than were
> Alcott and Thoreau, and he could not well have received less
> sympathy here than he did at home.

If fortune had taken one of the best political and social
observers of his day to the Boston of Charles Eliot Norton
and Oliver Wendell Holmes, or to Lincoln's Washington in
the tense summer of 1863—as it took Leslie Stephen—he would
have acquired a juster and closer appreciation of the relation
between leadership and democracy and between social mobility
and social responsibility, which might have affected his later
thoughts profoundly.

Chapter 7

THE HIDDEN REPUBLIC

The characteristic dangers of great nations, like the Roman, or the English, which have a long history of continuous creation, is that they may at last fail from not comprehending the great institutions they have created.
Essay on Lord Althorp

I

IN May, 1865 a new periodical was launched by Anthony Trollope, Cotter Morison and Chapman and Hall. *The Fortnightly Review* was a fresh experiment in English journalism for it was to be a combined literary review and magazine, with the novel device of signed articles, a lively counterpoise to Thackeray's *Cornhill* and to the *Saturday* which Bagehot called "a nearly perfect embodiment of the corrective scepticism of a sleepy intellect". George Henry Lewes was to be Editor (he lasted only a year and a half before the young John Morley took it over and transformed it into an influential monthly), and since his editorial ability was doubtful the founders were unsure of its success. It was therefore with relief that George Eliot (who had become a close friend of Bagehot's) wrote in her diary for June 25th that "G. dined at Greenwich with multitude of so-called writers for *The Saturday*. He heard much commendation of *The Fortnightly,* especially of Bagehot's articles, which last is reassuring after Mr. Trollope's strong objections." It was in this fashion, in chapters and sections spread out over nearly two years that *The English Constitution,* the work on which Bagehot's fame principally rests, began to make its appearance into the world.

It was small wonder that it was the center of comment, and well beyond Greenwich. Though the mid-Victorians were more accustomed to new ideas—in distinction to new facts—than we are today, they could not but catch their breath when informed in cold print that "We have in England an elective first magistrate as truly as the Americans have an elective first magistrate" . . . "A change has taken place in the structure of our society exactly analogous to the change in our polity. A Republic has insinuated itself beneath the folds of Monarchy." The impact of this challenge to established notions was all the greater because what Bagehot said was what many people had come to suspect, without being able to formulate their suspicions. As Leslie Stephen said of him, "He was not only clearing away a mass of useless formulae, but also making a discovery, and the rarest kind of discovery, that of the already known."

Since Mr. St. John-Stevas' fine new edition of *The English Constitution* and Bagehot's other political writings has recently been published, a detailed examination of its conclusions, where they are still valid and where they have been outdated by events, would be out of place in this study of Bagehot himself. They have suffered at times in the past ninety years from being treated with *too much* respect, from being regarded as an authoritative guide to the detailed workings of the modern Constitution, like Erskine May or Anson, instead of being accepted for what Bagehot intended, a glance behind the veil at the realities of power as they existed at the end of the thirty-five year period which separated the first from the second Reform Bill. To treat *The English Constitution* as a guidebook to the workings of the constitution is to miss the most original and valuable aspect of it, namely Bagehot's description of the social structure and climate which produced the constitutional system of Victoria's day and enabled it to function.

The idea of writing a book to unravel the mysteries of British government appears to have been forming in his mind for a long time. The contrast between the omnipotence which the country people in Somerset still attributed to the Crown and the nobility, and the reality as he saw it each week in London had impressed him for some years. The prevalence of the belief that the excellence of the British constitution rested on the

separation of power between Crown, Lords and Commons
intrigued him the more he studied the American political
scene where a constitution which then creaked at every joint
had been erected on a similar principle. A few attempts had
been made to re-assess the roles and relative power of Queen,
Prime Minister and Commons: de Lolme's *Constitution of
England* had made an effort to distinguish between the effective
and ornamental parts of the Constitution, but that had been
written in the year of the American Revolution when the two
still coincided more closely; and the latest book of importance,
Mill's *Representative Government,* while English in its context
was too abstract in its conceptions, to explain what was actually
going on. To describe the constitution as it really functioned
needed the eye of a journalist not a philosopher.

Bagehot's method was to reject the historical approach, the
narrative of "freedom broadening down from precedent to
precedent" or the legal analysis of Blackstone, which prevented
the Victorians from seeing how they had travelled towards a
political democracy. For as he said at the opening of his first
chapter "an ancient and ever altering constitution is like an
old man who still wears with attached fondness clothes in the
fashion of his youth: what you see of him is the same: what
you do not see is wholly altered". With the ironic simplicity of
Hans Andersen's child, he set out to describe what the old man
looked like without his clothes.

Two theories of the English Constitution, he began, still
had immense influence. One was the division of powers between legislative, executive and judiciary—that each was en-
trusted to an entirely different set of people: the other, deriving
from Montesquieu was that of "checks and balances", of the
monarchical, the aristocratic and the democratic element, each
with a share of sovereignty. Thus most English people cherished the belief that you could only reproduce such a constitutional system where all three elements existed in society.

These conceptions, he pointed out, overlooked the distinction between "the dignified" and "the efficient" elements in
any constitution. Both were indispensable: the former by

historical accretion had given government the necessary authority, reverence and force; the latter employed it. The dignified part of the English Constitution was very old and complex: the efficient part "is decidedly simple and rather modern". Its secret was the almost complete fusion of executive and legislative power through the "hyphen" of the Cabinet. The Queen was the head of the dignified part of the constitution, the Prime Minister of the efficient part. "The Cabinet, in a word, is a board of control chosen by the legislature, out of persons whom it trusts and knows, to rule the nation . . . A Cabinet is a combining committee—a *hyphen* which joins, a *buckle* which fastens, the legislative part of the State to the executive part of the State." Useful though the House of Lords might be as a reservoir of Cabinet Ministers, the ruling influence in its formation had passed to the lower house. Only when the virtually unfettered sovereignty of the Cabinet was recognised was it possible to see why the British and the American system had diverged so widely: the strict division of powers between the executive President and the legislative Congress tended to paralyze both, to bar the flexible interaction between policy and administration which modern government necessitated, and, by making it impossible for the legislative to turn out the executive and vice versa, to reduce the Congress's sense of responsibility and the level of man who sought to enter it.

Bagehot assaulted his audience with this argument in his first chapter, and in the rest of the book he set out to reinforce it by examining each institution in turn. Summarized thus, the argument seems to us—and has for three generations—nothing but the baldest common sense (though Bagehot's description of the Cabinet as merely a committee of the legislature has been more widely contested in recent years). But few people until then had understood—and certainly no one had described—the true nature of the change that had begun to develop under Pitt and had gathered momentum ever since.* Montesquieu and Locke still permeated the teaching of constitutional theory for the educated, the formalities of the "Queen's Government"

---

* W. E. Hearn's *Government of England* which also took a fresh look at established institutions was published in the same year.

and the "Queen's Ministers" were still so readily accepted by the uneducated, that most people thought in terms of loyal and disrespectful Prime Ministers—of loyal Wellingtons and Melbournes, or impudent Palmerstons—rather than saw them and their Cabinets as the sovereign beings they really were, whose difference lay in the way they used their power and the tact with which they handled the nominal sovereign.

Similarly, de Tocqueville and others had focussed British attention on the democratic basis of the American political system, as the principal reason why the systems of government had become so different on either side of the Atlantic. It was Bagehot who pointed out that it was not so much the difference in the franchise, as the different way in which the balance of power had developed within the central governments of the two countries, that constituted the real divergence. "The Americans of 1787 thought they were copying the English Constitution, but they were contriving a contrast with it. Just as the American is the type of *composite* Governments, in which the supreme power is divided between many bodies and functionaries, so the English is the type of *simple* constitutions, in which the ultimate power upon all questions is in the hands of the same persons." Certainly, most of the efforts that have been made in the United States, from Woodrow Wilson onwards, to overcome the difficulties of the separation of executive and legislative power—strengthening the Cabinet, making it responsible to Congress as well as to the President, or having its members directly elected—have taken as their starting point Bagehot's analysis of the role of the Cabinet as the hyphen.

Bagehot's treatment of the Monarchy, his description of its social as well as its constitutional function and utility, contains some of the best known of his aphorisms. Moreover, it brings out the conflict between his Cavalier instincts and his Whig reasoning, which still dominates the attitude of most intelligent Englishmen towards the Crown, the fruitful conflict of imagination and common sense. It is small wonder that whenever there is an outburst of criticism of the Monarchy, Bagehot is the most widely quoted authority.

First, he tackles the formal role of the Crown. "The use of

the Queen, in a dignified capacity is incalculable." She still represents the tribal instinct within us. "Most people when they read that the Queen walked on the slope at Windsor—that the Prince of Wales went to the Derby—have imagined that too much thought and prominence were given to little things. But they have been in error; and it is nice to trace how the actions of a retired widow and an unemployed youth become of such importance."

He gives four reasons why the British monarchy produces a strong government. In the first place, "it is an intelligible government: . . . The Greek legislator had not to combine in his polity men like the laborers of Somerset, and men like Mr. Grote. He had not to deal with a community in which primitive barbarism lay as a recognised basis to acquired civilization. *We have.* We have no slaves to keep down by special terrors and independent legislation. But we have whole classes unable to comprehend the idea of a constitution—unable to feel the least attachment to impersonal laws." (This anticipates the "cake of custom" argument of *Physics and Politics*.) "A family on the throne is an interesting idea also. It brings down the pride of sovereignty to the level of petty life . . . The women—one half the human race at least—care fifty times more for a marriage than a ministry."* "Royalty is a government in which the attention of the nation is concentrated on one person doing interesting actions."

Moreover the British Crown brings the government the strength of religion, and a mystic sanction beyond visible ones. Then the Queen is the head of society, and though the Court may be very dull, and the structure of society aristocratic and hydra-headed, it prevents a divorce between society and government. But most important, the Crown "acts as a *disguise*. It

---

* Mr. Richard Hoggart writing ninety years later of the attitude of the industrial working class towards the Crown confirms Bagehot's judgment. "As an institution, it is scarcely thought of by the working classes; they are not royalists by principle." But "since they are 'personalists' and dramatists they are more interested in a few individual members of the Royal Family, than in the less colourful figures of parliamentary government." *The Uses of Literacy* (London: Chatto and Windus, 1957), p. 92.

enables our real rulers to change without heedless people
knowing it. The masses of Englishmen are not fit for elective
government: if they knew how near they were to it, they would
be surprised, and almost tremble." The mystery and secrecy
that hedged the Crown were of immense importance as even
Liberals now acknowledged. "When there is a select committee
on the Queen the charm of royalty will be gone. Its mystery is
its life. We must not let in daylight upon magic."

Bagehot wrote at a time when the Court was becoming progressively less popular, as Victoria withdrew further and further into widowhood. The argument he puts forward for it, is
in fact a utilitarian one, that it is a useful instrument that can
not yet be dispensed with. Even its most mystic qualities have a
utilitarian purpose. Sometimes his pre-occupation with its
utility in strengthening government against the mob appears
also to support the charges of illiberalism that have been made
against him. But France had gone through two revolutionary
changes of constitution in his life-time, and the United States,
the archetype of Republican government, had only just emerged
from a murderous civil war which had been fought to save its
authority. In *The Economist,* he opposed Dilke's Republican-
ism solely on the grounds that "This is a very small and very
crowded country to try experiments in, and until education
has made them a little safer they are better let alone." And
again, "It (the monarchy) must endure if the constitution is to
be maintained, and if it is not maintained till the people are
educated, say fifty years hence, the British Empire will suffer a
shock such as it may not be able to survive." In this as in other
aspects of the constitution, he envisaged a much closer parallel
between changes in its internal balance and its external form
than has been the case.*

When he came to describe the actual influence of the Crown
on government he was much less ready to respect convention.

* "In 1870 perhaps the most general, though secret opinion among
thoughtful observers was that the virtues of its wearer would preserve the
Crown for one successor, hardly for more than one." G. M. Young,
Portrait of an Age, Early Victorian England (London: Oxford University
Press, 1934).

Queen Victoria, he accepted, had a considerable influence on policy, and Prince Albert had won the respect of the Liberal politicians who, as the heirs of Whiggery, of the quarrel between Fox and George III, had most dreaded it. But he was skeptical about the real contribution of the modern Crown to the efficacy of government. He argued that the effect of the party struggle within parliament is generally to throw up the best man as leader and Prime Minister, through "the preservative self-denial" of minority groups. But sometimes it may not, owing to strife within parties. Can the Crown through its power to designate an individual to form a government contribute to a resolution of these conflicts? Only if the monarch is a person of discernment and can pick a statesman whom the moderate elements will eventually rally around. But his training is likely to prevent him from acquiring that discernment.

"If at a period of complex and protracted division of parties, such as are sure to occur often and last long in every enduring Parliamentary government, the extrinsic force of royal selection were always exercised discreetly, it would be a political benefit of incalculable value. But will it be so exercised? A constitutional sovereign must in the common course of government be a man of but common ability. I am afraid, looking to the early acquired feebleness of hereditary dynasties, that we must expect him to be a man of inferior ability." "For the most part, a constitutional king is a *damaged* common man; not forced to business by necessity as a despot often is, but yet spoiled for business by most of the temptations which spoil a despot." This is a stern judgment, though it has a cruel ring of prophecy in so far as the two Edwards are concerned. But it was made under the shadow of Prince Albert's death, for whose wisdom, if not his tact, Bagehot and his friends had great admiration, and who, he acknowledged, "had the rare gifts of a constitutional monarch". And it was made before it had become clear, even to the informed insider like Bagehot, that Victoria possessed any of those gifts herself, or was anything more than a self-willed and stupid middle-aged widow with a German accent. But he did point out that "in the course of a long reign a sagacious king would acquire an experience with which few Ministers could contend". Those who, like the late L. S. Amery, have criticised him for undervaluing the role of the Crown in the choice of Prime Ministers, as evidenced by Victoria's choice of Rosebery over Harcourt or King George V's of Baldwin over Curzon—or for that matter Queen Elizabeth's of Mr. Macmillan over Mr. Butler—have overlooked the wide provision that he made for the future.

There were two developments he did not foresee. The first was the new importance that the Crown would acquire as the symbolic link in a chain of independent nations within a Commonwealth. Indeed with a mid-Victorian Liberal's distrust of any continuing colonial connection, he would have been highly dubious about the idea if it had been propounded to him. The other was the rise of a popular press under the leadership of Northcliffe thirty years after his death, and the invention of the rotogravure photograph, which made the faces and habits of royalty familiar in every home, put them on a par with the stars of entertainment and invested them with a glamor that would have been inconceivable in the 1860's. Ninety years ago probably only one English person in a hundred knew what Queen Victoria really looked like (the coloured tin types in so many English working class homes date from the Silver Jubilee) and Bagehot himself elsewhere recounted a conversation with a Somerset countryman during the Crimean War who envisaged her as a formidable Pallas Athene who was personally setting out to do battle with the Czar in the midst of Russia.

But nothing, in the intervening years, has diminished the accuracy of his definition of the modern sovereign's rights with respect to the Prime Minister and the Government: "the right to be consulted, the right to encourage, the right to warn. And a king of great sense and sagacity would want no others. He would find that having no others would enable him to use these with singular effect."

There is no evidence that Bagehot's views or definitions of the powers of the Crown were ever read by the "unemployed youth" even when he succeeded to them in his old age.* But in 1894 King George V, then Duke of York, was given *The English Constitution* to read and carefully analyzed it. There exists a school notebook among his papers at Windsor, in which he summarised its arguments in his own handwriting. "In these few notes," says his biographer, Sir Harold Nicolson, "the Duke crystallised the functions and duties of a constitutional monarch which, when he came to the throne, he applied with consistent faithfulness." It is interesting that he repeated Bagehot's emphasis on the dignified capacity of the crown and on its business capacity, but omitted any reference to the third of Bagehot's trilogy, its mystic capacity.

On one point—the reserve powers of the Crown—Bagehot's opinion remained until recently of crucial importance, in common with those of Hearn, Dicey and Low, for the good reason that no one, including the Crown and its own advisers, was sure how strong they were. The question which slumbered unanswered throughout Victoria's reign but fell upon the head of Bagehot's royal student to decide, was whether the Crown still possessed the power to dismiss a government with a parliamentary majority and appeal to the people by dissolving parliament, as William IV had done with the Melbourne ministry in 1834. Queen Victoria believed that she possessed the power but became increasingly dubious as to whether she could use it unless there was complete certainty of being vindicated by the electorate, for fear of harming the Crown itself. Earlier authorities such as Hallam had asserted the right, Erskine May and others had hedged their denial of it with so many qualifications as to make their definitions almost valueless to a hard pressed monarch.

Bagehot accepted that the right of dismissal still existed in the shadows but characteristically centered the question of its use on the judgment and quality of the monarch. To use it

* Sir David Keir has pointed out in *The Constitutional History of Modern Britain* (London: A. & C. Black, 1946), pp. 484-7 that Bagehot's description of the limitations on the prerogative were more accurate as prophecy than contemporary analysis. Queen Victoria would not have accepted them in principle.

"with efficiency", he said, "they must be able to perceive that the Parliament is wrong, and that the nation knows it is wrong. Now to know that Parliament is wrong, a man must be, if not a great statesman, yet a considerable statesman—a statesman of some sort". "The preponderant probability is that on a great occasion the Premier and Parliament will really be wiser than the king . . . Principle shows that the power of dismissing a Government with which Parliament is satisfied and of dissolving that parliament upon an appeal to the people, is not a power which a common hereditary monarch will in the long run be able beneficially to exercise. Accordingly this power has almost, if not quite, dropped out of the reality of our constitution." If Queen Victoria dismissed a ministry it would strike terror, he said "like a volcanic eruption from Primrose Hill".

It is not surprising that King George V, faced, in the crisis of 1910 and 1911, with demands that he dismiss the Asquith government at the very beginning of his reign and in circumstances of great temptation, should turn from weightier authorities to this simple human advice, and use Bagehot, first to rebut Asquith's advice that the power of dismissal had fallen into complete desuetude, and then, reflecting that he was after all only a common heredity monarch, to decide not to use it. Bagehot would undoubtedly have acknowledged King George V as a "sagacious king", an exception to the common run of hereditary monarchs. "The only fit material for a constitutional king is a prince who begins early to reign—who in his youth is superior to pleasure—who in his youth is willing to labour—who has by nature a genius for discretion. Such things are among God's greatest gifts, but they are also among his rarest."

Bagehot went farther than some of his contemporaries in asserting that the power to refuse a dissolution to a Prime Minister defeated in the House of Commons could now hardly be used. As he foresaw on this and other questions of the prerogative, the issue might be put to a much severer test in the relationship between colonial governors, on whom the formal but not the mystical powers of the Crown had been devolved,

and their legislatures. It was in fact the crisis caused in 1926 by
the refusal of the unfortunate Lord Byng, the Governor-
General of Canada, of a dissolution to the Prime Minister,
Mr. Mackenzie King, and his invitation to the opposition
leader to form a government to whom he immediately granted
one, that finally resolved the argument against the Crown.

II

Bagehot's treatment of the House of Lords shows a very
acute perception of the shaky foundation on which its far
from negligible power rested—a perception that was the more
remarkable since in many ways the great houses, Derbys and
Cecils, Bedfords, Portlands and Wesminsters, were at the height
of their influence in the sixties, far richer than a generation
earlier, with an immense accretion of industrial and urban
wealth to broad acres that had revived in value but had not
yet begun to decline again.* Moreover, the mid-Victorian
aristocracy had shed the dissipation of their grandfathers and
had grown rather than diminished in respect. As Mr. G. M.
Young has written "By exercise, temperance and plebeian
alliance, the spindle shanked lord of Fielding had become the
ancestor of an invigorated race."

For all his doubts of the real utility of the Crown, Bagehot
had no animosity towards the aristocracy. Though he had
none of Mallock's mystic reverence for them, he shared in full
what Gladstone called the Englishman's "sneaking kindness
for a lord". In *The English Constitution,* he pointed out that
they still had three useful functions to perform. With the
Crown, they helped in their dignified capacity to strengthen
the sense of government. "The office of an order of nobility is

---

* The Local Government Return of 1876 seemed to show that just under
one acre in every two of the United Kingdom was owned by a member of
the nobility, one in every eight by a duke. Even if this figure is re-worked
to include only the land of direct holders of Titles rather than their
families, the figure is between a fifth and seventh. A. S. Turberville, *The
House of Lords in the Age of Reform* (London: Faber and Faber, 1958),
pp. 408-9.

to impose on the common people—not necessarily to impose on them what is untrue, yet less what is hurtful; but still to impose on their quiescent imaginations what would not otherwise be there." He approved of its continuing existence, moreover, for preventing the idolatry of mere wealth and the rule of plutocracy, and for opposing idolatry of rank to idolatry of office, to the rule of the functionaries which the Victorian Englishman found so distasteful in France and Prussia. In England "a big grocer despises the exciseman; and what in many countries would be thought impossible, the exciseman envies the grocer". He accepted that this continuing political responsibility had made the British aristocracy dull "but a good government is well worth a great deal of social dullness".

Mr. Young, who has penetrated further beneath the surface of Victorian life than any writer since Bagehot, has pointed out in one of his most famous passages that "it is easier to frame a defence or an indictment of the Victorian attitude to aristocracy than to understand why, in a money making age, opinion was, on the whole, more deferential to birth than to money, and why, in a mobile and progressive society, most regard was to be had to the element which represented immobility, tradition and the past. Perhaps the statement will be found to include the solution. The English *bourgeoisie* had never been isolated long enough to frame, except in the spheres of comfort and carnal morality, ideals and standards of its own. It was imitative. A nation, hammered into unity by a strong crown, had ended by putting the powers of the Crown into Commission, and the great houses in succeeding to the royal authority, had acquired, and imparted to the lesser houses, something of the mysterious ascendancy of the royal symbol. For a hundred years they ruled, and almost reigned, over an England of villages and little towns. The new urban civilisation was rapidly creating a tradition of civic benevolence and government, but it had no tradition of civic magnificence. To be anything, to be recognised as anything, to feel himself as anything in the State at large, the rich English townsman, unless he was a man of remarkable gifts and character, had still to escape from the seat and source of his wealth; to learn a new dialect and new interests; and he was more likely to magnify than to belittle the virtues of the life into which he and his wife yearned to be admitted, the life, beyond wealth, of power and consideration in the land." The merchant Bagehots escaping from the house over the bank at Langport to Herd's Hill, the merchant Wilsons escaping from Dulwich to the wide sweeps of Claverton were very much a part of this process.

But Bagehot made a firm distinction between the social prestige of the aristocracy and the power of the House of Lords. It has never had as much power as the Commons since Walpole's day, for at each serious conflict between the chambers, the undoubted power of the Prime Minister to use the royal prerogative of creating peers in order to swamp the recalcitrant majority has forced the upper house to give way. 1832 broke the powers of the Lords over the Commons. "Before that Act it (the Lords) was, if not a directing Chamber, at least a Chamber of Directors* . . . Since the Reform Act the House of Lords has become a revising and suspending house . . . The House has ceased to be one of latent directors, and has become one of temporary rejectors and palpable alterers. It is the sole claim of the Duke of Wellington to the name of a statesman, that he presided over this change." Quoting Wellington's advice to Derby during the Corn Law crisis of 1846, that in the last resort the Lords must give way if the people are determined, he says: "The common notion evidently fails, that it is a bulwark against imminent revolution . . . In fact the House of Lords, as a House, is not a bulwark that will keep out revolution, but an index that revolution is unlikely. Resting as it does upon old deference, and inveterate homage, it shows that the spasm of new forces, the outbreak of new agencies, which we call revolution, is for the time simply impossible. So long as many old leaves linger

* Hallam writing before the Reform Act explicitly stated that constitutional harmony depended on the fact that one chamber contained the younger sons, the other the elder sons of the nobility. Even in 1860, 108 members of the House of Commons were either sons of peers or heirs to peerages.

on the November trees, you know that there has been little frost and no wind; just so while the House of Lords retains much power, you may know that there is no desperate discontent in the country, no wild agency likely to cause a great demolition."

When the Lords jibbed at the Irish Church Bill in 1869 he wrote in *The Economist* "To suppose that twenty or thirty noblemen can rule the English nation would be ridiculous, and above all things an aristocracy must not be ridiculous . . . The prestige of a privileged order is like the credit of a bank: if you do but discuss whether a bank is bad or good the bank will stop, and so of an aristocracy: if you have to prove that it *ought* to be obeyed, it will not be obeyed."

Much as he valued the revising function of the upper house, Bagehot, looking ahead, could see that it was becoming progressively unfitted for even this limited task. All but a few of its members were too apathetic to give close attention to legislation, its make-up was too uniform to be in touch with modern events, and being hereditary it contained men of only average ability. This was a business age—"what grows upon the world is a certain matter-of-factness"—"and there is no educated being less likely to know business, worse placed for knowing business than a young lord. Business is really more agreeable than pleasure; it interests the whole mind, the aggregate nature of man more continuously, and more deeply. But it does not *look* as if it did . . . It is as great a difficulty to learn business in a palace as it is to learn agriculture in a park."

For this reason he wanted to see the intelligent business man and the new aristocracy of intellect whose evolution has been so carefully explored by Mr. Noel Annan—and to which he himself belonged—represented in the Lords. In the introduction to the Second Edition of *The English Constitution* which he wrote in 1872 to bring it up to date after the Second Reform Act of 1867 and the clash between Lords and Commons in 1870 over the abolition of purchase in the Army, he pointed out that since the House of Commons had become even more plutocratic and less aristocratic in tone since 1867, it would be

folly on the part of the aristocracy if it did not take the plutocracy into partnership. "In all countries new wealth is ready to
worship old wealth, if old wealth will only let it; and I need
not say that in England new wealth is eager in its worship . . .
Nothing can be more politically useful than such homage, if it
be skilfully used; no folly can be idler than to repel and reject
it." To keep the Lords in tune with the changing social structure of the nation, he strongly advocated the creation of life
peerages—not to swamp the Lords in a sudden crisis, but to
give the nation "a larger command of able leisure". His conclusion has the sad ring of true prophecy. "The danger of the
House of Commons is, perhaps, that it will be reformed too
rashly: the danger of the House of Lords certainly is, that it
may never be reformed . . . If most of its members neglect
their duties, if all its members continue to be of one class,
and that not quite the best; if its doors are shut against genius
that cannot found a family, and ability which has not five
thousand pounds a year, its power will be less year by year,
and at last be gone, as so much kingly power is gone—no one
knows how. Its danger is not in assassination but atrophy;
not in abolition but decline." Though the plutocracy and
the aristocracy began the process of fusion even in his lifetime,
he did not foresee that the process of imitation would be carried a step further and that the former would acquire most of
the political vices of the latter, thus hastening the decline of
the upper house which he had prophesied. But like many of his
contemporaries he would have been amazed that the Lords
should have survived another 90 years without the introduction—except for law lords—of life peerages.

III

Bagehot had no close connections with the Court, he had
only a limited acquaintance among the influential members of
the House of Lords, but he knew his House of Commons as
intimately as a man can from the gallery and political dinner
tables. Yet, curiously, his analysis of the House of Commons

and its functions is less perceptive than his description of the role of the Crown and the Lords.

His power of illumination did not desert him, and his chapter on the House of Commons contains some of the most delightful phrases in all his writing. "Of all odd forms of government, the oddest really is government by a *public meeting*." "Nobody will understand Parliament government who fancies it an easy thing, a natural thing, a thing not needing explanation. You have not a perception of the first elements in this matter till you know that government by a *club* is a standing wonder." And of the Tory back benchers "A cynical politician is said to have watched the long row of county members, so fresh and respectable looking, and muttered, 'By Jove, they are the finest brute votes in Europe'."

Nor have most of his definitions of the real functions of the House been wholly outdated. He points out that unlike the Crown and the Lords, its dignified aspect, though useful is less important, "its office is not to win power by awing mankind, but to use power in governing mankind". The four functions are: *elective,* to choose the nation's leader as the American electoral college chooses (or was then supposed to choose) the President: *expressive,* "it is its office to express the mind of the English people": *teaching,* "it ought to teach the nation what it does not know": *informing,* to lay grievances before the people as it had once laid them before the sovereign. "Lastly, there is the function of legislation, of which of course it would be preposterous to deny the great importance, and which I only deny to be *as* important as the executive management of the whole State, or the political education given by Parliament to the whole nation." A modern writer might arrange the last four in a different pattern: the expressive function, the parliamentary question and the adjournment debate, has become more important in an age of complicated, bureaucratic government: the informing function perhaps holds its own: the teaching function has largely passed outside parliament to the party political broadcast, the television address and the newspaper article.

But Bagehot's emphasis on the importance of the elective function of the House, its role in creating and maintaining a national leader and executive, was wide of the mark even when he wrote. His very natural mistake was to assume that the confused pattern of politics which had dominated his manhood from the fall of Peel in 1846 onwards, when party lines had been fragmented and blurred and all depended on coalitions of relatively small groups as in the Third and Fourth French Republics, was now permanently embedded in English political life. He admitted that party was the essence of the House, "bone of its bone, breath of its breath", that party discipline, enforced by deference and the fear of dissolution were essential to its efficient functions. But he still thought in terms of a spectrum, Conservatives, Peelites, Whigs, Liberal Radicals, out of the center of which governments were formed. "If happily, by its intelligence and attractiveness, a Cabinet can gain a hold upon the great middle part of parliament, it will continue to exist notwithstanding the hatching of small plots . . ." He approved of this, being by nature a cross-bencher himself, and one reason for his opposition to electoral reform was his fear that a wider franchise would lead to a more highly disciplined two party system which would shift the power of choosing the executive from the House itself to the party organization. Even in the second thoughts he set down in the Introduction of 1872, he did not clearly apprehend that this was already happening, that Gladstone and Disraeli were polarizing the political forces within the nation, each building up sources of strength independent of the House of Commons.

However he did modify his views, and concede that the world was not going his way. In an article in *The Economist* in 1871, he acknowledged that Gladstone's ability to draw his strength directly from the people heralded a new era in English politics. "It marks the coming of the time when it will be one of the most important qualifications of a Prime Minister to exert a direct control over the masses—when the ability to reach them, not as his views may be filtered through an intermediate class of writers, but *directly* by the vitality of his own mind, will give a vast advantage in the political race to any statesman . . . As far as our own tastes go, we might prefer the sort of statesman who could only reach the nation through comparatively select audiences like Parliament, whose power is reserved for the higher regions of statesmanship . . . (In future) there will be a very strong disposition on the part of the masses to believe what the Prime Minister says of Parliament more easily than what Parliament says of the Prime Minister." Three years later, he acknowledged that the idea of a middle party, a coalition of the center, had now become impossible.

He was appalled that the House might lose its power of making and unmaking ministries, that it might pass to some amorphous or extreme body of public opinion. He has been accused of failing to foresee the emergence of the modern party system in the House: it would be truer to say that he saw what was coming, disliked it intensely, and used his great powers of analysis and advocacy to try and point out the dangers. "Constituency government," he wrote in *The English Constitution* "is the precise opposite of Parliamentary government. It is the judgement of immoderate persons far from the scene of action, instead of the government of moderate persons close to the scene of action." And ten years later, he went further, "The power of the constituencies is too great. They are fast reducing the members, especially the weaker sort of them, to delegates. There is already, in many places, a committee which telegraphs to London, hoping that their members will vote this way or that, and the member is unwilling not to do so, because at the next election, if offended, the committee may, perchance, turn the scale against him. And this dependence weakens the intellectual influence of Parliament."

His preoccupation with moderation also led him to oppose the extension of the franchise. It was impossible at that moment to write on the constitution without getting involved in the debate. For the book had not been long under way in *The Fortnightly* when Palmerston died and the Russell cabinet let it be known that they were drawing up a new reform bill,

and the period during which it was being written and published coincided with that of the most heated public and
parliamentary debates on reform.

Bagehot's views on the franchise—his opposition to an extension at that time of the vote to the urban householder or
below—coincided in practical effect with those of Cranborne
and Carnarvon who eventually resigned from the Tory Cabinet
in 1867 when Disraeli picked the measure up from the ir-
resolute Whigs in order to dish them. But he had arrived at
his view by a much subtler process of reason and observation
than the ordinary Conservative, for what *The Quarterly* called
"Eldonine", fear of change and of the masses, did not weigh
heavily upon him, no heavier at least than upon Matthew
Arnold.

Ten years earlier he had written a series of articles in the
Saturday in which he attempted to throw a new light on the
problem of government by demagogues. Government is a dull
affair except in moments of great crisis. "You cannot have a
Chatham in time of peace—you cannot storm a Redan in
Somersetshire. There is no room for glorious daring in times of
placid happiness . . . It has been the bane of many countries
which have tried to obtain freedom, but failed in the attempt,
that they have regarded popular government rather as a means
of intellectual excitement than as an implement of political
work." The English fortunately have a high natural resistance
to Bonapartism; to personal rule "The English idea is a committee—we are born with a belief in a green cloth, clean pens,
and twelve men with grey hair." "Nature has provided against
the restlessness of genius by the obstinacy of stupidity . . . We
have been governed for the longest periods and with the
greatest ease, by men who are essentially common men—men
who never said anything which anyone in an omnibus could
not understand," though the price that is paid for this is too
much deference to habit and too little fresh thought. "What
mankind really wishes to economise is thought." But the
necessary foundation of the English system by which common men can govern, and which is not constantly looking

for the strong man, for Carlyle's heroes, is a high degree of intelligence and experience on the part of the electorate, so that it is not confused by demagogy.

He carried this argument a stage further in his essay on *Parliamentary Reform* (1859) and his History of the *Unreformed Parliament* (1860), and finally restated it with an additional argument in *The English Constitution*. The reason why Cabinet Governments work in Britain—this indirect election of the real rulers—which in fact involves abdication by the numerical majority in favour of an *élite*—is that England is a deferential nation. The deference is paid to the actors in the theatrical procession, the Crown and the aristocracy, leaving the real rulers who are "secreted in second class carriages" to get on with the task of governing.

"The middle classes—the ordinary majority of educated men—are in the present day the despotic power in England." "Public opinion nowadays is the opinion of the bald headed men at the back of the omnibus." "It is *not* the opinion of the aristocratical classes as such, or of the most educated or refined classes as such; it is simply the opinion of the mass of educated, but still commonplace mankind." In a system of pure democracy these dull sensible men would lose their influence.

Accepting as he did Burke's view that it was the function of the House of Commons to express the public interest rather than to reflect it in detail—"You have an equal representation because you have men equally interested in the prosperity of the whole, who are involved in the general interest and the general sympathy"—he feared that any general widening of the franchise would swamp the influence of the plain hardworking men who ran the country. And he rooted his argument against the "democratic theory" in the very quality of deference which made cabinet government valuable. To admit male adult suffrage would mean the disappearance of the small boroughs and the kind of independent minded members they sent to Westminster. In the big towns it would mean the dominance of the representatives of the artisans "not

possibly of the best of the artisans, who are a select and intellectual class, but of the common order of work people" and
thereby the effective disfranchising of the urban middle class.
But in the country districts where the standard of education
was much lower, it would merely increase the influence of the
squire and the magistrates. So that instead of having a House
of more or less like minded people, it would be made of
opposites; "one would have the prejudices of town artisans
and the others the prejudices of county magistrates", a more
militant Radicalism confronting a less intelligent Conservatism.*

He was fully aware that the distribution of seats under the
1832 Reform Act was now out of date and in need of overhaul,
since great changes in the distribution of wealth and population and taken place in the intervening thirty-five years. The
countryside was over-represented at the expense of the new
industrial areas. The North of England was under-represented
at the expense of the South: Ireland was pitifully represented,
Scotland hardly at all. What he wanted was to restore by a
logical redistribution of seats, one of the accidental virtues of
the chaotic system before 1832, namely the enfranchisement of
a limited number of purely working class areas, so that it could
have a number of its own spokesmen at Westminster as, in
the old days, it had through the Scot and Lot franchises, the
Westminster seat and other means. Just as the earlier theory
of the constitution had ensured that each of the great trades
should have their spokesmen, so "a great many feelings have
gathered among the town artisans—a peculiar intellectual
life has sprung up among them. They believe they have in-

* ". . . unless Reformers are very careful and foreseeing in their operations,
unless they are vigilant and sagacious to provide substitutes for what they
propose to destroy or change, measures which are devised in the popular
interests and intended to give preponderance to popular views, may end
in being aristocratic in their practical operation to a wholly unexpected
degree. A Ministry composed of Peers and landed gentry, with a House
of Commons composed of Radicals, Railway directors, elderly local celebri-
ties and county magnates, is not exactly the combination which thoughtful
and learned liberals would most desire to bring about." Politics as a Profession: *The Economist*, June 17th, 1865.

terests which are misconceived or neglected, that they know
something which others do not know, that the thoughts of
Parliament are not as their thoughts. They ought to be allowed to try to convince Parliament; their notions ought to
be stated as those of other classes are stated; their advocates
ought to be heard as other people's advocates are heard." It
is much the same argument that he used for admitting the
plutocracy and the new aristocracy of brains into the Lords by
means of life peerages.

Bagehot wished, as it were, to put 1885 ahead of 1867, to
tackle the redistribution of seats before contemplating a
marked extension of the franchise. He did not rule out the
possibility that political equality might one day be attainable
in England. But the strength of his feeling about the unwisdom of Disraeli's "leap in the dark", his fear that it would lead
to the dictatorship of party, his apprehension that henceforth
politics would become a scramble on the part of the Tories for
the urban worker's vote, on the part of the Liberal for that of
the agricultural worker, can be judged from the fact in his
Introduction to the Second Edition in 1872, all the humor
and irony which he elsewhere brought to political analysis
deserted him. Much of his later political writing has what he
called "the cold and guarded melancholy" of de Tocqueville.
His distrust of Disraeli, who, he hinted, was not above taking
a leaf out of the notebook of Napoleon III and creating a
plebiscitory dictatorship, took sharper form. This was not
blimpishness, not a feeling of being sold out to the class enemy,
but the reverse—distaste for those who would use the political
power of the working class without accepting the social revolution this implied—; contempt for the cheap jack with a
false historical perspective—"the light hack in a ploughing
match"—who for a temporary advantage was prepared to
undermine a political and social structure that had been so
lovingly and patiently devised over the years.

However here again, his open mindedness allowed him to
revise his opinions. Although in the year before he died he
wrote darkly in *The Economist* of "those Tory radicals who

may have got hold of real force but have not the slightest notion how to ascertain the law of that force's expansion", he did admit in an unpublished fragment, *The Chances for a Long Conservative Regime,* written in 1874, that so far the practical effect of the Second Reform Act on the composition of the House of Commons had been very small. Since the floodgates had been lowered, he also saw no reason why there should not be a limited franchise for women, for they were often more prudent and reflective than men.

IV

Bagehot's views on the extension of the franchise and his re-statement of the ancient conception of the function and basis of the House of Commons are of importance, because it was almost the last time that it was seriously put forward by a political writer of the first rank before the inevitable pressure for political equality swept it aside in the seventies and eighties. The fact that this corporatist view of democracy, that it is the function of the legislative to reflect interests rather than represent people, together with his emphasis on the indispensable political role of an intellectual *élite,* was put forward so lucidly so late as it were in European history, has led some writers to classify Bagehot with Mosca and Pareto as one of the unconscious forbears of Fascism.* Certainly there is not a little Bagehot, his irony and psychological realism twisted into moral assertions about the right to subordinate the working class, in the literature of twentieth century authoritarianism. What he did not see, or if he saw did not accept, was that in a democracy

* But those who have made this charge are apt to forget that he never carried this argument to the length of arguing for a legislature made up entirely of special interests. In *The Economist* of July 22nd, 1865, commenting on Oxford's rejection of Gladstone, he wrote "There ought to be some special constituencies in Parliament for every such special type of thought—some for the shipowner, some for the manufacturer, some for the landlord, some for the clergy; but there ought to be a vastly greater number of constituencies of no aberrant type, no eccentric idiosyncrasy, which simply represent the common voice of educated men, which must hear what the commissioned advocates of classes allege, weigh their arguments, estimate their often conflicting assertions, and in the last resort decide."

the question "which interests should be represented" is of its own nature incapable of an agreed answer, and that the rule of numbers must in the end prevail from the lack of any acceptable alternative.

But in his own day he was only trying to give practical expression to a widespread uneasiness among intelligent and thoughtful people as well as among plainer members of the middle class about the implications of extending political power to the working class. Even Bright and his fellow enthusiasts for a reform bill, were only interested in widening the franchise in order to give a vote to the remainder of the middle class: they had little interest in enfranchising the working class as such. Eldonine "genuine, hearty craven fear" was only one cause of this sense of alarm, though the Hyde Park riots of July, 1866 and the weak behavior of the authorities before "the mob" had heightened it. De Tocqueville's grim picture of the kind of society produced by Jacksonian democracy in America lay heavily upon the minds of the cultivated, and the handful of people who, like Leslie Stephen, could give a fairer perspective on the realities of American society were not then influential. Most important of all, Mill, both in his *Essay in Liberty* and in *Representative Government,* had brought out the fundamental dilemma of a progressive society, the encroachment of a mass culture on liberty.

Compared to the frantic gesticulations of Carlyle, his attitude was judicious. Compared to the Canute-like attempts of George Eliot to implore, through her radical hero Felix Holt, the newly enfranchised workers not to employ their powers until they had acquired more culture, he was eminently realistic. And even in his gloomiest moments he never wrote anything as panic-stricken as the quotation from his father which Matthew Arnold first inserted in *Culture and Anarchy*—though he excised it from the later editions. "As for rioting the old Roman way of dealing with *that* is always the right one; flog the rank and file and fling the ringleaders from the Tarpeian Rock."

He was as fully aware as his contemporaries that three

generations of neglect had left the British working class one of the most brutish in Europe. He shared the forebodings of the "old Liberals"—Goschen and Sidgwick, Henry Maine and Fitzjames Stephen—about the future pattern of British politics. "I can conceive of nothing more corrupting or worse for a set of poor ignorant people than that two combinations of well-taught and rich men should constantly offer to defer to their decision, and compete for the office of executing it." The High Tory dream of a new alliance between the aristocracy and the working class had for him the grotesque quality of a nightmare. And like Arnold he was fighting for time. "Our University," he told the electors of London University in his election address of 1867, "has shown upon what principles a sound and sensible culture can be given to young men sincerely bred in different religious creeds, without sacrificing either the faith to the culture or the culture to the faith. For myself, I believe that the experiment is capable of indefinite development. The sudden extension of the franchise is one of those facts 'of the first magnitude' which are never long resisted. After the first Reform Act the cry was 'Register! Register! Register!' The cry should now be 'Educate! Educate! Educate!' The State will have to intervene far more widely than is as yet thought ere the problem of wide education in a mixed society is solved." But he could not accept education as the panacea.

Moreover, he was concerned to an even greater extent than many of his contemporaries—one might almost say obsessed— with the problem of authority in the modern state. In his treatment of the monarchy, of the aristocracy, of the machinery of government, he lays so great a stress on their utility as devices for exacting obedience, that at times his description of the England of 1867 sounds more like the England of 1667. It seems hard to believe that the stable, reasonably contented, prosperous and united country which so deeply impressed visitors like Taine, could fall apart as easily as Bagehot suggested. It is true that there is a certain nervousness in his description of the ailments of the British body politic. But he had been twenty in 1846, the year that the structure of politics had collapsed, and his early twenties had been spent in watching the march and countermarch of government and revolution in Europe. His buoyancy and his tolerance reflect the recovered confidence of the fifties and sixties, of his own early middle age. But compared to Gladstone on the one hand who had surveyed "the dangerous years" from the vantage point of both experience and of maturity, or of the younger generation of Liberals—Morley, Bryce and their kind who had been children during these searching years—his attitude to political change in England always carried the implicit warning, "It is not true that it couldn't happen here."

In part, also, this apparent preoccupation with the survival of government and leadership was a by-product of his particular analytical method—of his ability to dismantle institutions to show how they really worked. His method allowed him to take nothing for granted, not even that an old and strong society would continue and prosper. And that he was able to do this—to describe the British Constitution in the half bantering fashion that revealed truths which had hitherto been concealed by their obviousness—was a symptom that the prestige of government was in fact declining, that the problem of authority was in fact a real one.

But where Bagehot differed from many of his contemporaries, most particularly Matthew Arnold, was in his strong and continuing belief in his own class—not the middle class as such, but the intellectual, the devoted, the hard working core of it. As a school inspector Arnold saw the Victorian middle class at its worst, as a banker and an editor Bagehot saw it at its best. Pride in their achievements made him view with gloom the ending of what he regarded as their too brief hegemony of power, particularly as it was only they who understood the most fruitful applied science of the day—economics. He did not confuse the awakening sense of protest against the crudeness and philistinism of Victorian middle class culture with an indictment of their political leadership, any more than he was prepared to take the fitful rumblings of the working class for anarchy. Government had become a hard, difficult business which needed able and industrious men to provide the administrative efficiency in which Britain was beginning to lag. It was not enough to staff the civil service with men of his own kind, even if they did "regard the parliamentary statesmen who are set to rule over them much as the Bengalees regard the English—as persons who are less intelligent and less instructed than themselves, but who nevertheless are to be obeyed". A good bureaucracy was no substitute for an informed and energetic House of Commons, for effective leadership was now inseparable from public confidence. Whatever their shortcomings as the agents of a truly civilized community, he believed that the upper middle class were for the time being most likely to throw up the men who had the stuff of statesmanship, "a manly utterance of clear conclusions".

There is much in *The English Constitution* that is ephemeral. But there is a great deal in Bagehot's political thought which is not. Quite apart from his description of the real balance of the constitution, his comments on English politics, if taken as a whole, contain one of the earliest, if not the clearest, formulations of modern liberalism in its widest sense, namely that the political structure of a nation can only be studied, understood or changed in conjunction with its social structure. He wanted a middle class franchise and a powerful House of Commons because he wanted the men of his own kind to lead Britain: to advocate a more democratic political structure without being ready to accept the accompanying social changes was, he knew, cynical and unrealistic.

Chapter 8

ANIMATED MODERATION

"All the world wants to know about science; there is an irritable accumulated curiosity in us and about us, such as history never saw equalled . . . An instinct of revision is felt to be abroad in human opinion, of which thinking men want to know the direction, and wish, if they could, to see the end."   *Essay on Matthew Arnold*

I

ELIE HALÉVY, the great historian, was first made aware of the special quality of the country to which he devoted his life's scholarship, through being shown by his father a handful of English coins each with the same sovereign's profile repeated in different guises—swan necked, matronly, veiled, imperial—for decade after decade. But the appearance of continuity which Victoria imparted to the last sixty years of the nineteenth century is well recognized to be quite deceptive. The years between 1865 and 1870 form a watershed of ideas, of aims, and a rent in the atmosphere of the times that is as clearly marked as if some great cataclysm had occurred. For Frenchmen, for Americans, for Prussians the alteration in their fortunes and their lives could be traced to great and dramatic happenings. But even in England which had known neither defeat nor civil war nor victory, the outward signs of change were as numerous, if less crushing, and carried as heavy an implication for the future.

The crash of Overend, Gurney in 1866 which profoundly shook the confidence of the middle class; the Reform Act of the following year, which the dullest baronet could see was the first step, as 1832 had not been, to universal suffrage and the uncharted wastes of democracy; the British North America Act which contained the germ of the modern Commonwealth; the revival of Fenianism and the long delayed entry of the Irish question into the heart of the political stage; the reappearance of the cattle plague and the re-casting of the American sword into a ploughshare which together foreshadowed the long decline of British agriculture; the consolidation and triumph of Prussian power—the events of these five years were clamorous enough to impress even the most unobservant.

The lull between the age of repeal and that age of construction which Bagehot had enjoined upon Gladstone to initiate and make his own was suddenly over, the plateau of prosperous isolationism was as suddenly left behind for a land in which, like the pioneer crossing the Continental Divide, "from here on up the hills don't get any higher, but the hollows get deeper and deeper". And with it went much of the eccentricity and humor, and also much of the flippancy and neglect of the middle years. Between the death of Palmerston in 1865 and the death of Derby in 1869, between Appomatox and Sedan, between the death of Thackeray in 1863 and the death of Dickens in 1870, the mood, the preoccupations, the color almost of English life seemed to change perceptibly. The arrival of Jowett in the Master's Lodgings at Balliol, the opening of the Civil Service to competitive examination, the beginning of Morley's editorship of *The Fortnightly,* all occurred within a few years of each other, all in their different ways the presages of modern England.

Sensitive people were aware how greatly the context of English life was altering. "We are most of us earnest with Mr. Gladstone's," wrote Bagehot in 1868; "we were most of us *not* so earnest in the time of Lord Palmerston. The change is what everyone feels, though no one can define it." Palmerston himself, Derby and Cobden, Mill and Grote, Faraday and Livingstone, Crabb Robinson and Charles Kean, all died within a few years of each other. When, in 1872, he wrote his Introduction to the Second Edition of *The English Constitution,* Bagehot tried to dispel the idea that it was the Reform Act alone which had changed the face of English life and politics.

> The change since 1865 is a change not in one point but in a thousand points; it is a change not of particular details but of

pervading spirit. We are now quarrelling as to the minor details of an Education Act; in Lord Palmerston's time no such Act could have passed. In Lord Palmerston's time Sir George Grey said that the disestablishment of the Irish Church would be an "act of Revolution"; it has now been disestablished by great majorities with Sir George Grey himself assenting. A new world has arisen which is not as the old world, and we naturally ascribe the change to the Reform Act. But this is a complete mistake. If there had been no Reform Act at all there would, nevertheless, have been a great change in English politics. There has been a change of the sort which, above all, generates other changes—a change of generation.

For the Reform Act had not only registered this change of generation, but having settled one great area of dispute, even temporarily, had left room for the discussion of new questions.

A political country is like an American forest; you have only to cut down the old trees, and immediately new trees come up to replace them; the seeds were waiting in the ground, and they began to grow as soon as the withdrawal of the old ones brought in light and air. These new questions of themselves would have made a new atmosphere, new parties, new debates.

The lives of individual men, even clever and informed men, do not necessarily alter with a changing political or social rhythm. The reverse is more often true. Yet for Bagehot the change in the nation's general preoccupations did correspond with a change in the pattern of his own life, and the balance of his interests. In 1867 he was forty-one, little changed in appearance from the young country banker who had made love to Eliza ten years before. He was now something of a figure in London, for *The Economist* had been growing in influence through the early years of his editorship, and his own arguments against introducing universal suffrage at that time had been widely quoted in the debate on the Reform Bill. His only serious disappointment had been his failure to get into Parliament. For most of those ten years he had lived a life of immense activity, posting between London and the West Country, between the City, the Strand and Whitehall, writing, directing a bank, arguing, his remarkable power of association enabling him to weave the thread of a conversation with a Somerset yokel on Langport Station into an editorial on foreign policy, or one with George Eliot into an observation on the money market. He was a by-word for absent-mindedness and at a family wedding mislaid his brother-in-law's will.* He seemed to condense several men's lives into his own; a breathless figure, slightly late for his appointments, appealing for the forgiveness of hostess or cabinet minister; making illegible records of a conversation or phrase in a succession of diminutive notebooks that he always carried; just catching the Taunton train to slump into the corner of a carriage with a pad or a proof; or peering through his eyeglass at the latest Bank of England figures in the office at 340 Strand—refuting in his own life his remark about Brougham that "he who runs may *read,* but it does not seem likely that he will think".

Though he took plenty of holidays—journeys through Normandy or the Dolomites, or quiet disappearances with Eliza to English watering places when he had a particularly thorny piece of writing to work on—there is little of the period's sense of still summer afternoon in his essays or letters: of

> *roses that down the alleys shine afar,*
> *and open, jasmine muffled lattices,*
> *and grapes under the dreaming garden trees*
> *and the full moon, and the white evening star.*

* Whenever Walter was on the scene, and whatever the occurrence might be, some funny little incident would happen connected with him which tickled the fancy and gave a welcome quaint flavour to the solemnities. Such incidents remain fixed fast in the memory whatever else is forgotten. On the day of my marriage, after returning from the church, we (the bride and bridegroom) retired with Walter into his study to sign our wills and eat a quiet luncheon, there being at the breakfast a vast assemblage of relations and old friends. The wills, however, were not forthcoming. Walter had had charge of them, but at the critical moment could not produce them. Ultimately they emerged from the butler's pantry. 'The wills are found', he said. 'They went down to be brushed with my evening clothes'." Mrs. Russell Barrington, Life of Walter Bagehot (London: Longmans, 1915), p. 406.

or of its peacefulness:

> *geranium, lychis, rose arrayed*
> *the windows all wide open thrown;*
> *and someone in the study played*
> *the Wedding March of Mendelsohn.*

But at Christmas 1867, an especially cold and foggy winter, he fell seriously ill, presumably with pneumonia, and throughout the winter he was too weak to work, or at times even to read. He recovered slowly, but the superhuman energy and the high spirits did not return, and for the rest of his life he had to husband his strength. Mountstuart Grant Duff who knew him only in these later years found it difficult to believe that he had ever been a hunting man. At *The Economist* he engaged Robert Giffen as his first full time assistant, and handed over to him the weekly article on the money market and the technical economic commentaries, while keeping general economic and political affairs for his own province. For three years his health was unpredictable and precarious, though he would never admit himself beaten, and one could not guess that *The Economist's* close analysis of the descent of Prussia on Austria and France, or of Gladstone's first government, were written by a frail man, now often having to dictate his editorials from a couch.

And further to quench his spirits and seal off his youth, his gay *distrait* mother died at last in 1870. He hated the fact that her family and friends looked on her death as a merciful release, for, mad though she was, he had learnt how to penetrate into the strange world where her mind so often wandered. Moreover, their roles had become transferred, and in her later years she had, in a sense, become his child, to be protected and understood, and he felt her death the more keenly for having no children of his own.* Whether her death revived

---

* I can find no trace in Eliza's near illegible diaries of any decision not to have children or of any mishap. But there are a number of allusions both in *Physics and Politics* and the *Economic Studies* which suggest that Bagehot thought that he, or perhaps both of them, were incapable of having children. They occur when he discusses population problems,

the fears about his own sanity that he had undoubtedly suffered as a young man, it is impossible to judge. But the father
of one of the present residents of Langport used to tell him
that about this time Bagehot would roam the lanes on horseback talking aloud to himself, and that the farmers and
farmhands would leave their ploughs and flocks and hide
under the hedgerows to catch what he was saying. When he
walked down the street at Langport, it was with his eyes on
the ground.

Politics did not lose its fascination for him after 1867. But
his interests altered in two ways: he became increasingly absorbed in economic theory as opposed to economic news, as the
depression of the money market in the late sixties and the
onset of wider depression a few years later forced him to re-
examine many of the assumptions on which the City and the
Government had operated. In 1871 he began *Lombard Street*
to knock some sense into the heads of the bankers and voters,
and thereafter his ambition to be considered a serious economist grew with each year.

The other effect that enforced leisure and low spirits had
upon him was to enhance his interest in speculative problems.
His association with *The Economist* had transformed him from
enfant terrible into a man of affairs: bad health and the
frustration of political opportunity turned his restless mind
back to the problems which had engaged it sporadically since
his schooldays.

He started to write *Physics and Politics* as soon as *The
English Constitution* was completed. It began to appear, like
its predecessor, as instalments in *The Fortnightly* in November,

---

where he fastens on to the popular fallacy, which was even then disputed,
that intellectuals were less fertile than those who did not engage in much
mental activity. "An incessant action of the brain often seems to diminish
the multiplying power", "There is only a certain quantity of force in the
female frame, and if that force, is invested, so to say, in one way, it cannot
be used in another", "Anxiety, as has been said, does so tell, and we have
seen that there is reason to believe that it much tends to slacken the
growth of population; and probably, any of the higher exercises of the
mind, which cause, as they all do, obscure and subtle pain, have a similar
effect". (*Works*, Vol. VII, p. 172 and pp. 218-19.)

1867 though it was not published as a book until 1872. It was never as widely read in England in his own day as his other works, but it has probably had the most pervasive influence of any of them. Beside the vast tomes in which Spencer set down his social theories, it is a mere pamphlet, no longer than a novel—and as racy—which can be read in a long evening. He did not intend it to be a comprehensive explanation of the origins of societies or the laws which govern their progress: it was not the first attempt at a link between the new discoveries in science and psychology and the study of political societies: and some of the assumptions on which its conclusions are based have since been disputed or out-dated. But it marks as clear a watershed of ideas as *Essays and Reviews*. For when he wrote it, it was still possible to consider political institutions purely in moral terms without reference to the level of political consciousness and cohesion of the societies for whom they were intended. But, as Sir Ernest Barker has written, "ever since Bagehot wrote *Physics and Politics,* political theorists have turned social psychologists; they have approached the facts of group-life on the assumption that these facts are facts of group-consciousness, which it is their problem to describe and explain by means of the method which a natural science uses in order to describe and explain the facts of matter". In all movements of ideas, there is a place for the brilliant guess: *Physics and Politics* is like a cavalry foray that captures a commanding position in order that the slower moving infantry may later consolidate it.

The book itself represented the conjunction of two of Bagehot's keenest private interests. One was a fascination with the social and political structure of England and France. Ever since he had stood upon the barricades in Paris and had seen, on that quiet, sinister morning, an old and complex society atomized into its individual molecules, he had been unable to take his comfortable English surroundings for granted. "We unconsciously assume around us the existence of a great miscellaneous social machine working to our hands, and not only supplying our wants, but even telling and deciding when those

wants shall come." But how was the machine put together
and made to run in the first place? How did people come to
trust each other sufficiently to leave protection to the police,
or obey the Queen's government, or discount each other's bills?
His knowledge of the City and its vast network of transactions
resting solely on confidence, sharpened his Socratic sense of
wonder. He was no positivist but Burke's answer that we must
venerate where we cannot comprehend had never satisfied him,
in secular matters at any rate.

The other was an interest in science and the scientific
method. Having escaped Oxford and Newman, he had no
predisposition to distrust the bearing of frogs and newts and
paleolithic skulls upon human origins or destiny. Moreover,
he had had, partly at London but particularly at Bristol College, as thorough a scientific grounding as an English education could provide. His literary essays had been considerably
influenced by his reading in Dugald Stewart and the earlier
psychologists: and Sir Herbert Read has pointed out that
his attempts to classify the various kinds of literary genius into,
for instance, the symmetrical, the regular and the irregular,
Plato, Chaucer or Shakespeare, explored ground that was later
consolidated by Jung's *Psychological Types*.

But during his own adult lifetime the great advances in
biology and physiology had begun to have a profound effect
upon the study of social as well as individual psychology.
Carpenter, who had taught him at Bristol, had opened, with
the publication in 1852 of his *Principles of Human Physiology*,
a quarter century which carried the study of human behavior
further than it had progressed in the previous two centuries.
Herbert Spencer, with whom he was on terms of acquaintance-
ship, he had followed carefully. He had accepted from Spencer
the theory of the transmission of acquired characteristics which
Spencer had accepted from Lamarck. He was a friend of Sir
Joseph Hooker, the great botanist, who had induced Darwin
to publish *The Origin of Species*. The great forward leap at
the end of the fifties when Darwin and Wallace both produced
their papers on evolution and natural selection had come at a

time when his interests were turning from literature to the study of political and economic behavior, and had made a profound impression on him. According to Hutton he devoured their books as well as Huxley's *Principles of Physiology*. Huxley's views on imitation, that the reflex desire to conform is one of the foundations of society, had confirmed his own surmises.

But *Physics and Politics* is not a commentary on the scientific discoveries of his time (it only mentions Darwin once and it was finished before *The Descent of Man* was published). It is an attempt to explore the revolutionary implications for historians and sociologists of the idea of civilization as an evolutionary process. What appears to have stimulated him to crystallize his ideas was not so much Darwin as the spate of books on primitive society in the years immediately before he sat down to write: Maine's *Ancient Law,* Lyell's *Antiquity of Man*, Huxley's *Man's Place in Nature,* and Lubbock's *Pre-historic Times*. It was their revelations of the vast gap in thought, in habit, in consciousness, and, above all, in mutual confidence, between primitive society and the web at whose center he himself dwelt, that set his mind to work.

The question to which Bagehot set out to find at least the beginnings of an answer was this: if the theory of natural selection is correct, how did man pass from the brute level to the highly complex and restrained social level of existence? The new knowledge of pre-history and primitive man "has dispelled the dreams of other days as to a primitive high civilization". Enough was now known to be certain that the ascent of all societies has been from a period that preceded any concept of law, of social organisation, of nationhood and of anything but the most primitive morality. How did *homo sapiens* succeed in thus pulling himself up by his boot straps. "Man, being the strongest of all animals, differs from the rest: he was obliged to be his own domesticator."

This was not the first time the question had been asked, and before attempting to answer it Bagehot showed the way in which the new advances in physiology and the other sciences had made it possible to provide a better answer. In the first place, the effect of the new biology "is that man himself has, to the eye of science, become an antiquity". The history of his first development was to be found in his physical structure, and consequently the emphasis was on those characteristics which he has inherited and transmitted. Second, the new knowledge of the nervous system and the stress it laid upon reflex action in the individual gave a clue to the development of society. He quoted Huxley to show that this was the basis of education in the individual, and Maudsley to show that it was the basis of the increasing skill and differentiation of function within the group. This notion of a transmitted nerve element thus provided a physical explanation of social progress enabling each generation to make "nicer music from finer chords".

Finally, despite the new emphasis on the transmission of physical characteristics, moral causes played an essential part in the process of development. "It is the action of the will that causes the unconscious habit; it is the continual effect of the beginning that creates the hoarded energy of the end; it is the silent toil of the first generation that becomes the transmitted aptitude of the next. Here physical causes do not create the moral, but moral create the physical; here the beginning is by the higher energy, the conservation and propagation only by the lower."

The knowledge which Bagehot drew on, and the terms of reference which he set for himself, mark a final break with the older necessitarianism, the concept of a mathematically determined universal order in which man finds his level. The idea that the individual has a double heritage, part psychological, part physical, had involved, in the twenty years before he wrote, a radical recasting of all the accepted ideas of the origins of man, of the noble savage and the Golden Age, that had come down from the eighteenth century. But in 1867 Bagehot was exploring uncharted seas, for Darwin had not yet cast his theory of natural selection in any wider terms than the individual. In attempting a new explanation of the development of group life and of political societies, he was venturing beyond the accepted views of his contemporaries, not only in applying the idea of the transmission of acquired characteristics to the group as well as the individual, but in casting the process on the plane of mind rather than body, of asserting that social development implied the transmission of acquired mental characteristics and attitudes to law and custom. It was from the new anthropology, notably Maine, Lubbock and M'Clennan, that he drew his authority, and in this he is on our side of the dividing line between modern political thought and the older inductive political thinkers.

II

The central argument of *Physics and Politics* is that there have been three broad stages in the development of man from primitive, atomistic life to a complex modern society. The first is the age before the dawn of most recorded history when nothing that can be described as political society is discernible, "the preliminary age". The second is the stage of fixed, customary polity, "the fightng age". And the third is the present stage of flexible polity which we take as much for granted as the air we breathe, "the age of discussion". The transition from the first to the second stage required the development of a rigid, inviolable law—what Bagehot called the "cake of custom"—in order to weld the units, which at first owed no higher loyalty than family, into a strong society. But the very virtues which were most useful for this purpose, for the creation of unitary societies, militated directly against the transition from the second to the third stage, to a freer, more varied and original society. It was the failure of certain nations, like the Chinese, thus to break the mould that their ancestors had found necessary to create, which accounted for the contrast between progressive and arrested civilizations.

Bagehot was not primarily concerned with the transition from the first to the second stage, from the primitive to customary polity. Too little was known about it for any amateur to shed much fresh light. In any case, since he had taken the theory of evolution for his starting point, he was entitled to assume the truth of its assertion that, over the course of thousands of years of prehistory, man had acquired an instinctive loyalty both to an ethnic and to a family group, and that he had arrived at the threshold of history with a rudimentary instinct for social coherence. Once there the critical problem became one of obedience to a rule—the object of social organisation was to bake this "cake of custom".

> In early times the quantity of government is much more important than its quality. What you want is a comprehensive rule binding men together, making them do much the same things, telling them what to expect of each other—fashioning them alike and keeping them so . . . To gain that rule, what may be called the impressive elements of a polity are incomparably more important than its useful elements. How to get the obedience of men is the hard problem; what you do with that obedience is less critical.

Several elements combine to bake the mould hard. There is law itself: there is status, the "net of custom caught men in distinct spots, and kept each where he stood". But two causes worked for cohesion more than any others. One was war. Bagehot did not share the belief of many of his contemporaries that skill in the peaceful arts, commerce and industry, was the principal reason why some nations evolved faster than others. These factors, in his view, only came into operation at a much later stage. War with its emphasis on loyalty, courage and obedience was an essential tool of customary society, and progress in war and civilization went side by side. The reason why backward nations had remained so, was often that they had been isolated from the main areas of conflict, just as the forwardness of Europe, was explicable in terms of the constant process of conflict, conquest and assimilation that had gone on there. Survival of the fittest did not, in this context, mean the dominance of a strong physical type but of a group that has been more successful than its neighbors in producing a high state of internal discipline. Athens to modern eyes might have achieved a higher form of government than Rome or Sparta "But to the 'Philistines' of those days Athens was of a lower order. She was beaten; she lost the great visible game which is all that short sighted contemporaries know". Bagehot was prepared to equate the most successful military nations with those which had the greatest flair for political development—not necessarily the most highly civilised—since military prowess involved the encouragement of originality, the diversification of skill, and keeping of superstition to a minimum.

The other ingredient in the cake was imitation, which by impelling men and groups—how he did not claim to know— to conform to the most successful type within their range of experience, set a style which, for him, was the principal ingredient in the formation of national character. This is so disputed a question that it is worth a separate glance a little later.

But given success in creating a disciplined customary society,

"the great difficulty which history records is not that of the first step, but that of the second step. What is most evident is not the difficulty of getting a fixed law, but getting out of a fixed law. No one will ever comprehend the arrested civilizations unless he sees the strict dilemma of early society. Either men had no law at all, and lived in confused tribes, hardly hanging together, or they had to obtain a fixed law by processes of incredible difficulty. Those who surmounted that difficulty soon destroyed all those that lay in their way who did not. And then they themselves were caught in their own yoke. The customary discipline which could only be imposed on any early men by terrible sanctions, continued with those sanctions, and killed out of the whole society the propensities to variation which are the principle of progress. Experience shows how incredibly difficult it is to get men really to encourage the principle of originality." "One of the greatest pains to human nature is the pain of a new ideal."

How then did civilization ever become unfrozen?

To this history gives a very clear and a very remarkable answer. It is that the change from the age of status to the age

of choice was first made in states where the government was
to a great and a growing extent a government by discussion, and
where the subjects of that discussion were in some degree
abstract, or, as we should say, matters of principle.

But Bagehot did not pretend to know *why* certain nations and
kinds of national character developed a greater aptitude for
discussion than others. Obviously the smaller the political unit,
the easier discussion came. But no simple theory of climate,
physical surroundings or race gives the answer, and freedom
from external pressure gives the wrong answer since the need
to acquire military strength often provided the necessary element of variation. He accepted Maine's view that the expansion
and definition of the family as a means of counsel and education was one factor in the process, to which he added a second,
the capacity for gradual change—the progress from the age of
custom to the age of discussion was never achieved by revolution—and a third, the gradual expansion of the number of
subjects on which it was possible to hold that "opinion was
optional".

Once the process began to operate, the advantages of polity
which admitted discussion accelerated its formation. One effect
of this variation was the growth of leisure, possibly through
certain "provisional institutions" like oligarchy or slavery,
which enabled some men in the community to sit still and
think.

> If it had not been for quiet people who sat still and studied
> the sections of the cone, if other quiet people had not sat still
> and studied the theory of infinitesimals, or other quiet people
> had not sat still and worked out the doctrine of chances, the
> most "dreamy moonshine", as the purely practical mind would
> consider, of all human pursuits . . . modern life could not have
> existed. Ages of sedentary, quiet thinking people were required
> before that noisy existence began, and without those pale pre-
> liminary students it never could have been brought into being.

There is no doubt that he meant *Physics and Politics* to be
a much larger book, applying his suggestion of three stages
of social growth not only to political but to economic behavior

and organization as well. His breakdown in health not only made him write it more slowly than he had intended, over nearly five years rather than a year or so, but also forced him to modify its scope. In consequence, it was published after Darwin's *Descent of Man* and at a time when the originality of his conceptions had been somewhat blunted.*

He succeeded, however, in fully developing the most interesting idea which the book contains, man's propensity to unconscious imitation as one explanation for the early development of societies. And as long as the theory of imitation remained part of the main corpus of psychological thought, that is to say until the early part of this century, his description of how it worked was more convincing than that of his successors who took up the idea and developed it further, Tarde, Le Bon or William James.

The instinct for conformity—in one place he calls it conscious, elsewhere unconscious—was one of man's strongest, both in the days when it was politically essential, namely in a customary society, and later when it came to act as a necessary brake on that propensity to variation which was indispensable to progress.

> There is a cynical doctrine that men would rather be accused of wickedness than of *gaucherie*. And this is but another way of saying that the bad coyping of predominant manners is felt to be more of a disgrace than common consideration would account for its being, since *gaucherie* in all but extravagant cases is not an offence against religion or morals, but is simply bad imitation.

It was characteristic of his style that he was prepared to argue this point not only on broad grounds of historical

* Darwin's refinement of the idea of evolution in *The Descent of Man* is in close parallel with the theme of *Physics and Politics*. "Important as the struggle for existence has been and even still is, yet as far as the higher parts of man's nature is concerned, there are other agents more important. For the moral qualities are advanced either directly or indirectly much more through the effect of habit, the reasoning powers, instruction, religion, etc., than through natural selection: though to the latter agency we owe the social instincts which afford the basis for the development of the moral sense."

evidence but from homely examples as well. Conformity was
a current that one could trace throughout early history; but
it could also be seen in the metamorphosis of the contemporary
Englishman in Australia or America where he swiftly acquired
entirely different idols. Even in England itself any one who
requires would find:

> even in these days of assimilation, parish peculiarities which
> arose, no doubt, from some old accident, and have been heed-
> fully preserved by customary copying. A national character is
> but the successful parish character.

Look, he added, more closely around you.

> The bane of philosophy is pomposity: people will not see
> that small things are the miniatures of greater, and it seems a
> loss of abstract dignity to freshen their minds by object lessons
> from what they know. But every boarding school changes as a
> nation changes. Most of us may remember thinking: "How
> odd it is that this 'half' should be so unlike last 'half': now we
> never go out of bounds, last half we were always going; now
> we play rounders, then we played prisoner's base"; and so
> through all the easy life of that time.

Look at the way fashion changes: at the way a whole newspaper, like *The Times,* catches the editorial style of one member of the staff. Look at politics: "We are most of us earnest
with Mr. Gladstone: we were most of us not so earnest in the
time of Lord Palmerston."

> The infection of imitation catches men in their most in-
> ward and intellectual part—their creed . . . Insensibly and as
> by a sort of magic, the kind of manner which a man catches
> eats into him, and makes him in the end what at first he only
> seems.

There is something of his own experience, the odd man out
who could never fully accept the predominant pattern of
ideals of any society in which he moved, literary, political
or commercial in this sentence:

> There is much quiet intellectual persecution among "reason-
> able" men; a cautious person hesitates before he tells them

anything new, for if he gets a name for such things he will be
called "flighty" and in times of decision he will not be attended
to.

Imitationism was a theory capable only of a limited usefulness until sociology had grown firmer roots in anthropology
and biology. For the past generation or so there has probably
been more agreement with Huxley than with Bagehot that
imitation is one important factor in the formation of national
character, but only one. Bagehot's contribution, even in over-
stressing its role, was to establish how potent a force it is and
how much it contributes to the irrationality of national character and customs. Weissman's demolition of Lamarck's theory
of the inheritance of acquired characteristics a few years after
Bagehot's death did not really invalidate his point, for he was
not arguing so much from biological data as from the evidence
of national mood or atmosphere, by the process of imitation,
and the effect upon the strength and destiny of nations of
changes in the "leader image", the kind of men who set the
tone and created the ideal. It is the argument of a professional
observer of life rather than of an amateur scientist; and in it
he came very close to formulating a theory of the group unconscious, a generation before Adler and Jung.

There also is a great deal of his own predilections in his
treatment of the Age of Discussion. It was his own setting, the
atmosphere he liked, and he personally had no nostalgia for
more heroic days, despite his worship of Scott. The great virtue
of discussion was that it kept "the ruinous force of the will"
at bay. The duty which it laid upon political leaders was to
fight a constant battle against the instinct for action for its
own sake, inherited from the stage of civilization when action
formed the whole of policy. This premium on thought would
in time, he considered, also produce a check on population by
diverting sexual activity into other channels, a naïve belief
which he acquired from Spencer.

Moreover, a polity of discussion should tend to produce a
new type of man capable of a new quality which Bagehot
called "animated moderation", "a union of spur and bridle",
"of life with measure, of spirit with reasonableness". The

English produced the type of man in more abundant measure than other races by the nature of their public life.

> It is plain that a government by popular discussion tends to produce this quality. A strong idiosyncratic mind, violently disposed to extremes of opinion, is soon weeded out of political life, and a bodiless thinker, an ineffectual scholar, cannot even live there for a day. A vigorous moderateness in mind and body is the rule of a polity which works by discussion; and upon the whole, it is the kind of temper most suited to the active life of such a being as man, in such a world as the present one.

At the end of *Physics and Politics* he disclaimed any intention of writing a panegyric on liberty but nevertheless he devoted the whole of his last chapter on "Verifiable Progress" to stating his own definition of the meaning of liberty—the opportunity and the ability to sieve all subjects to a fine grain before action is decided upon. This is the essential condition of progress. "Nature does not ever wear her most useful secrets on her sleeve." The instinct for action which modern man bore as an inheritance from an earlier day when it had more value than thought and which tended to ruin judgments, political, commercial or private, could best be restrained by an intensive and prolonged discussion. It was no wonder that he found Sir George Cornewall Lewis, the vegetable, whose preference was for talking all round a subject in order that it might be decided that action after all was unnecessary, so sympathetic a friend.

"Bagehot held," said Hutton, "with Sir George Lewis that men in modern days do a great deal too much; that half the public actions, and a great many of the private actions of men had better never have been done; that modern statesmen and modern peoples are far too willing to burden themselves with responsibilities. He held, too, that men have not yet sufficiently verified the principles on which action ought to proceed, and that until they have done so, it would be better far to act less." The ghost of Clough still dwelt at his elbow.

By the same token he opposed with all his forcefulness Carlyle's revolt against discussion, the denunciation of Parliamentary government as "national palaver" or of Parliament as a talking shop.

> They add up the hours that are consumed in it, and the speeches which are made in it, and they sigh for a time when England might again be ruled, as it once was, by a Cromwell— that is, when an eager, absolute man might do exactly what other eager men wished, and do it immediately . . . They are all distinct admissions that a polity of discussion is the greatest hindrance to the inherited mistake of human nature, to the desire to act promptly, which in a simple age is so excellent, but which in a later and complex time leads to so much evil.

Energy had not diminished, he pointed out, whatever the detractors of parliamentary government might say. Whenever something had had to be done, when a war had to be fought, or a great commercial venture was to be undertaken, it was done as well as ever. If there was a more widespread atmosphere of doubt, "it is a great benefit; and it is to the incessant prevalence of detective discussion that our doubts are due".

> Liberty is the strengthening and developing power—the light and heat of political nature; and when some "Caesarism" exhibits as it sometimes will an originality of mind, it is only because it has managed to make its own the products of past free times or neighbouring free countries.

The English Constitution ended upon a note of settled melancholy, exhibiting what Mr. T. G. Pearson has rightly called Bagehot's "political hypochondria" about too fast and careless a pace of reform and legislation, and his almost morbid fear "of the bungling fingers of the political surgeon, cutting and slicing the flesh which was so much more delicate than any of the surgeons Bagehot knew could ever appreciate." *Physics and Politics,* however, has a more cheerful conclusion, for in the interval between the two books he had arrived at his own definition of progress which to a certain extent liberated him from nostalgia for the more oligarchic polity that had existed between the two Reform Bills. The new scientific knowledge gave him a basis on which to build a superstructure of belief

that if discussion of the great subjects of today could be kept
vigorous and uninhibited, the deficiencies of the political
leaders he saw around him, the demagogy of Gladstone, the
triviality of Disraeli, the hasty remedies of radicals and philanthropists could be made good. What he was really after
was "piecemeal social engineering", a generation before the
Fabians, for he had none of the fears of the older Liberals of
of state action as such.*

> If, therefore, a nation is able to gain the benefit of custom
> without the cost—if after ages of waiting a nation can have
> order and choice together—at once the fatal clog is removed,
> and the ordinary springs of progress as in a modern community
> we conceive them, begin their elastic action.

Order and choice—they formed the central dilemma of the
century, a stiff requirement for any political society to meet.
Bagehot was clear that the English could possess them, while
the French had achieved only choice without order, the Prussians order without choice. For the time being discussion was
a prerogative only of the upper and middle classes; the rest
of the nation was held together not by the considered judgment of individuals but by deference and imitation; it dwelt
as it were in a different era, in the age of custom which the
governing class had moved beyond. If the State would now
take the problem of mass education seriously, as he was urging
on the electors of London University three years before
Forster's Act, there was a reasonable prospect that the circle
of discussion could be gradually expanded, as more and more
of the electorate acquired "the fine judgement" which was
necessary. Deference, which he regarded as a means to an end,

* His election address at London University takes a modern liberal's view
of the State "The English State is but another name for the English
people. From countless causes the age of great cities requires a strong
government. The due extension of the functions of the State in super-
intending the health and in lessening the vice and misery of our larger
towns must receive speedy attention from a Parliament in which most of
the inhabitants of those towns are for the first time represented. The
co-operative, if not the compulsory agency, of the State ought, too, to be
used far more than now in applying to our complicated society those
results of science which are new to this age."

not as a social virtue in itself, would become less important. Bagehot arrived at the position of the later Victorian liberals by a road of his own, illuminated by little or no idealism except for a coherent and intelligent society. His mistake was to confuse means with ends. His persistent weakness was that he could only show the rules by which societies progress: he gave no clue as to what all this discussion should be about, or to what vision of society, to what moral end, to what relationship of the individual to the group, it should be addressed.

Bagehot is free of the vice of "historicism", the attempt to impose an external pattern upon history. Though clearly the "preliminary age", "the fighting age" and "the age of discussion" correspond broadly to the period before the Roman Empire, to Romanesque and medieval civilization, and to Europe since the Reformation, he does not attempt to link his analysis loosely to actual events or eras. At first reading this lessens the force of his argument, until one realizes that he was writing as much about contemporary societies as about their origins, since all nations have at different levels of group consciousness the characteristics of all three phases. It was fortunate that he did not attempt to project his thesis on the actual course of history, for it would have brought him very close to the errors of the Whig interpretation. In the same way that he identified rather than exalted social deference, he never sought to raise the irrational in national beliefs, "muddling through" in Imperial or in domestic policy, to the status of a positive virtue, as Seeley and his successors did.

Physics and Politics was not as widely read in England in his own generation as Bagehot's other writings. But it was translated into French and Russian and five other languages, and his influence as a social psychologist was greater in Europe than in England. The proponents in France of the theory of unconscious imitation, Gabriel Tarde and Gustave Le Bon proved their own theories by incorporating a great deal of Bagehot's views without acknowledging their source. It was not until William James, Graham Wallas and Trotter, that the importance of Bagehot's views on social behavior and his delineation of the irrational basis of social beliefs were intelligently criticized. The later Victorian psychologists were much more concerned with behavior than with consciousness, and it was not until after the beginning of the century that the growing interest in the social importance of the myth, stimulated mostly by European and American rather than British researches, together with the widening acceptance of the view that man has a cultural as well as a biological inheritance however transmitted, made people look back at the origin of the train of ideas which has engrossed us ever since, and thus to Bagehot.*

III

The fluency with which Bagehot could develop an argument, the wealth of illustration, the friendly view he took of

* In from *Luther to Hitler*, (London: Harrap, 1946), Professor W. M. McGovern lays a heavy onus on the Social Darwinists, and in particular on Bagehot and Gumplowicz, as the foster parents of Fascism and what he calls "etatism". He attaches considerable importance to the fact that Bagehot carried the Darwinian theory of the struggle for existence and the survival of the fittest from the plane of the individual human being to that of the group, and that he believed that those groups which in a customary society survived and progressed were the most highly disciplined. Other American writers following the same train of ideas have equated Bagehot's respect for the military virtues of societies in an earlier age with a glorification of militarism. The most recent has written "This military bias probably reflected his identification with the *élite* of his day and his endorsement of the imperialism and military puissance of England." (Leonard Ostlund, *Social Science*, April, 1956.)

Certainly, one can find overtones of Bagehot in the writings of Mussolini, Rosenberg and Hitler, as Professor McGovern has done, but this is merely another way of saying that the twentieth century fascists took what suited them from the researches of the Victorians into the irrational and evolutionary origins of modern societies and social beliefs, and deliberately perverted them into a contemporary ideal and ethic, to suit their own ends.

Bagehot, it should be remembered, was not an Imperialist, and believed in his own day in keeping the military under the firmest of civilian controls. He differs from some of his contemporaries in according to the military virtues a high place in the development of successful modern societies, but it is "the age of discussion", the civil age, which forms the kernel of *Physics and Politics*. Nor for that matter did he believe in an *élite*, in the sense of a closed and privileged ruling class. He believed in a certain type of man rather than a class of man, as the ideal instrument of power in a modern society.

human nature, can deceive one into thinking that his writing was the product of a simple and uncomplicated nature, a man of "common sense raised to the power of genius". It is perhaps the impression that he hoped to leave upon his readers. He was not a simple man, but one who had achieved simplicity of expression by a severe process of restraint and intellectual discipline, who recognized, as he wrote when he was thirty, that "Deep under the surface of the intellect lies the *stratum* of the passions, of the intense, peculiar, simple impulses which constitute the heart of man; there is the eager essence, the primitive desiring being." Logically, the bent of his interests in science, in criticism, in the examination of the myth for the reality should have led him away from orthodox religion. Bristol and London, Greg and George Eliot, Spencer and Morley, the places and people whose influence he acknowledged would, with the strong exception of Hutton, have inclined a simpler man either to some form of agnosticism or rationalism. Moreover, few people except the specialists had immersed themselves so deeply in the new anthropology and the widening circle of discovery and conviction about man's origin which culminated in the *Origin of Species*. Yet the development of his religious views took an entirely different course from those of, say, Huxley or Leslie Stephen, and he became as he grew older not only a more convinced Christian but closer to the High Anglicans whose influence he had been so thankful to escape in youth.

Mr. Noel Annan in his study of Leslie Stephen, distinguishes three central positions which Stephen developed as an agnostic once he had lost his rather wintry Christian faith. "Firstly, dogmatic religious systems are unreal: secondly, evidence does not support belief in God's existence: thirdly, religion demoralises society." Throughout his later life Bagehot recognized the strength of these assertions and set out to combat them where he could, or to deny them where he could not, for the reason that he felt that belief in God was essential to his own sanity and survival.

Kant had made a much deeper impression on him at school than any other philosopher, and Kant's distinction between the world accessible to the senses and the world accessible only to the moral faculties, compelled him to remain according to Hutton, "in spite of the rather antagonistic influence of the able, scientific group of men from whom he learned so much—a thorough transcendentalist." In 1862, the year that Stephen resigned his Cambridge fellowship in despair, Bagehot published his own attempt to deal with the first of the agnostic assertions, that dogmatic religion is unreal. *The Ignorance of Man* goes in fact a very long way towards accepting it. The best the theologians could do, he thought, was to "show, not, indeed, that an omnipotent Being created the universe, but that an able being has been (so to say) about it". Natural theology could do little to remove the primitive dilemma, that to admit the existence of Providence as "an adjusting agency" is to admit the existence of an arbitrary rewarder and withholder of rewards while the essence of morality is disinterestedness. For the agnostic this proposition was good enough. But for Bagehot, to whom belief was an inner necessity, as it was for Burke and for de Tocqueville, is was an argument not for the non-existence of God but for man's inability to comprehend the moral part of God's nature. Man's ignorance was in fact his salvation.

> It shows us that a latent Providence, a confused life, an odd material world, an existence broken short in the midst, and on a sudden, are not real difficulties but real helps: that they, or something like them, are essential conditions of a moral life to a subordinate being.

"Lift not the painted veil" had been one of his favourite quotations as a young man, and this fascination with man's ignorance of God remained with him. "A clear, precise discriminating intellect," he suddenly bursts out against Jeffrey in *The First Edinburgh Reviewers,* "shrinks at once from the symbolic, the unbounded, the indefinite. The misfortune is that mysticism is true."

He grew more skeptical about a great deal of the historical evidence for Christianity as he grew older, much to Hutton's

disapproval. But Darwin did not shake him, as it shook
Stephen or confirmed Huxley in his agnosticism. He did not
accept the view that evolution had made a fundamental breach
in the metaphysical basis of Christianity by showing that
chance alone produces order. Nor did he believe that the evidence that progress is the result of minute accidental variations
in the species destroyed belief in a Supreme Being who ruled
a rational universe by keeping order among its diverse and
conflicting elements. For Bagehot "the new principle is seen
to be fatal to mere outworks of religion, not to religion itself". In fact, to a mind with a natural bent towards religious
belief, the principle of evolution in its broad effects was scientific confirmation of the existence of a creative mind behind
the universe. The idea of steady biological progress freed a
mind like Bagehot's from the idea of a universal order based
on checks and balances, or on analogies drawn from the physical sciences, which had haunted the eighteenth century.

Desmond MacCarthy pointed out that Stephen, unlike
Clough, never associated religion with emotion, since for him
morality did not involve the emotions. Bagehot belongs with
Clough in this respect. His religious upbringing had been
undertaken by his mother rather than his gentle Unitarian
father and from the first it had become involved in his intense,
imaginative private world. Hutton doubted whether the "religious affections were very strong in Bagehot's mind, but the
primitive religious instincts certainly were". Before his marriage he had gone through a brief period of skepticism, though
"I say that I am only lazy in believing". When they were engaged he wrote to Eliza:

> The faith of young men is rather *tentative*. Some points of
> course are very fixed, but a good many are wavering, are rather
> tendencies than conclusions. I have perhaps an unusual degree
> of this myself. From my father and mother being of different—I
> am afraid I might say—opposite sentiments on many points, I
> was never taught any scheme of doctrine as an absolute certainty
> in the way most people are . . . What I have made out is a good
> deal of my own doing. I have always had an indistinct feeling

that my inner life has been to harsh and vacant to give me an abiding hold of some parts of religion.

But guilt worked powerfully upon his mind. "Conscience is the condemnation of ourselves," he wrote in his remarkable study of Bishop Butler (when he was twenty-seven),

We expect a penalty. As the Greek proverb teaches, "where there is shame there is fear"; where there is the deep and intimate anxiety of guilt—the feeling which has driven murderers, and other than murderers, forth to wastes, and rocks and stones and tempests—we see, as it were, in a single complex and indivisible sensation, the pain and sense of guilt, and the painful anticipation of its punishment. How to be free from this, is the question.

And after a graphic description of the bloodier heathen methods of propitiation he wrote:

Of course it is not this kind of fanaticism that we impute to a prelate of the English Church: human sacrifices are not respectable, and Achilles was not rector of Stanhope (Butler). But though costume and the circumstances of life change, the human heart does not: its feelings remain. The same anxiety, the same consciousness of personal sin, which led in barbarous times to what has been described, show themselves in civilized life as well.

How could this "intense, eating, abiding supremacy of conscience" as an intuitive force be kept in balance with the conception of a God, who is the author of light and giver of concord. It was an old question, to which Bagehot tried all his life to form his own answer. He abjured Sydney Smith and the well-fed liberal divines who "have endeavored to petrify into a theory, a pure and placid disposition". Like Matthew Arnold he despised Calvinism for blunting the sense of beauty in religion—"there is nothing like Calvinism for generating indifference"—as he disliked Thomas Arnold for overstimulating for his own purposes the consciences of the sensitive young. In his study of Cowper, and the effect upon his sanity of the Calvinism of the Reverend Newton, there is an echo of his own fears, a recollection of what the stern Estlins and Priors had succeeded in doing to the balance of his mother's mind. Conscience, for Bagehot, as for Butler, was "a daily companion, a close anxiety".

Yet the religion of beauty "of week days as well as Sundays, or 'cakes and ale' as well as of pews and altar cloths" held him even faster than the religion of fear. It was the root of the gentle flirtation with the Catholic Church which he carried on throughout most of his life. As a young man he wrote an atrocious poem to the Church, and such poetry as he attemped was directly inspired by Newman, his favorite contemporary poet. They never appear to have met, though it was partly Bagehot's admiration which encouraged Newman to re-publish his poems separately from *Lyra Apostolica,* in which they had first appeared. Among Hutton's correspondence with Newman, is a letter from the Oratorian of Edgbaston, written at the time of their publication in 1867, asking Hutton to forward a copy to Bagehot, "because I do not know his address, and still more because I think you will be so kind as to explain to him what otherwise may seem an abrupt introduction of myself to his notice".

Though Bagehot would have denied emphatically Stephen's third proposition, that religion demoralizes society—in *Physics and Politics,* he contended that it accelerates the development of politically mature societies by promoting "confidence in the universe" and thereby the conquest of rational ideas over myths—his Catholic leanings were not dictated by his conservatism. In the *Letters on the Coup d'état* he had written a strong defence of the Church as the only element of social stability in a nation temporarily unfitted for parliamentary government, and a counterpoise to "the feverish excitement, the feeble vanities and the dogmatic impatience of an over-intellectual generation".

> The poorest priest in the remotest region of the Basses Alpes has more power over men's souls than human cultivation. His ill mouthed masses move women's souls—can you? . . . Idol for idol, the *de*throned is better than the *un*throned.

But in his more mature writings he never pressed this line of argument. He was considerably irritated by the crass anti-Romanism of the English middle class. "When an Englishman sees anything in religion which he does not like, he always, *prima facie,* imputes it to the Pope." But his respect for the social authority of the Roman Catholic Church in Europe did not lead him to cast the Church of England for a similar role. Despite his belief in the social utility of deference, he had very little respect for the Anglican clergy as a social instrument.*

He distrusted Newman's disregard of the element of evidence. What Newman contributed to his private life and private doubts was absolute faith which, by liberating him from the dark places of his own mind, enabled him to dwell on the imaginative and romantic aspect of worship.

"In every step of religious argument we require the assumption, the belief, the faith if the word is better, in an absolutely *perfect* Being—in whom and by whom we are, who is omnipotent at well as most holy, who moves on the face of the whole world and ruleth all things by the word of His power. If we grant this, the difficulty of the opposition between what we have called the natural and supernatural religion is removed; and without granting it, that difficulty is perhaps insuperable." Unlike George Eliot whose fundamental conservatism also made faith a deep psychological necessity, he was able to direct his own need towards an orthodox creed.

Religion was for Bagehot a very private matter. He trekked across London to mass at St. Albans, Holborn—unaccompained it would seem by Eliza. He was a member of that curious body, The Metaphysical Society in which Sir James Knowles, a most unmetaphysical architect but an unrelenting lion hunter, each month collected the ablest antagonists of the day in Willis's Rooms, and induced them

* Just before he died Bagehot was staying at Knebworth in company with Mountstuart Grant Duff. As they were walking through the great gates Bagehot turned to Duff and said: "Ah they have got the church in the grounds. I like that. It is well that the tenants should not be *quite* sure that the Landlord's power stops with this world."

to argue. Tennyson and Cardinal Manning, Gladstone and Huxley, Dean Stanley and Wilfred Ward, Morley and Gasquet, Martineau and Frederick Harrison, Seeley and Mark Pattison, Balfour, Ruskin, Froude and many others were pitted against each other in what Maitland called "showy tournaments". It was characteristic of the duality of his own nature, that when the discussions turned on points of metaphysics, Bagehot was one of the most ardent debunkers of any elaborate hypothesis put forward, taunting Ruskin or Gladstone to make good their assertions about possibility, probability and certainty. But when the conversation turned to religion he drew back. The only paper he read to it, "The Emotion of Conviction", ended with these words:

> Intense convictions make a memory for themselves, and if they can be kept to the truths of which there is good evidence, they give a readiness of intellect, a confidence in action, a consistency of character, which are not to be had without them.

And as a younger man he gave one clear hint of the privacy of his own feelings:

> There is much of mankind that a man can only learn from himself. Behind every man's external life, which he leads in company, there is another which he leads alone, and which he carries with him apart. We see but one aspect of our neighbour, as we see but one side of the moon; in either case there is also a dark half, which is unknown to us. We all come down to dinner, but each has a room to himself.

Chapter 9

MEN AND MONEY

"Men of business have a solid judgement—a wonderful
guessing power of what is going to happen—each in his
own trade; but they have never practised themselves in
reasoning out their judgements and in supporting their
guesses by argument: probably if they did so some of the
finer and correcter parts of their anticipations would
vanish. They are like the sensible lady to whom Coleridge said: 'Madam, I accept your conclusion, but you
must let me find the logic for it'." *Economic Studies.*

I

THE compass of knowledge was still just small enough,
ninety years ago, for a man of great intellectual vigor,
one who thought "business more amusing than pleasure",
to form views on all the great questions of the day. But,
though Bagehot might have his private trains of thought,
he had no ivory tower on which he could retreat, even had
he wished for one. He was neither a don nor the holder of a
sinecure, but the Editor of a weekly paper whose judgments
affected the behavior of markets, the views of government
departments and the tenor of parliamentary debates. The
new sciences were his private hobby, literature his recreation
and religion his solace; but his working week was absorbed
primarily in economic problems. If he has descended into the
reference books under other headings than "economist",
it is because of his diversity and energy. It is as analyst of
economic behavior that he would have expected to be judged.

By the time he reached *The Economist* in 1859, much of
the radical fire and sense of the urgency of social reform
which had marked his review of Mill's *Principles* in 1848,
had evaporated—as to a certain extent they had in Mill
himself. The England of the late fifties and early sixties
was a more prosperous place with a better distribution of

income than any man, reading the signs of 1848, could have dared to hope. Californian and Australian gold had helped to set in motion a period of cheap money and economic expansion throughout the world, which the policies of governments, in the existing climate of opinion, could never have accomplished. In the first half of the fifties, wages rose by 16 per cent in England, and by the middle of the next decade they were on an average between 20 and 25 per cent higher than those of 1848, even in the older trades, while bread had risen only 12 per cent above the very low prices of the years immediately after Repeal. The middle and upper classes were patently better off in the early sixties than they had been a decade earlier, the working class less securely so but with a widening range of alternative jobs. The restrictive effects of the panic of 1857 and of the Crimea and Mutiny years had been offset by the impetus which the extension of limited liability to joint stock banking in 1858, the introduction of the Bessemer process in steel smelting, and Gladstone's Companies Act of 1861 had given to credit, to enterprise and to basic industry. Only the blight on the Lancashire cotton industry, which the blockade of the South involved, restrained the economy from developing even faster. The task of the Editor of *The Economist* was not to preach nostrums, but to act as one of the guardians of an economy that was if anything expanding too fast, to evolve practical means of foretelling the economic weather, and to differentiate between frenzy and activity.

Bagehot accepted Wilson's rigid Liberalism on only one point of economic policy—free trade and protection. He had always admired his father-in-law for his work in making Free Trade an economic, rather than a class or a moral issue, during the years of the League. He continued to defend and advocate Free Trade, not only through its triumphant years, but when, as the depression of the mid-seventies gathered weight, the clamor for Protection began to rise again.

He was always a supporter of the income tax, a subject on which he disagreed with Gladstone. *The Economist* had supported Gladstone's introduction of the tax, both in principle and as the best security for the maintenance of free trade. But one of Bagehot's first duties as Editor was to lead the last forlorn charge against the Budget of 1861 and the injustice of taxing earned and unearned incomes on the same scale—an injustice "much discussed in the fifties", wrote Sir John Clapham, "of which it is not unfair to say that Gladstone's will and prestige, and they alone, perpetuated it for half a century". One of Bagehot's first actions on taking over the paper had been to write privately to Gladstone to try and find out the basis on which his financial policy would be conducted, now that he was back at the Exchequer after his period in exile. He received back a letter on November 29th, 1859, that is a model of the master's double talk, (and also indirect conflict with his Prime Minister's rearmament policy).

> All matters in these departments for the coming session are as yet in embryo, and I know nothing to guide a journalist at this time except general principles. If I had a journal, I would, with the amount of reserve I might find necessary, and no more, aim at showing again and again the profitableness of remissions which reproduce revenue by enriching the people; and this in quiet comparison with vast outlay on military establishments, which especially when suddenly and violently enlarged, tend in many ways to produce the very evil they aim at averting.

Though he remained very close to Gladstone on other financial questions, he felt no obligation to support his taxation policy, and ten years after 1861 he took a leading hand in the discrediting of Robert Lowe's attempt to abolish the income tax and impose a match tax instead. In general, *The Economist* under Bagehot took a modern view of taxation, that a buoyant and expanding economy, tapped by a judicious system of low general taxation, was a more important objective of official policy than concentration on making minor savings in expenditure.

Bagehot, however, had his share of idiocyncracies, a modest

ration of which has apparently been allotted to most of his successors. One was his belief, which was consistent with his confidence in governmental action, that the question of nationalizing the railways should be re-opened. Wilson, though he had tried to control the railway mania of 1846, had opposed state interference with the railways. Bagehot thought nationalization well worth considering.

> a transfer of the ownership of the railways to the Government might be made so as to diminish their danger, economise their cost, and augment their utility. It would be very difficult so to transfer, we know. But when great results are *possible,* we should carefully examine whether they are not also *attainable.*

Another, embodied in a pamphlet of 1868 written during his illness and enforced light duty, was for a universal coinage, a subject much discussed in those days as a means of facilitating international trade. He argued for converting the pound sterling from 960 to 1,000 farthings, thus taking a step further the decimalization of the English coinage, to which the introduction of the florin in 1849 had been intended as the first move. Most English experts were in favor of an interchangeable ten franc-eight shilling coin and a one pound-twenty-five franc coin. At a time when the pound was the strongest currency of all, Bagehot's suggestion that it should adapt itself to the decimal system rather than the reverse, was a bold one. His argument assumed, as perhaps it was entitled to in an age of expanding gold production and when the American greenback seemed merely a temporary aberration, that a universal gold standard and the parties it sustained were immutable: any Frenchman today must read with nostalgia of an idea for making one pound and twenty-five francs into the same coin.

He took a leading part, at the end of his life, in a long dead controversy over the role of silver. In a series of articles for *The Economist* in 1876 which he circulated as a pamphlet, and in evidence before Goschen's Select Committee on the subject, he opposed Jevon's contention that the retention of silver along with gold in the world's currencies would help to keep the value of both metals steady; and his arguments had a good deal of influence over the official view that a bimetallic standard was impossible unless every country adopted it. True to his anti-imperial views, he was little moved by the principal reason for the contemporary concern in London with the depreciation of the world price of silver, namely its effect on Indian finances and trade.

One of the best of his literary critics wrote:

> Bagehot suffered from economic degeneration of the heart. For the "still, sad music of humanity" he had no ear. Shakespeare's scorn of the rude mechanicals is music to him, and in any discussion of capital and labour, he is not only on the side of capital—as he might reasonably be—but he is patently contemptuous of Labour as no true economist should be.

Only a very superficial reading of what he wrote could endorse this charge. It is true that Bagehot was by training and environment a banker and that he knew very little about industry. Though he had the banker's liberalism and responsiveness to change as compared with the more embattled attitude of the employer of labor, he lacked the industrialist's first-hand knowledge of working class psychology and his necessary feeling for the human equation in industry, (though he deplored the increasing remoteness of the employer from his work people, and his steady retreat into a "monarchical position" behind a desk and papers). He also felt somewhat out of sympathy, as one who remembered the real hard times of the forties, with the emotional attitude towards the industrial problems of the day which he discerned in his younger Liberal friends, finding it necessary to remind them that in a highly developed economy the capitalist also can suffer as much from economic maladjustments as the worker.

> "It is true that the distress of the labourer is much more conspicuous, and that he advertises it; he goes about saying 'I am starving, and it is the tyranny of capital which is killing me'. But it is also true that the capitalist is in danger of ruin and that he conceals it. If he cannot complete contracts which he

has made, if he has to stay out of a return from his business longer than he can afford, he is ruined. But he will never say this, because it may injure his credit and quicken the coming of the evil. He will lie awake with anxiety till his hair turns prematurely grey, and till deep lines of care form on his brow, but will say nothing. And it is necessary to insist on this now, because our current literature—some even of our gravest economic literature—is dangerously tainted with superficial sentiment." For him the employer was "the general of the army: he fixes on the plan of operation, organizes its means, and superintends its execution . . . Everything depends on the correctness of the unseen decisions, on the secret sagacity of the determining mind."

But redressing the balance of sentiment was one thing; being opposed to the legitimate claims of labor was quite another. As Professor W. W. Rostow has written in his study of Bagehot as an economist, "*The Economist* was not simply the hard-bitten advocate of the mid-Victorian capitalist." At the beginning of his editorship, when the Nine Hour Movement was strong, he admitted the right of labor to wage an organized fight for a larger share in profits, and though he did not accept the current argument that the employer would get as much value out of a man in nine hours as in ten, he was quite prepared to accept the loss. *The Economist* kept a close check on the extent of the hardship which the Civil War caused in the Lancashire cotton districts. Throughout the trade union agitations of the sixties, Bagehot had many harsh things to say about what he considered to be the undemocratic way in which union decisions were arrived at, but he defended the unions, even during the great Tyneside strike of 1871, as the necessary means of equalizing the otherwise hopelessly unequal bargaining position of the individual worker, just as he accepted that the Factory Acts had been a proven success.*

* The following extract from *The Economist* of October 7th, 1871, is a fair sample of Bagehot's views. "*The Strikes.* In saying that the one demand deserves no more sympathy than the other we do not wish to be misunderstood. We have no objection whatever to the aspiration of the workmen for more wages. We believe and are glad that the tendency of the conditions of industry at the present moment, with the constant ex-

Finally, he continued Wilson's support for the Co-operatives. It is true that, as Harold Laski wrote of him, "he had nothing of that heedless, and instinctive, generosity which in men like Lincoln, Cobden and Bright symbolized the essential morality of democratic endeavour". But though Laski's suggestion that "his confidence in men ceased—perhaps from professional bias—below that stratum in society where the privilege of a bank account begins" has a grain of truth, it overlooks the extent to which Bagehot tried to balance his own natural apprehensions.

A comparison between Jevons and Bagehot is interesting in this respect. They came from somewhat similar backgrounds, including University College, except that Jevon's father was a Liverpool engineer and he had grown up in closer contact with the working class. (His mother was the daughter of the great William Roscoe, and he was thus the first cousin of Bagehot's poet friend.) Jevons had a more highly developed social conscience: "the amusements of the masses . . . have been frowned upon and condemned and eventually suppressed by a dominant aristocracy. . . . It seems to be thought that the end of life is accomplished if there be bread and beef to eat, beer to drink, beds to sleep in, and chapels to attend on Sunday. . . . It is hardly too much to say that the right to dwell freely in a grimy street, to drink freely in the neighbouring public house, and to walk freely between the high walled parks and the jealously preserved estates of our landowners, is all that the just and equal laws of England secure to the mass of the people." But Jevons, with his mathematical approach to economics, at first opposed and later only reluctantly accepted the necessity for trade unions. Bagehot accepted the necessity of col-

---

tension of machinery and accumulation of capital which we witness, is towards a most material elevation of skilled labourers in the scale of living—an elevation far surpassing what has actually been accomplished during the last thirty years. What we object to is the inappropriateness of the methods selected to accelerate the inevitable end, methods so inappropriate as in reality to retard it while inflicting serious damage on the whole community; and we certainly do not think those methods are excused because the demand for more pay is itself disguised as a demand for shorter hours of labour."

lective bargaining, because, knowing the realities of politics at first-hand, he was aware that a sense of social responsibility is no substitute for pressure.

The years during which Bagehot edited and managed *The Economist,* from September, 1859 to March, 1877 were broadly the years of mid-Victorian prosperity. During that time money wages rose by 40 per cent and even allowing for unemployment real wages rose by 30 per cent. The population of the United Kingdom increased by 30 per cent, the output of coal was exactly doubled. But they were not years of even progress. At the time he assumed control of the paper, the British economy was recovering from the relatively mild set back of 1857 and was beginning to expand rapidly in production and in confidence. This period came to a sudden end in 1866 when the panic caused by the crash of Overend, Gurney, "like a spark falling on tinder", revealed that industry and the credit structure had become over-extended. There followed two sluggish years, then the great boom of 1868 to 1873, and then the first stage of the Great Depression which haunted the rest of the nineteenth century with rapidly falling wages and prices. Bagehot was thus the leading weekly commentator on the British economy during two major trade cycles. As he conceived it, this gave him a dual responsibility: to keep a sharp eye on the movements of the various economic indices, and to evolve for his readers an intelligible theoretical basis for judging why prices, production or wages were likely to rise or fall.

He did not bring to the second of these responsibilities any hard and fast views. What distinguished him from his contemporaries, many of whom still looked on depressions or crises as acts of fate like thunderstorms, was a knowledge of the relation between psychological and purely economic factors, between the state of mind of the business community and its actions. Two years before he became Editor, he had attempted an analysis of the crisis of 1857 in an article in the *National* which contained the germ of the ideas that eventually flowered in *Lombard Street.* Everyone at that time was casting around for scapegoats for a panic which had originated in America, and even sensible men like Cardwell were blaming it on the mismanagement of the United States' currency. "In fact," wrote Bagehot, "it was nothing but the result of an over-extension of credit. Our capital is clothed in a soft web of confidence and opinion: on a sudden it may be stripped bare and with pain to our prosperity." The French alone of all the great trading nations had been almost exempt from its effects, because they trusted each other so little that they carried on most of their trade in cash. "Our own system of commerce is precisely the reverse. A certain energy of enterprise is the life of England. Our buoyant temperament drives us into action; our firm judgment makes us steady in real danger; our solid courage is inapprehensive of fanciful risk; *an impassive want of enjoyment in that which we are prompts us to try to be better than we are.*" This is an inversion, to make the same point, of his famous remark in *Lombard Street,* "All people are most credulous when they are most happy."

His analysis of the trade cycle, as he evolved it in Chapter VI of *Lombard Street,* "Why Lombard Street is often very dull, and sometimes very excited", centers very largely round the problem of confidence. "Our current political economy does not sufficiently take account of *time* as an element in trade operations." He believed there were two elements to this proposition. Different industries were much more closely interdependent than was supposed, since in a complex economy like England most people were now producing for the consumption of others. The effect of a depression in any single trade ramified throughout the rest of the economy though it might take a long time to do so. Agriculture was the prime example: if corn was dear, first clothing, then liquor, then machinery, then one trade after another began to suffer in turn, the full effect taking two or three years to work itself out.

The other element was expectations about the future, operating through the institutions of credit.

> Credit—the disposition of one man to trust another—is singularly varying. In England, after a great calamity, every-

body is suspicious of everybody; as soon as that calamity is forgotten, everybody again confides in everybody.

This was a state of affairs peculiar to the Britain of the seventies, where credit and confidence were as real an instrument of
expansion as a run of good harvests.

But the general mild prosperity thus engendered brought
into play a third factor, namely idle savings, tempted out by
the prospect of a good return. This set new enterprises of
marginal value in motion, with a consequent strain on the
relatively inelastic resources of the basic industries, drove
prices up and created a prosperity "precarious as far as it is
real, and transitory in so far as it is fictitious". Then some
extraneous event or a bad harvest produced a loss of confidence: money cheapened as industrial or commercial demand
fell off: credit began to improve as the "remembrance of
disaster becomes fainter and fainter" until eventually the
irritation of John Bull with 2 per cent revived the adventurous
and a good harvest started the whole process in motion again.

Professor W. W. Rostow, (on whose analysis of Bagehot's
views on the trade cycle in his *British Economy in the Nineteenth Century* I have drawn with gratitude), has commented
that "the terms of this dynamic system are familiar and modern
with two exceptions: the considerable role of the
harvests and the absence of the Hamlet of current theories—
the marginal productivity of capital". In the important part
he assigned to harvests Bagehot was unlucky in terms of the
durability of his analysis. For though the harvest had played
the part he described throughout his own lifetime, despite the
effects of Repeal, the year in which he published *Lombard
Street*—1873—was the very one in which the English harvest
ceased to have a decisive effect on the British economy as a
whole.

With regard to the productivity of capital, Professor Rostow
suggests that when he wrote Bagehot was entitled to assume
that "the opportunities for profitable private investment were
ample, and that the worst that had to be dealt with was the
relatively mild irregularity of the rate at which they were

exploited in an economy where investment decisions were taken by individuals, acting under self defeating common impulses. . . ."

One of Bagehot's most important contributions to the relative stability of the mid-Victorian years, was his effort to control the too easily revived complacency of the mid-Victorian capitalist and investor. Being concerned by training and position more with the financial than the industrial aspects of recovery and decline, he concentrated a great deal of his attention on trying to show the necessity for an even balance between savings and investment. In 1863 when confidence was building up rapidly, as the inevitability of the South's defeat set a time limit on the drag created by Lancashire, he wrote, "The savings of the country are constantly swelling the loanable capital to be disposed of, and, unless an increasing trade gives a new opening to our new resources, there will be a momentary superfluity, and a momentary depression in the money market in the value of capital for brief periods." If, at any time British industry could not absorb the high level of savings filtering into the market from a prosperous bourgeoisie it was desirable that they should be lent to capital-hungry foreign countries to avoid distorting the British capital market. And when a speculative boom appeared to be in the making, he warned his readers sharply of what was certain to happen. Two years before the crash of Overend, Gurney, and as the boom caused by the rise of the new limited liabilities companies gathered speed, *The Economist* began to sound a steady note of warning against the danger of "blind money"—he coined the phrase—rushing into every trade that asked for it. He was well aware how internally rotten Overend's itself had become, and had only welcomed its transformation into a limited company because the firm "would now have to publish an account of the nature of their business". But he could not, without risking legal action, go further, and after the terrible Black Thursday and Friday of May 10th and 11th, 1866, when "The Corner House"—the greatest private firm in England, that had sometimes seemed to rival and outshine the

Bank itself—failed for five million pounds, the day when "the doors of the most respectable Banking Houses were besieged . . . and throngs heaving and tumbling about Lombard Street made that narrow thoroughfare impassable", he wrote a pitiless epitaph.

> "In six years" the immensely rich partners "lost all their own wealth, sold the business to the company, and then lost a large part of the company's capital. And these losses were made in a manner so reckless and so foolish, that one would think a child who lent money in the City of London would have lent it better."

In the same way he was warning his readers against the seductions of the boom in foreign bonds, mostly Japanese and Spanish, in 1870. Giffen, his assistant, wrote that:

> it was his conspicuous honour to have "spotted" the danger of these loans long before the public were sensible of it; in fact almost from the time the loans began.

Interested though he was in money and the making of it—for as a young man, bored in the counting house at Langport, he used to dabble his hands in the till full of sovereigns to cheer himself up—he had a strong personal hatred of speculation for its own sake. This was reinforced by the fact that he was a frugal man who had disliked spending too much ever since boyhood, and therefore had no temptation to turn a quick pound. "As times go," he wrote in an essay on French banking,

> the making of money by work is perhaps the most innocent employment of man: but no passion is so dangerous as an avarice which is at the same time inactive and intense.

A flutter on the stock exchange was the amateur's temptation which drove good savings into dubious channels. The year after the Overend crash he was offering this solace to the country vicars and retired majors who had been so badly bitten.

> The fact is, that there is a real pleasure to the mind in slight pecuniary danger. It has the character of gambling and the delight of gambling; and to that temptation experience shows very quiet, grave looking people are often susceptible.

The strong gambler's streak in his own temperament, he sublimated by playing cards, especially bezique.

By the time he had been ten years at *The Economist*, Bagehot had lived through three major financial crises, 1847, 1857 and 1866, and the intimate knowledge of English commercial history which he had culled from his father and uncles and from a wide reading had made the earlier crises in the century almost as familiar. In the light of his own analysis he had no belief that the swinks of the trade cycle could be eliminated, but the conviction grew on him that their effects might be mitigated and such panics avoided by a more responsible policy on the part of the Bank of England.

II

The belief that the Bank of England did not fully understand or live up to the responsibilities which had revolved on it as the London money market became more and more highly organized, had been germinating in his mind for a long time. In his own youth the great question had been whether Peel's Bank Act of 1844, which divided the Bank into separate Banking and Issuing Departments and fixed at a basic fourteen million pounds the latter's power to issue notes not covered by gold, was sound or would achieve its objects of preventing currency excesses by safeguarding the convertibilty of the note issue. Bagehot had entered the lists briefly in an article in the *Prospective* in 1848, in which, true to his training in the principles of Ricardo and the Bullionists, he had defended the Act against the strong criticisms of Tooke, the historian of prices, and the milder comments of James Wilson, his future father-in-law, who favored the Act but thought it would provide no safeguard against panics.

But by the time of his marriage, when the Government had

had to suspend the Bank Act for the second time in ten years in order to enable the Bank to replenish its banking reserve by the issue of notes beyond the statutory limit, and to extend still further credits to allay a general *sauve qui peut* rush for cash, Bagehot had become of a mind with Wilson. What already concerned him was not whether the rules by which the Bank's note-issuing policy should be changed, but whether its banking policy was adequate to its position, not merely as the most privileged bank, but as the bankers' bank.

> "The authorities of the Bank can hardly be permitted to abdicate all responsibility at these times—to manage in ordinary periods as they did in the year 1847, so as to aggravate the intensity of a great crisis" (by indiscriminate lending): "and then, in the moment of the most harassing difficulty, to devolve the entire care of the banking community upon the executive government," he wrote the year after the 1857 crisis.

As London became the financial capital of the world throughout the sixties, he became increasingly concerned at the fact that many influential people in the City continued to regard the Bank as merely *primus inter pares* with the joint stock banks and discount houses which had grown up around it, with special privileges and duties in the matter of note issue and the government accounts, but with no special responsibilities to the money market, the government or the nation, as *the* Central Bank, the sole holder of the nation's banking reserve. His thoughts on the subject became crystallized when he was invited to Paris to give oral evidence before a French official commission which was then studying the question of Central Banking. When he praised Henry Holland, the Governor, in *The Economist* for acknowledging this responsibility in the crisis of 1866, he was attacked in a pamphlet by Thomson Hankey, a former Governor: "the more the conduct of the affairs of the Bank is made to assimilate to the conduct of every other well managed bank in the United Kingdom, the better for the Bank and the better for the community at large". But Hankey in Bagehot's eyes was living in a forgotten world while the telegraph and the steamboat were knitting the world markets together into a sensitive web, when a quarter of the world's trade was British and when London was acquiring liabilities to a much wider sterling area even than the Empire.*

When France collapsed in 1870 and the Bank of France suspended cash payments, London began to fill up with "hot" money from all over the world and a new speculative boom seemed to threaten: already some of the storm signals of another 1866 crisis were flying. Bagehot could confine himself to the anonymity of *The Economist* leading articles no longer. He sat down that autumn to write a book that, as Keynes once put it, would "knock two or three fundamental truths into the heads of City magnates". He meant to write *Lombard Street* at a sitting, for he had all the arguments and facts at his command. But his health and the preoccupations of the paper, of his mother's death and of revising *The English Constitution,* forced him to lay it continually aside, so that it was not published until the spring of 1873. What he had clearly intended was a piece of pure advocacy, and he feared that "a slowly written book on a living and changing subject is apt a little to want in unity". In fact the writing of it more slowly carried him into a psychological analysis of the behavior of the City which turned a pamphlet into a classic.

Lombard Street, though it has been read by four generations of students and economists all round the world, was aimed at a very small audience—the solemn, rather limited men who converged each day from Surrey and the Chilterns and Belgravia upon the square mile east of Temple Bar. "It is not easy to rouse men of business to the task" (of rethinking their systems). "They let the tide of business float before them: they make money or strive to do so while it passes, and they are unwilling to think where it is going." Robert Giffen said that Bagehot "had always some typical City man in his mind's eye; a man not skilled in literature or the turning of phrases,

* "Hankey complains that he sees nothing of you. It is a connection worth cultivating" Wilson had written to his son-in-law from India in July, 1860. Bagehot it would seem thought otherwise, though their social relations were pleasant enough, and they dined often in each other's houses.

with a limited vocabulary and knowledge of theory, but keen as to facts, and reading for the sake of information and guidance respecting what vitally concerned him". To drive his meaning home he abandoned the clever phrase and the good quotation, and used strong simple words. "He was never content with having the meaning there provided the words were delicately and nicely weighed; the meaning must shine through the words; and he detested all writing which gave a false impression . . . he was always amused to come up from the City and give me in a sentence—the City says you think so and so—the meaning of a long article on which I had laboured, perhaps using many figures."

His first objective was to prove to the City that the Bank of England was a Central Bank, not merely in having the largest note issue, but in having become the bankers' bank, the repository of the banking reserve of the whole country, whose interest and lending policy affected the whole credit structure of the country and indeed the world. He was not the first to have seen this: Goschen's book on the international aspect of the Bank's responsibilities had appeared twelve years earlier. But it was not an easy idea even for an open-minded business man to grasp. Historically, the Bank had developed as an ordinary capitalist business, primarily concerned with financing merchant enterprise, and with certain special privileges, such as its joint stock structure, (and, after the Gordon riots, a platoon of Guards to safeguard its vaults each night) extracted from the Government at various periods of financial stress. There was the explicit authority of Peel, at the time of the separation of the Issuing and Banking Department in 1844, that the latter was to be "governed on precisely the same principle as any other body dealing with Bank of England notes". In the United States the attempt to create a central bank had been abandoned nearly forty years earlier, and on the continent the new Reichsbank and the Bank of France behaved, apart from their note issuing privileges, like ordinary deposit bankers, with no responsibilities for the control of their capital markets.

Bagehot's attachment to *laissez faire* made him disposed to a "natural system" in which each bank kept its own reserves of gold and legal tender, (as in the United States before the days of the Federal Reserve) though he held to this view with none of the dogmatism of Herbert Spencer. "A republic with many competitors of a size or sizes suitable to the business, is the constitution of every trade if left to itself, and of banking as much as any other." But "you might as well, or better, try to alter the English monarchy and substitute a republic, as to alter the present constitution of the English Money Market, founded on the Bank of England, and substitute for it a system in which each bank shall keep its own reserve. There is no force to be found adequate to so vast a reconstruction and so vast a destruction, and therefore it is useless proposing them."

For there were two facts of recent history that could not be controverted. As London's money market had become more highly organized, a smaller and smaller proportion of the resources of its component banks and discount houses could be allowed to lie idle as reserves, and the only real reserve in the country was the deposits of the bankers with the Banking Department of The Bank of England, whose liabilities were of the order of three times greater than its assets. "In consequence all our credit system depends on the Bank of England for its security. On the wisdom of the Directors of that one joint stock company, it depends whether *England shall be solvent or insolvent* . . . The Directors of the Bank are, therefore, in fact, if not in name, trustees for the public, to keep a banking reserve on their behalf . . . But so far from there being a distinct undertaking on the part of the Bank directors to perform this duty, many of them would scarcely acknowledge it, and some" (e.g. Hankey) "altogether deny it." The effect of the Bank's failure to recognize the central position which it now held in the money market—that is was not just a bank but The Bank—was that in times of crises it always moved too slowly.

What did he propose to do about this situation? A multiple reserve system was out of the question. "Credit in business is like loyalty in Government. You must take what you can find of it, and work with it if possible." Should the Government acquire control of the Bank as in France, especially as historically it had done much to make it predominant over all other banks. Earlier he had toyed with the idea of its nationalization, but by 1870 he had decided that this would lead to jobbery, and to a fluctuating policy "as chance majorities and the strength of parties decide". Three obvious remedies suggested themselves to him: that there should be an explicit recognition on the part of the Bank's directors that they were the real trustees of national stability; that the government of the Bank should be strengthened; and that the demands of the rest of the banking system on the Bank itself should be reduced.

In Bagehot's day, and for half a century after it, the Court of the Bank of England was entirely made up of part-time directors, the Governor and Deputy Governor being appointed in rotation. It took, he estimated, some twenty years on the Court to reach the chair, and its most powerful members were those who had passed it. In consequence "the young part of the board is the fluctuating part, and the old part is the permanent part; and therefore it is not surprising that the young part has little influence. The Bank directors may be blamed for many things, but they cannot be blamed for the changeableness and exciteability of a neocracy." Nor could the professional London bankers, by ancient custom, become Directors. "In theory nothing could be worse than this government for a bank—a shifting executive; a board of directors chosen too young for it to be known whether they are able; a committee of management in which seniority is the necessary qualification, and old age the common result; and no trained bankers anywhere."

He admitted that the government was committed to the hilt to the soundness of the Bank: "the position of the Chancellor of the Exchequer in our Money Market is that of one who deposits largely in it, who created it, and who demoralised it". But "no English statesman would consent to be responsible for the choice of the Governor of the Bank of England. After every panic, the Opposition would say in Parliament that the calamity had been 'grieviously aggravated', if not wholly caused, by the 'gross misconduct' of the Governor appointed by the Ministry." Bagehot would have read with appreciation the proceedings of the Bank Rate Tribunal of 1957.

His own solution was the appointment of a full-time Deputy Governor, on the analogy of the Permanent Under Secretary in a government department, a trained banker who would bring some expertise to the counsels of the merchant directors, a man of "fair position" who would not have to say "Sir" to the Governor. It was not until the Norman revolution of the nineteen-twenties that Bagehot's suggestion eventually bore fruit.

But his suggestions for a reform of the government of the Bank were secondary to his insistence on the need to reform its policy and its attitude. His central argument was that the Bank, as the lender of last resort, must keep a larger gold reserve in good times than had been its practice; respond sensitively to drains upon it, especially from abroad, through its interest rate policy; and when a crisis arose act much faster than was its wont, lending freely on good securities to sustain the general credit while discriminating against bad securities rather than letting the whole credit structure collapse. Like the good pamphleteer that he was, he supported this argument from every angle, by historical explanation of how it was that the Bank of England had come to be the holder of the bankers' reserves, by analysis of its behavior in past crises, and by a dissection of the various components of the money market, joint stock banks, private banks, bill brokers, to show their complete dependence on the Bank, and how little it could afford to let them get into deep water. All led back to the same simple proposition. "A panic, in a word, is a species of neuralgia, and according to the rules of science you must not starve it. The holders of the cash reserve must be ready not only to keep it for their own liabilities, but to advance it most freely for the liabilities of others."

He was not prepared to answer his own characteristic question, "How much?" by telling the Bank just what reserve it should keep. No rule of thumb, such as the old idea that one third of total liabilities would suffice, could be accepted since the nature of these liabilities varied so much. If a foreign government withdrew a large quantity of money from the private banks of London, as the Germans just had, it affected the Bank of England doubly since it forced it to make greater advances to the private banks from reduced means. For his own day he was prepared to set the right figures at a minimum of eleven million pounds, instead of the average of eight million pounds which had prevailed in the previous decade. But his central point was that what he called the "apprehension minimum", the point at which a "vague fright and timorousness" began to creep over the market, varied according to a number of external and internal factors. It was the job of the Bank to keep its reserves above a figure that in the last analysis could only be determined by a day to day knowledge. If they did this, they would not have to use the reserve: if they did not it would prove inadequate. Since the Bank of England was a central and not an ordinary bank, "errors of excess are innocuous, but errors of defect are destructive".

There are some blind spots in *Lombard Street*. Though Bagehot noted the growth of the check system and the diffusion of joint stock banking, he did not perceive that these developments were making it possible for trade to expand without an increase in the note issue. Secondly, later historians have shown that the Bank, whatever it might say, was in fact becoming more responsive to its duties than he gave it credit for. Part of the force of Bagehot's argument for a larger reserve derived from the fact that the Bank appeared to be unable to exert effective control over the market rate of interest; its own Bank rate, it was contended, merely followed instead of determining the market rate. In fact, research has shown that the Bank, by the sale and purchase of securities, was in the late sixties groping its way towards a technique of influencing interest rates and did keep a closer day to day watch on "the apprehension minimum" than Bagehot was aware of. Professor R. S. Sayers has recently written that in the early seventies:

> Bank Rate, once it was reflected in market rate, was quite a potent instrument for strengthening the reserve quickly and so overcoming any temporary strain . . . These sources of strength in London's position were in some degree perceived by Goschen already in 1861; but their importance was increasing rapidly in the succeeding years, and they were not given quite their due weight by Bagehot when he wrote a decade later. If he had fully appreciated them he would still have wanted a stronger governance of the Bank of England to enforce a strong Bank Rate policy, but he could scarcely have worried quite so much about the size of the reserve.

There was not doubt about the effect of *Lombard Street*. Hankey remained on the Court of the Bank for another twenty years, but no one could ever again be taken seriously in the assertion that the Bank of England was just another London bank. Though it took another generation and the Baring crisis of 1890 before his views were finally accepted in the City, the professional economists, notably Jevons, were immediately aware that he had made a great stride forward in the theory of central banking, and the ailing Cairnes, the leading academic economist of the day, incorporated large parts of Bagehot's argument in his *Leading Principles*.* Gladstone wrote to Bagehot that he knew "not most whether to admire its clearness or its force".†

But *Lombard Street* would long ago have been relegated

---

* The exception being Bonamy Price, the Drummond Professor of Political Economy at Oxford, who in a virulent review in *Fraser's Magazine* attacked Bagehot's slur on the good name of the Bank.

† *Life,* p. 416. Fifty-eight years later, the report of one of the most powerful bodies that has ever examined the British economy—the Macmillan Committee of which Keynes, Ernest Bevin and Lord Brand were members—said in its historical introduction: "That there is a distinction between the code of behaviour appropriate to a commercial bank and that appropriate to a central bank was recognised as early as 1797, was a bone of contention between practical authorities for nearly three-quarters of a century thereafter, and was finally established with unanswerable brilliance and cogency by Walter Bagehot in 1873." Comd., 3897, *The State of the British Economy* (London: H.M.S.O., 1931), p. 15.

to the top shelves as an interesting source for the historian of a forgotten controversy, instead of remaining a beacon in a waste of arid and complex literature, were it not for Bagehot's literary power. Keynes, who was no admirer of Bagehot as a literary critic or as a theoretical economist, wrote of *Lombard Street*: "No book on banking and the money market has ever attained such a position—an undying classic, outliving the facts it describes and the controversies to which it contributes by reason of its author's sweet persuasive ways, it is a perfect example of a certain kind of English writing, and its truth of human nature. It lives by goodness, art and truth, the three immortals, born by accident as it were, out of a plain description of an ephemeral fact." And elsewhere that "little of the sort has ever been attempted equal to the psychological observations of English men of business. No other economist has had either the gifts or the opportunity."

Bagehot's secret is that, like Keynes, he took business men seriously: he did not treat them and their processes of thought with the mild contempt which some academic economists cannot keep out of their descriptions of business psychology. "Business is really a profession often requiring for its practice quite as much knowledge, and quite as much skill, as law and medicine . . . he has a revenue from talent as well as from money." The portraits he drew in *Lombard Street* of the rapidly expanding joint stock banks, of the old established but decaying private banks, and of the bill brokers, are almost as fresh today as they were eighty years ago. Of the boards of the big joint stock banks with their quota of peers and notables: "There are very many men of good means, of great sagacity, and great experience in business who are obliged to be in the City every day, and to remain there during the day, but who have very much time on their hands . . . Accordingly, many excellent men of business are quite ready to become members of the boards of directors, and to attend to business of companies, a good deal for the employment's sake." Of the attraction of the old private banks whose day was past: "Banking is a watchful but not a laborious trade. A banker, even in a large business, can feel pretty sure that all his transactions are sound, and yet have much spare mind:" but also of the secrecy of their accounts and operations which made it difficult for them to bring in new blood and created "the constant difficulty of an hereditary government".

His picture of the changes that were affecting the structure of banking is an epitome of mid-Victorian England: "This increasingly democratic structure of English commerce is very unpopular in many quarters, and its effects are no doubt exceedingly mixed. On the one hand, it prevents the long duration of great families of merchant princes, such as those of Venice and Genoa, who inherited nice cultivation as well as great wealth, and who, to some extent, combined the tastes of an aristocracy with the insight and verve of men of business. These are pushed out, so to say, by the dirty crowd of little men. After a generation or two, they retire into idle luxury . . . When we scrutinise the impaired reputation of English goods, we find it is the fault of new men with little money of their own . . . But these defects and others in the democratic structure of commerce are compensated by one great excellence. No country of great hereditary trade, no European country at least, was ever so little 'sleepy', to use the only fit word, as England . . . The rough and vulgar structure of English commerce is the secret of its life: for it contains 'the propensity to variation', which, in the social as in the animal kingdom, is the principle of progress."

"In the constant and chronic borrowing, Lombard Street is the great go-between. It is the sort of standing broker between quiet saving districts of the country and the active employing districts. . . . Deposits are made with the bankers and bill brokers in Lombard Street by the bankers of such counties as Somersetshire and Hampshire, and those bankers and bill brokers, employ them in the discount of bills from Yorkshire and Lancashire. Lombard Street is thus a perpetual agent between the two great divisions of England. . . ."

Despite the fact that Bagehot was himself involved in this process, as Vice Chairman of Stuckeys, the largest collector of

the money of the "quiet saving districts", he preferred the
freedom of the outsider rather than the bonhomie of the
insider, in his relations with the City. None of the great City
figures of his day formed part of his circle of close friends.
Though he called once a week at The Bank of England, he was
much too caustic both in *The Economist* and in *Lombard
Street* about the Bank's shortcomings for him to be very
welcome in the Parlour. It must have been hard to forgive the
author of chapters 7 and 8 of *Lombard Street*. His composite
portrait of the Bank in the fifties and sixties, making a mystery
out of what should have been straightforward decisions—"the
business of banking ought to be simple: if it is *hard* it is
wrong"—nervous of the Press yet unwilling to make plain the
principles on which it acted, made as fresh reading in 1957,
when it had one of its rare moments of public scrutiny, as in
1873.

But in Whitehall *Lombard Street* set the seal on Bagehot's
growing influence. Gladstone had used Bagehot to test the
ground with the City at the time of his Bank Notes Issues Bill
in 1865, and among his papers is a note of that year to send a
private memorandum on his financial policy to selected members of the Government, to important peers, to influential
foreign observers such as Guizot, and to Bagehot. In the same
year, Bagehot had been invited by Rouher, the French Finance
Minister, to give his views to the Conseil Superieur on monetary circulation. In the crisis of 1866, he had been one of
the Treasury's principal sources of intelligence on feeling in
the City. Goschen, who had left the City for politics, had been
a close friend since the same time, and in 1873, when he was at
the Admiralty, he apparently rated Bagehot's influence so high
that, when his own family connections in the City told him
that Bagehot was overdramatizing the likelihood of another
financial crisis, he thought it wise to write at once to the
Prime Minister. Lord Welby, who was head of the Financial
branch of the Treasury for many years, said that Bagehot was
the only outsider who had ever thoroughly mastered British
financial machinery: "Indeed he understood the *machine* as

completely as we who had to work it. . . . Chancellors of the Exchequer attached great weight to the opinion of Mr. Bagehot."

At the end of his life he turned this position of respect to good account. For many years the Government's main instrument for financing its floating debt, the Exchequer Bill, which had been devised by Charles Montagu, William III's Chancellor, had been losing ground with the City and with the public. It was a cumbrous security, issued only twice a year, with a life of five years and an arbitarary rate of interest; and its unpopularity meant that the Government was paying well above the market rate of interest for its short-term loans. Gladstone had worried about the problem for a decade. But with the new education programme and the other social legislation of the seventies, the question of financing the Government's floating debt acquired a new urgency. Disraeli's Chancellor, Sir Stafford Northcote, decided that something must be done about it and in 1876 sent Welby to seek Bagehot's advice. Bagehot told him that the Treasury had the finest credit in the world, but no idea how to use it; he advised them to use a short-term security, redeemable in a matter of months, resembling as nearly as possible a commercial bill of exchange: "such a Bill would rank before a Bill of Barings". The advice was followed, the Treasury Bill immediately became popular, and for the last eighty years has been used—abused sometimes —as the Government's principal means of raising short-term money.

For the value that was put upon his judgment and discretion by the Treasury and for his willingness to lend a hand without any publicity or credit, Gladstone described him as for many years "a sort of supplementary Chancellor of the Exchequer".* It was characteristic of his modesty that it was not until Welby set down his recollections, some thirty years later, that his family or friends were aware that Bagehot had made this

---

* If the wording of Eliza's diaries is taken literally it appears that he was told about a change in Bank Rate in August 1866, and given the gist of Lowe's Budget speech of 1871, before either was published.

particular and direct contribution to the technique of government.

III

As he approached his fiftieth birthday, he had much to content him. At the paper Robert Giffen had proved a tower of strength, creating a foundation of solid record and observation of the economic scene, on which Bagehot could build one or two pungent articles each week. His health had recovered from the low years of his early forties, and he was now a delicate rather than a sick man, who could look forward to many years of useful life. Eliza and he had moved to Wimbledon in 1870 from the Wilsons' house in Belgravia in order that he could get some riding, for Eliza's pony phaeton, in addition to a brougham and a Victoria which they had had since they were married, did not satisfy his energies. But the pressure of life made living there difficult, and they decided in 1874 to settle permanently in Queens Gate Place, living in a rented house in Rutland Gate until it was ready. The new Conservative Government placed as much trust in him as had the Liberals. He was a member of Brooks's and Wyndhams and in 1875 he had been elected to the Athenaeum under Rule 2, for eminence in the arts and sciences, which in those days was a mark of eminence as coveted as a knighthood. *The English Constitution* was being quoted on every side, serious German and American scholars were poring over *Physics and Politics,* and *Lombard Street* had begun to achieve its purpose (it had already run through six editions).

But one powerful ambition remained unfulfilled—to make a permanent contribution to economic thought. Two reasons, in particular, impelled him to devote his diminishing ration of leisure to the attempt. After the turbulent controversies and advances of the first half of the century, very little had been accomplished since the publication of Mill's *Principles* twenty-five years earlier. Many people indeed doubted if there was anything more to be said on the subject. Jowett apparently believed that, except in the field of distribution, "Political

Economy like Benthamism had done its work," and Gladstone that the application of economics to public policy was almost complete. Galton, the sociologist, suggested that political economy be dropped from the curriculum of the British Association, and even the economists themselves admitted that there was something in what their fellows said. Most of the discussion of economic theory in the sixties and early seventies was either dominated by the dogmatic assumptions of the amateurs like Cobden, or suffered from the heavy hand of Mill, against whose economic psychology Bagehot had revolted at the age of twenty-two, and whose "monarchical influence" he had never since accepted. Jevons had begun the attempt to carry economic thought beyond Mill with the publication of his *Theory of Political Economy* in 1871, but Jevons's mathematical approach to the description of economic phenomena made no great appeal to Bagehot (whose quantitative sense accepted the value of using statistics to confirm the soundness of an economic hypothesis, but not the using of mathematical formulae to solve economic equations).

The second impelling force was the changing condition of the world. The financial crisis of 1873 had failed to materialize; but prices and wages were now falling rapidly, and though it could be argued that the British economy was still expanding, it was undeniable that Britain, now hard pressed by Germany and the United States, had ceased to dominate the world of trade and industry. Moreover, Britain's own economic fortunes were becoming more and more involved with those of India and what would now be called the "underdeveloped countries" (Giffen with fewer susceptibilities to consider called them "imperfectly civilised"). Yet British economists were still trying to frame universal laws in terms of purely British experience.

In the opening paragraphs of *Physics and Politics* Bagehot had written: "One peculiarity of this age is the acquisition of much physical knowledge . . . A new world of inventions—of railways and telegraphs—has grown up around us which we cannot help seeing: a new world of ideas is in the air and affects us, though we do not see it. A full estimate of these effects would require a great book, and I am sure I could not write it: but I think I may usefully show how upon one or two great points the new ideas are modifying two old sciences—politics and political economy."

Illness and other preoccupations had forced him to confine *Physics and Politics* to the development of political behavior alone. But in 1875, in what was demonstrably an even more rapidly changing world than 1867, in which the question of economic behavior in other societies had acquired a fresh and practical urgency, in which the assumptions of the classical economists stood even more open to question, he determined to complete what he had begun.

The book he had in mind would consist of three distinct volumes. The first and most important was to be his own definition of the scope of political economy, and an attempt to show the modifications that were necessary to the assumptions of British economic thought when applied to economies in earlier stages of development than contemporary Britain; the second was to be a study of classical economic theory as exemplified in Adam Smith, Ricardo and Mill; and the third a series of portraits of the great economists.

The introduction to the first book appeared as "The Postulates of English Political Economy" in the *Fortnightly* in January and February, 1876. He then became diverted to a reappraisal of Adam Smith—in his centenary year—for Morley, with an eye to including it in the third volume. During the winter of 1875-6 he settled down to work again in earnest on the book, but no more was published before he died. Two years after his death, Hutton and his friends put together from the published and unpublished essays, a short volume and called it *Economic Studies*. Of the first book, he completed only the outlines of his ideas on the redefinition of political economy as a whole, together with the draft of chapters on the mobility of labor and capital, cost of production and of capital growth. Of the second, there are unfinished studies of Adam Smith, Ricardo and Malthus—Mill was never written—and of the third he had written only the portrait of Adam Smith.

Incomplete though it is—and in need of revision for Bagehot wrote fast and rewrote at leisure—there is enough in *Economic Studies* to make clear what he was attempting. His concern was not with restating the fundamental axioms of classical economics after Mill, as Jevons and now Marshall were attempting to do, but to provide English economic thought with a firmer anchor to the real world, and to lift the siege of political economy from the assault of the other new social sciences, (which had so occupied Cairnes), by redefining the limits of its usefulness.

It suffered, he thought, because its pretentions were too great:

> It has been put forward, not as a theory of the principal causes affecting wealth in *certain* societies, but as a theory of the principal, sometimes even of all, the causes affecting wealth in *every* society.

The axioms of the English school were in fact applicable only to "a society of grown up competitive commerce".

> In my judgement we need—not that the authority of our Political Economy should be impugned, but that it should be *minimized* . . . that its sovereignty should be upheld, but its frontiers marked.

As a result of the search for universal laws, the English economists:

> "have been too content to remain in the 'abstract', and to shrink from concrete notions, because they could not but feel that many of the most obvious phenomena of many nations did not look much like their abstractions". "Our Political Economy is not a questionable thing of unlimited extent, but a most certain and useful thing of limited extent."

One consequence of this tendency to abstraction was a failure of communication between expert and layman.

> Anyone who tries to express varied meanings on complex things with a scanty vocabulary of fastened senses, will find that his style grows cumbrous without being accurate, that he has to

use long periphrases for common thoughts, and that after all
he does not come out right, for he is half his time falling back
into the senses which fit the case in hand best, and these are
sometimes one, sometimes another, and almost always different
from his "hard and fast" sense.

With this as his starting point he had begun to take the
several postulates of the classical economists, in order to show
how many purely English—or at least European—assumptions they involved, how "unnatural" and complex a stage of
social development was required for the free transferability of
capital and labor, and similarly how much the structure and
nature of a capitalist organization had changed even in recent
years. The two chapters on the growth of capital and the cost
of production are, as one would expect, the most finished, for
they were the two aspects of economic theory closest to his
own experience.

He was not an enemy of abstract concepts, for a deductive
method of reasoning seemed to him to be forced on the
economist by the complexity of his material. "If you attempt
to solve such problems without some apparatus of method,
you are as sure to fail as if you try to take a modern military
fortress—a Metz or a Belfort—by common assault." He had
no use for the extreme claims of the "historical" school. The
weakness, however, of the whole book, as to a lesser extent of
Physics and Politics, is that he explores the limitations of the
classical concepts of value, labor, capital and distribution, only
by showing their irrelevance to the primitive societies which
Maine, Galton and others had described, Australian aborigi-
nes, American Indians or Brahmins. He makes little attempt to
bridge the gulf between the pre-economic and highly complex
society; he is hardly concerned with crudely organized economies of his own day such as Italy, Russia or the American West.
He did not, it is true, set out to be an economic historian or
geographer, but by contrasting only the opposite ends of the
scale he fell into the trap of unrealism from which he was
trying to rescue his colleagues.

When he wrote of the great economists themselves, his judgment was unequivocal. Adam Smith "prepared the way for, though he did not found, the abstract science of political economy". "But what he did was much like the rough view of the first traveller who discovers a country; he saw some great outlines well, but he mistook others, and left out much. It was Ricardo who made the first map; who reduced the subjects into consecutive shape, and constructed what you can call a science." Mill "shaped with masterly literary skill the confused substance" of Senior and those who succeeded Ricardo "into a compact whole. He did not add a great deal which was his own, and some of what is due to him does not seem to me of great value . . . His remoteness from mercantile life, and I should say his enthusiastic character, eager after things far less sublunary than money, made him little likely to give finishing touches to a theory of 'the great commerce'. In fact he has not done so: much yet remains to be done in it as in all sciences. Mr. Mill, too, seems to me open to the charge of having widened the old Political Economy either too much or not enough."

Keynes thought economists interested him more than economics. Certainly the biographical portrait of Adam Smith is one of Bagehot's most enchanting, the description of his "lumbering *bonhomie* which amused and endeared him to those around him"; of the important chance event which removed him from his Glasgow professorship and the danger of being just a clever man feeding on too little experience, and sent him to France:

> on all economical matters the France of that time was a museum, stocked with the most important errors.

Malthus, "a mild pottering person" who stumbled on a revolution in economic thought, is perhaps the most finished sketch. But Ricardo "the true founder of abstract Political Economy" was for him the central figure, and he would have endorsed Keynes' considered judgment that "Ricardo was the greatest mind that found economics worthy of its powers". Bagehot had an interesting theory of how this unlikely figure,

a practical man of business, who had little education, who was
for much of his life closely occupied in a singularly absorbing
trade, and who made a fortune in that trade

came to acquire his capacity for abstraction. It was because he
operated on the Stock Exchange, where there is nothing tangi-
ble to handle, no appeal to the senses, but only debts and
promises.

"The ordinary human mind finds a great rest in fixing itself
on a concrete object, but neither the metaphysician nor the
stock jobber has any such means of repose. Both must make
their minds ache by fixing them intently on what they can
never see . . . If any man of business is to turn abstract thinker,
this is the one who should do so." "He did not go to Political
Economy—Political Economy, so to say, came to him . . . He
dealt with abstractions without knowing they were such; he
thoroughly believed he was dealing with real things."

If twenty years had not been shorn from his natural span of
life, could Bagehot have made an important contribution to
the development of economic thought? If one thinks in terms
of Ricardo, Marshall and Keynes, the answer is almost certainly
that he could not, despite his clear sightedness, his analytical
power—and his ambition to do so. The world was too much
with him, and he lacked the power of synthesis and abstraction
which he admired in others. But one thing emerges clearly
from *Economic Studies,* incomplete though it is. Bagehot did
not aspire to write a *Principles* or a *General Theory*; he wished
to write a new *Wealth of Nations.* The map makers could
come later. What first needed exploring and signposting was
the new economic country and its psychological climate—the
country created by central banks and trades unions, strong
nationalistic governments and colonial empires, big business
and urban proletariats—an expedition which would make
possible a revision by others of the laws of value, capital, distribution and taxation. It was his gifts as a cavalry scout,
as an observer, which he wished to contribute to economic
thought.

Chapter 10

VICTORIANUM MAXIME?

"The only thing I maintain is that I have a *spring* and
energy in my mind which enables me to take some hold
of good subjects and makes it natural and *inevitable* that
I should write on them. I do not think I write well, but
I write, as I speak in the way (I think) that is natural
to me, and the only chance in literature, as in life, is to
be yourself. If you try to be more you will be less."

Letter to Eliza

I

BAGEHOT felt less and less drawn to the ordinary round
of society as he grew older. Eliza's attempts to be a smart
intellectual hostess, a Lady Eastlake or Lady Augusta Stanley,
during the years at Upper Belgrave Street had petered out
since Walter hardly ever remembered to appear at her teas. He
had earned high praise for not slipping away to bed during a
ball which they had given, although Lady Waldegrave's parties
at Strawberry Hill with their queer mixture of people were
one of the few social occasions he never missed. He preferred
to intersect London life at many points, rather than to stand at
any of its centers.

In 1876 a keen-eyed young man from the North with the
right background for serious journalism, Burnley, Balliol and
the Bar, was given a job by Hutton on *The Spectator* with the
opportunity of contributing to *The Economist*. "The Bagehots
and Huttons and Townsends* were in my young days," wrote
Herbert Asquith in his memoirs,

> an interesting and in some ways an important group in the
> literary life of London. They could not be described as a

---

* Meredith Townsend was co-owner and Editor of *The Spectator* with
Hutton. He started life as a journalist in India, and had been sent by
James Wilson to Hutton when his health forced him to return to England
in 1859. They managed and edited the paper jointly until Hutton's death
in 1897, when St. Loe Strachey became Editor.

coterie or set, but they were a disputatious tribe, and rarely agreed with one another about anything except a few "fundamentals". Of the living writers they would have agreed in putting George Eliot in the front rank.

Bagehot had remained devoted to George Eliot; tea at The Priory was his favorite Sunday afternoon occupation now that his uncle Reynolds was dead, and he resisted any suggestion that she was not the greatest living novelist. But he did not choose to live in the world of letters. With Matthew Arnold he had long been on terms of respectful but not close friendship: there is an elusive hint in George Eliot's letters of a disagreement with Trollope: Lord Houghton and his friends he knew well, but was not one of the habitués of Fryston: Meredith was his own contemporary but their paths seem never to have crossed. Like Sir Henry Maine and Leslie Stephen he had always devoured novels and was for ever imploring his sisters-in-law to go to Smith's Library to get them for him. But now he used them more as an opiate, with a taste for Miss Braddon, for *Vixen, Joshua Haggard's Daughter* or *Only a Woman*, since economic analysis was absorbing more and more of his critical powers.

His tastes were changing, and throughout the seventies he became increasingly interested in the arts. Ruskin had made a deep impression though he was not prepared to accept Ruskin's passionate protests against the Philistines any more than he was prepared to accept Arnold's. Burne Jones had become a friend: and when Queens Gate Place was bought its furnishing was put into the hands of William Morris's firm. George Wardle, Morris's manager, was in charge, "but the great man himself, William Morris, is composing the drawing room, as he would an ode", while William de Morgan, the son of Bagehot's old professor at University College, was to do the tiles. Morris's autocratic views on every question of color, fabric and design amused him, though Morris was also characteristically slow. The blue damask silks for the drawing room curtains and covers were a year or more late in arriving, making the waiting house a chilly if aesthetically pure shell for its frail master.

His quality as a conversationalist, of combining trenchancy

with gentleness, what Smith Osler described as "his power of keeping up animation without combat", made him greatly sought after, but except for an occasional official function or a sporadic foray to the Metaphysical Society or the Political Economy Club, he reserved himself more and more for his friends and for the tribal life of the Wilson sisters. Friendship was the especial talent of the Victorians, as good fellowship had been that of an earlier age, but he was no collector of friends as Crabb Robinson had been. Among politicians, Lord Carnarvon, now back at the Colonial Office under Disraeli, was closer to him than any of the leaders of his own party. Morley and the new generation of Liberals were too earnest, too rational and too priggish for his taste. "I often ventured to say to him," wrote Morley, "you have only one defect; you do not feel the inherent power and glory of the principle of liberty." Bagehot's answer, fortunately for Morley, is not recorded, but the latter wrote to Eliza six months after Walter's death that he felt

> the impossibility of conveying to those who did not know him the originality, force, acuteness, and above all the quaint and whimsical humour of that striking genius.

With only one of the new political generation did he strike a close friendship: he met James Bryce, then Regius Professor of Civil Law at Oxford, at George Eliot's one Sunday afternoon in 1874, and they instantly took to each other. Perhaps it was Bryce's greater sophistication, his concern with a wider world than most of his Liberal contemporaries, that made him find Bagehot's doubts and irreverence about contemporary ideals stimulating rather than shocking; he wrote later of Bagehot that

> "one seemed to gain more profit as well as pleasure from a talk with him than with almost anyone else, all the more so because, however much one felt his superiority, it always remained conversation, and not, as so often with great talkers, a lecture or a declamation". "He put himself on a level with his interlocutor, and however much you might feel his superiority, he always

seemed to be receiving as well as giving, striking out thoughts from others as well as bringing them from his own store. Goldwin Smith was stately and impressive but rather chilling. Bishop Wilberforce was brilliant and witty, but even if he did not exactly talk for display he seemed not to care very much whether what he said was true or not, but only whether it shone. But Bagehot was always cheerful, natural, spontaneous, unaffected. You felt he was hunting for truth, and you enjoyed the sense that he allowed you to be his companion in the chase."

It was Bryce who was responsible for spreading Bagehot's reputation in the United States, and very probably it was his influence which gave Woodrow Wilson an admiration, amounting almost to idolatry, and certainly to conscious imitation, of his style and method of political analysis.*

The two Stephen brothers; Henry Fawcett, the only radical he could stand, who was one of his fellow examiners at University College; Auberon Herbert, Carnarvon's younger brother, who opposed every cherished Victorian institution from the monarchy to marriage; Henry Maine, whose judgment he revered; Francis Galton, the sociologist, who shared his passion for hunting; Arthur Stanley and Mountstuart Grant Duff; Mary Mohl, now well over eighty but still showering curses on successive French governments, came to dinner and listened to the gentle flow of epigrams. But it was for Hutton that the place of honor was always reserved. After thirty years of friendship, after having seen each in turn through bouts of depression and doubt, it mattered very little that they no longer agreed on many questions of religion and politics, for each understood the psychological balance of the other's mind. "I doubt if I ever received a letter from Mr. Bagehot in my life," wrote Meredith Townsend, Hutton's coadjutor. "If he had anything to say, he ran into *The Spectator*."

* The first attempt at a collected edition of Bagehot's works was made as a private venture by The Traveller's Insurance Company of Hartford, Connecticut, in 1889. His American reputation really dates, however, from Woodrow Wilson's articles on him in *The Atlantic Monthly* of November, 1895 and October, 1898.

Their offices were a few yards from each other, and each Thursday or Friday, after they had put their respective newspapers to bed, Bagehot and Hutton would hurry across Trafalgar Square to play hectic games of chess at the Athenaeum until the small hours.

As the wet winter of 1877 gave way to a cold bright March, he had a wide future to survey. He was at the height of his powers, or so Robert Giffen thought who had had the closest opportunity to study him at work. Having turned aside from *Economic Studies* to write *Lord Althorp*, he was now hard at work at these again. The Act which would put his Treasury Bill into effect was about to go before the House of Commons, and he had a private tip from Giffen, now a civil servant, that he was to be invited to be a member of the Stock Exchange Commission. Queens Gate Place was nearly finished despite the slowness of Morris, and his longing for children had been appeased by the existence of a small eight year old Barrington, whose rocking horse he considered the finest ornament in the house. "Hit him, he hasn't got any friends," the same nephew can remember his saying, on being confronted with a boiled egg.

Hutton, meeting him on March 19th, 1877, complimented him on his vigor and youthfulness and told him that he looked "less like a contemporary of my own than one of a younger generation". But the black beard and the high color had for many years concealed a weak chest, a recurring tendency to migraine and an unsuspected weak heart. "Pain is an awful thing," another child, the late Mrs. St. Loe Strachey, could remember his saying to her suddenly. On the following day, the 20th, he came down with a heavy lung cold. He wrote a characteristic note to Hutton:

> I think you must have had the evil eye when you complimented me on my appearance.

Yet he did not take it so lightly as he chose to pretend: one night during the previous week he had risen from bed to make his will, and before leaving *The Economist* office he had told one of his staff that he did not think he would get better.

But Easter was approaching, and his father must be fortified with company. So, delaying his departure for a few hours in order to vote for George Trevelyan, the son of Wilson's old enemy, at the Athenaeum, he set off with Eliza on the draughty, cold journey to Langport. He was a very sick man by the time he reached Herd's Hill late on the night of Tuesday the 20th, and his right lung had become congested. By the Friday a specialist from Taunton confided to Eliza that he was dangerously, but not hopelessly, ill, while the gentle patient played cribbage with an aunt who was nursing him. The following day, the 24th of March, he was slightly better and Eliza, herself in pain, lay by his side throughout the morning, cutting the pages of a new edition of *Rob Roy* for him. As the short afternoon drew in, he roused himself on his pillows, and when she tried to help him, said gently, "Let me have my own fidgets." He fell into a quiet sleep which deepened into death.

He was buried in Langport churchyard five days later, in a quiet ceremony which the *Langport Herald* recorded with an economy of language which would have delighted him.

> Old servants of the family acted as bearers and pall bearers. Adopting the reformed method of conducting funerals, now becoming very general, the emblems of mourning worn by the persons in attendance were of a quiet and simple character. The inhabitants generally testified their respect towards the deceased gentleman by closing their shops during the afternoon.

As became a Justice of the Peace and the Deputy-Recorder of the Borough, the Corporation of Langport followed his coffin in their robes.

Forty-two years later, in the year of the Versailles Peace Conference, their sons looked in surprise up Cheapside to the churchyard where a gaunt, spare figure, the President of the United States of America, stood in reverent contemplation of his master's grave.

II

"Those who had the good fortune to know him still remember him as perhaps the most original mind of his generation," wrote Lord Bryce towards the end of his own life. It is a stiff claim to sustain, for it was a generation which, as its narrowest definition, embraced Arnold and Buckle, George Eliot and Charlotte Bronte, Calverly and Clerk Maxwell. But as the mid-Victorian years have emerged into the clear light of history, and out of the twilight of the recent past from which Lytton Strachey judged their leading figures, it is a judgment that has been more widely accepted than challenged.

Yet he remains one of the most difficult figures in English letters to treat with justice. Since he was bold enough to venture with so much dash into four separate fields of scholar-ship and controversy, literature, politics, sociology and econom-ics, he has rightly been judged by the highest standards of each, and inevitably he has not held his place in the front rank of any. For the reason that Bryce gave, that his was an original not a great mind, that he was an explorer rather than a cartographer, let alone one of the rare thinkers who change the contours of the map itself, his achievements have become neglected once more careful and methodical minds have gone over the same ground.

He was not really a critic of literature in the accepted sense, for he brought no objective standard to bear upon either prose or poetry: he was a student of the minds of great writers, a different art. He did not aspire to be a political philosopher, and though *The English Constitution* has had as great an effect on the way in which those who must operate a parliamentary government look at the tool they have in their hands from Westminster via Canberra to Delhi and Ghana, as ever *L'Esprit des Lois* had on the European and American governments of an earlier day, it is notes on how to cultivate a flourishing tree rather than on how to plant. *Physics and Politics* is a remark-able book—perhaps the most brilliant study of social psychol-ogy of the whole nineteenth century—and in Sir Keith Feiling's phrase "whole libraries added since have done little more than elaborate Bagehot's single spies into battalions", but it falls short of his own aim for its concluding definition of verifiable progress has no permanent meaning. *Lombard Street* is one of the ablest pieces of special pleading ever written—the more so for being in a good cause—and a wonderful description of business psychology as well. But he died before he could make any permanent contribution to economic thought. The indictment of Bagehot is that his books are neither fish nor fowl, that they contain neither the fieldwork and precise observation of the social and the political scientist, a Lyell, Maine or Darwin on the one hand, or the prophetic insights of the reflective thinker, a Mill, a Tocqueville or even an Arnold, on the other.

Before deciding where this leaves him, there is one question which the diversity of his work must make one ask. Would his achievement have been greater if he had narrowed and concentrated his interests? He said of Nassau Senior:

> that he scattered and wasted in a semi-abstract discussion of practical topics, powers which were fit to have produced a lasting and considerable work of philosophy.

Was it true of himself? The answer quite simply must be—No. If he had stuck to literary criticism, he would have been only a good, rather than a great, critic, for as I have tried to show, the process of steeling himself to live in the real world had involved the atrophy of his sense of tragedy, and in consequence, as he said of Scott, he lacked "the consecrating power". If he had confined himself to political analysis, he could have achieved nothing finer than *The English Constitution* and his articles in *The Economist* taken together, because he wished only to modify and explain rather than recast the system which he found. If he had engrossed himself in social psychology, instead of moving on to *Lombard Street* and *Economic Studies,* he might have arrived at a more positive conclusion about the way and direction in which social progress is politically achieved, but the case-work on which a lasting hypothesis could be constructed was at that time very meagre. The promise of *Economic Studies* as a map of the new economic country of the last quarter of the nineteenth century was considerable, but Bagehot had few illusions that he possessed the powers of a great economic thinker. Indeed, one can regret that, rather than concentrating his talents, he did not diversify them even more and turn historian as well. For his mastery of character, the power of his studies of Bolingbroke, Pitt and Peel as well as of minor figures, the sense of historical proportion he displayed in his essay on Macaulay, his psychological realism, show that he had the makings of a great historian. Had he chosen, he could have reinterpreted the two centuries before his own, avoiding the historicism of Macaulay, with a balance and brilliance which would have left his reputation in no doubt. Giffen, indeed, had the impression that Bagehot's next ambition, once his economic trilogy was completed, was to write a political history of modern Britain.

But such speculations can be misleading if they obscure the unity of his method or lead to any neglect of the two important and enduring contributions which he did make, not only to English letters but to modern life itself—in the desire to comprehend, and the ability to elucidate, the workings of a complex society. Mr. G. M. Young in his short essay on Bagehot, "The Greatest Victorian" has written:

> We are looking for a man who was in and of his age, and who could have been of no other: a man with sympathy to share, and genius to judge, its sentiments and movements; a man not too illustrious or too consummate to be companionable, but one, nevertheless, whose ideas took root and are still bearing; whse influence, passing from one fit mind to another, could transmit, and can still impart, the most precious element in Victorian civilization, its robust and masculine sanity. Such a man there was: and I award the place to Walter Bagehot . . . *Victorianorum maximus,* no. But *Victorianum maxime* I still aver him to be.

My own reflections on Bagehot have led me to carry this judgment a stage further. His "robust and masculine sanity", though won at a certain price, relates him to his time: his opinions as contrasted with his doubts were for the most part those of his intelligent contemporaries, such as a man who listened as well as talked would acquire from the breakfast table of Gladstone and the dinner table of Dean Stanley, Lord Carnarvon or the Political Economy Club. But in the way in which he used his mind, his insights and his intuition, he was far ahead of his own day. There had been many excellent observers of the contemporary scene before him, from Chaucer down through Hazlitt. Bagehot was one of those rare men of real intellect who recognize that analysis is as worthy of a man's best powers as advocacy, that modern society has achieved a complexity which makes it as important to know where it stands and what its constituency is, as where it is going or where it should go. He is the true ancestor of our modern view that the knowledge of what a society is really like, what drives it, what checks it, what distorts its judgment, cannot be gleaned from statistics or mere facts alone, but is as much the province of the literary and imaginative arts as of the moral and metric sciences. If mid-twentieth-century England can be distinguished, at its best, from mid-Victorian England, at its best, by a certain toughness of mental fiber, by an enhanced ability to look reality in the eye, to distinguish between the formal and the effective, and to accept its own shortcomings without too much tragedy, then Bagehot has a claim to be called not only the perfect Victorian, but the first of our own contemporaries.

His other achievement, the formulation of a new prose style for the transmission of serious ideas, is easier to identify. There are thousands of people all over the world—not just in England, but in the United States, in India, wherever English is the language of ideas—who are, consciously or unconsciously, writing in Bagehot's style. What he did was to loosen and unmat the architectural form of serious prose which he had inherited by way of Macaulay from the Augustans, and to inject into the language of politics and economics some of the color and verve that Hazlitt and an earlier generation had developed for slighter themes.

At times his style seems so colloquial that it has the appearance of mere haste. Nevertheless he knew what he was doing, and he was ready to give this impression because he was in fact writing for his ordinary contemporaries.

> Writing for posterity is like writing on foreign post paper: you cannot say to a man at Calcutta what you would say to a man at Hackney: you think "the yellow man is a very long way off: this is fine paper, it will go by a ship" so you try to say something worthy of the ship, something noble, which will keep and travel.

Moreover he was writing about reality. "The manner of the *Decline and Fall* is the last which should be recommended for strict imitation. It is not a style in which you can tell the truth . . . Truth is of various kinds—grave, solemn, dignified, petty, low, ordinary: and an historian who has to tell the truth must be able to tell what is vulgar as well as what is great, what is little or what is amazing. Gibbon is at fault here. He *cannot* mention Asia *Minor* . . . Men on *The Times* feel this acutely: it is most difficult at first to say many things in a huge imperial manner."

As he slowly and deliberately shed the old ornate forms throughout his literary essays, he did not acquire what has been called the "neutral" Victorian style which replaced the older formal and the older plain rhythms of English prose. He had no horror of slang: he was the inventor of the word "padding" to mean filling out a paper or book.* He used American importations, and Giffen knew of an eminent German economist who deduced from Bagehot's style that he was a self-taught business man. He was prepared to sacrifice euphony and form, to use phrases in an odd way, sometimes in an awkward way, in order to drive his meaning home, for he had learned from Adam Smith that to be convincing, especially to an unimaginative business man, it was essential to be graphic. "The fancy tires if you appeal only to the fancy: the understanding is aware of its dulness, if you appeal only to the understanding: the curiosity is soon satiated unless you pique it with variety."

* The letter to Crabb Robinson on page 75 is almost certainly the first time the word appeared in that meaning in the English language.

Professor Dover Wilson has said of Matthew Arnold that he was "the most delicate ironist of the Victorian era". But irony by itself was often Arnold's undoing, as the host of earnest people who misunderstood the message of *Culture and Anarchy* and *Friendship's Garland* bear witness. Bagehot was a less subtle ironist than Arnold, for his humor was more earthy, and at all costs it was essential to be clear. His writing became plainer as he grew older because he grappled more and more with subjects where flights of imagery or colorful language might confuse rather than enhance his meaning. Since he had an exceptionally clear mind, he had no respect for jargon or for the hubris of those writers, particularly in his own field, who believe that their reputation is advanced by devising a private language. The following sentence is from a recent book by an influential and original American social scientist:

> The spread of other-directed patterns beyond the metro-politan centers is often due to the influence of opinion leaders who have learned these patterns while away at high school, at college, or on a job, and who continue to keep in touch with the newer values through the mass media, which in turn support their efforts with their local "constituency".

And Bagehot on the same subject: "This gave English country life a motley picturesqueness then, which it wants now, when London ideas shoot out every morning, and carry on the wings of the railroad, a uniform creed to each cranny of the king-dom, north and south, east and west . . . There is little oddity in county towns now: they are detached scraps of great places." Or more simply: "I want to bring home to others what every new observation of society brings more and more freshly to myself—that this unconscious imitation and encouragement of appreciated character, and this equally unconscious shrinking from and persecution of disliked character, is the main force which moulds and fashions men in society as we now see it."

But forcefulness is not style, nor is the mastery of metaphor and illustration. Bagehot had in varying measures the qualities which F. L. Lucas has suggested as the elements of style: char-acter, simplicity, humor, vitality, and above all the twin marks of courtesy towards the reader—clarity and brevity. Despite the trenchancy and originality of his books and longer essays, Bagehot was at his best in *The Economist,* when he was working under pressure, within a defined compass, writing, as he thought an editor should, "as a trustee for the subscribers". What Matthew Arnold called "his concern for the *simple truth*", with the accent as much on the first as on the second word, has been the test of great journalists—J. A. Spender and C. P. Scott, Walter Lippmann, Geoffrey Crowther—ever since. It is hardly surprising that the prose style he developed as a journalist, with its irony and restrained use of paradox, its proportion and simplicity, its slum clearance of irrelevant ideas, its fine balance between reverence and impudence, between humor and gravity, should have made him a model for three generations of journalists, teachers, officials, diplomats or any writer who must elucidate a complex subject and bring an inert idea to life.

Here is Bagehot at his most characteristic.

The British community is sound in wind and limb, it has an immense accumulation of subconscious judgement, it rarely makes a very stupid mistake, prudence is its middle name—but it moves slowly. This is not true of public affairs alone. From all over the country, the story at the present time is the same: there is no active discontent, but also no sparkle or enthusiasm for anything but the various ways of consuming leisure. It would be dangerous to write this mood off merely as a temporary phenomenon of exhaustion; many millions of individuals are in better health and spirits today than they have ever been. Besides, the same phenomena were all too visible when the excuse of exhaustion did not exist. The probability is that it is a more permanent state . . . The causes that lead to the decay of the enterprising spirit in nations are obscure and often intangible; but they are quite decisive nonetheless, as has been shown a hundred times in past history. Britain finds herself today between two great competitors, both of whom, in their different ways, keep a sharp edge on the motives that lead to action . . . Both the Russian and the American economies are, avowedly and deliberately, carrot and stick economies: the British is rapidly becoming a sugar-candy economy.

That, however, was written not by Bagehot, but by his seventh successor at *The Economist,* and not in 1876 but in 1946.

III

He was the fruit of a rare and dwindling stock, pure southern English. For a century and a half the seats of power in Britain, in politics, in business, in journalism, have passed increasingly to the Scots, the Welsh, the Irish and the North Countrymen. What he called "the lazy and genial south", those who live below the invisible Mason-Dixon line which runs somewhere between Thames and Severn have been content to be conquered and have produced fewer champions of their own. Bagehot was one of them. His enjoying instinct, his contentment and conservatism, his naturalism, his feeling for old forms and customs, the sublimated and practical romantic in him, come from this strain. And he shared a quality of cheerful mental vigor with two other great southern Englishmen of the past century—Richard Cobden of Sussex, and Ernest Bevin of Somerset. A distrust of sophistry, a taste for irony rather than wit, a preference for example over dogma, differentiate his kind from the Welsh, the Irish and the Scots strains in the complex character called British—though like many southern Englishman he felt an instinctive attraction for the Scots and an instinctive fear of his own formidable and energetic countryman to the north of Trent. He was a very English figure; he was by temperament deeply distrustful of most things German, insensitive to the promise of the United States, and unsympathetic to the social and political dilemmas of France— all English characteristics. But his insularity came only partially from pride in Britain's political and economic achievements, for he saw as clearly as Arnold how Britain was beginning to fall behind the march of other nations in the sixties and seventies, and more from a passionate attachment to his own land. The highest tribute that he could pay the landscape of northern Spain was that "it is a sort of better Devonshire".

Though he was not a representative figure, he stands in the true line of descent of one great Western tradition—no special possession of England but more apt to flower there—that of the amateur. It was characteristic of his mind that he should have pressed for abolishing the distinction between barristers and solicitors, for he had a conviction of the unity of experience, and he refused to be intimidated by the growing fragmentation of knowledge into hydra-headed forms of expertise, from framing and expressing his own opinions. His occasional slipshod judgments and his many inaccuracies were a personal weakness, for his haste and lack of precision would have made him a careless man even if he had ever lifted a pen. But by treading as an intelligent and informed amateur in the land of the specialist, by having the courage of his insight, by using one form of experience to comprehend another, he not only threw new light on ancient questions of human behavior but helped lay the foundations of a bridge, that is in need of repair today, between the expert and the lay mind.

Yet for all his insularity his life was more than just the fine flowering of the English temperament, his achievement wider than that of the brilliant and studious amateur. The conquest of his mind over his apprehensions, the contrast between the conservatism of his instincts and the open-mindedness of his judgments as an influential editor and writer, give him an enduring place among the contenders for the open society. Harold Laski's tribute to Acton and de Tocqueville applies also to Bagehot.

"Liberalism is the expression less of a creed than of a temperament. It implies a passion for liberty; and that the passion may be compelling it requires a power to be tolerant, even sceptical, about opinions and tendencies you hold to be dangerous, which is one of the rarest of human qualities. To be conscientious about facts which tell against your desire, to be calm and detached in the presence of events by which, within yourself, you are deeply moved, to admit the inevitability of change and, as a consequence, the impermanence of all matters of social constitution, to recognize that history gives no sanction to any dogmas which claim an absolute value—these, I venture to think, are the very heart of the liberal temper."

To those who knew him in his forties, he seemed a figure uniquely gifted and resolved, worthy of Sir Walter Raleigh's later phrase on Shakespeare, a "man cast in the antique mold of humanity, equable, alert and gay". But this balance had been won by victories in a private campaign against himself, against arrogance, against intellectual pride and folly, against circumstance, against dejection and ill health. In the course of the campaign, he had achieved not only simplicity and modesty but gentleness. The search for reality had left him, not with a harsh but with a profoundly sympathetic mind, so that an hour in his company became a recollection men carried with them all their lives. "Talking to him," Roscoe had once said in their youth, "was like riding a horse with a perfect mouth."

NOTES AND REFERENCES

INTRODUCTION

p. 9   John Foster Dulles.
Sir Edward Fry, one of his closest friends at school and university, was the leader of the British Delegation to the Hague Conference of 1907.

p. 10   official life. Mrs. Russell Barrington, *Life of Walter Bagehot* (London: Longmans, 1914). It was published as Vol. X of Mrs. Russell Barrington, *Works and Life of Walter Bagehot* (London: Longmans, 1915). It is from this edition that all references to Bagehot's writings are drawn.

p. 10   separate book. Mrs. Russell Barrington, *The Love Letters of Walter Bagehot and Eliza Wilson* (London: Faber, 1933).

p. 11   "about himself." Augustine Birrell, *Miscellanies* (London: Stock, 1901), p. 117.

CHAPTER 1

p. 15   "face of God." *Victoria County History of Somerset* (London: Constable, 1906), Vol. II, p. 213.

p. 18   fortunes. The information on Stuckey's Bank is drawn largely from Phillip T. Saunders, *Stuckey's Bank* (Taunton: The Wessex Press, 1928).

p. 20   for the season. Rev. David Melville Ross, *Langport and its Church* (Langport: Herald Press, 1911).

p. 21   "obtain it." R. H. Hutton, *Memoir* [Mrs. Russell Barrington, *Works and Life of Walter Bagehot*] (London: Longmans, 1915), Vol. I, p. 33.

p. 21   that it is not larger. *Life,* p. 97.

p. 24   adventurous of knights. *Works,* Vol. I, p. 189.

p. 26   his own thoughts. *Life,* p. 82.

p. 27   in the early fifties. I am greatly indebted to Mr. Bryan Little for the information on Bristol College.

p. 31   *the empire of himself.* These extracts are from letters in the possession of Mr. Robert Bagehot Porch (referred to hereafter as Unpublished letters).

p. 32   had been there. *Life,* p. 65.

p. 32   "always noticeable." *Life,* p. 85.

CHAPTER 2

p. 34   practical occupation. *Works,* Vol. I, pp. 177-8.

p. 34   Oxford or Cambridge. Hale Bellot, *University College, London (1826-1926)* (London: University of London Press, 1929).

p. 35   familiar inhabitants. Unpublished letters, October 23rd, 1942, September 2nd, 1846.

p. 35   cry with laughing. *Ibid.*

p. 36   nearly over. *Works,* Vol. VII, p. 291. He forestalled by a century one of the great controversies of American education.

p. 37   Dr. Hoppus *immediately. Life,* p. 102. I have quoted from the original letter and have used slightly different parts of it from Mrs. Barrington.

p. 37   middle thirties. "W. C. Roscoe whose verse is at least interesting, and has been thought something more, is critically not negligible." George Saintsbury, *History of Criticism* (Edinburgh: Blackwood, 1904), Vol. III, p. 514.

p. 38   de Morgan. *Memoir (Works),* Vol. I, p. 3.

p. 39   "with much tact." Unpublished letter, September, 1846.

p. 39. "at college." *Memoir* (*Works*), Vol. I, p. 6.

p. 40 without a college. *Works,* Vol. I, p. 170.

p. 40 Oxford Street. *Memoir* (*Works*), Vol. I, p. 4.

p. 41 "by his own eyes." *Life,* p. 85.

p. 42 for such pursuits. Unpublished letter, May 7th, 1845.

p. 42 all his generation. *Memoir* (*Works*), Vol. I, pp. 11-12.
See Chapter 8.

p. 43 William Roscoe. *Works,* Vol. VIII, p. 146.

p. 44 physical condition. *Works,* Vol. VIII, p. 188.

p. 46 external marks of genius. Edith J. Morley (ed.), *Books
and their Writers, Henry Crabb Robinson* (London: Dent,
1938), pp. 688-9.

p. 46 "Schiller and Goethe." *Works,* Vol. V, p. 53.

p. 49 is not his forte. Unpublished letters.

p. 50 passion for it. *Memoir* (*Works*), Vol. I, p. 22.

p. 50 Who knows? Quoted. *Ibid.,* p. 21.

p. 50 sad, unquiet nature. "Mr. Clough's Poems," *The National Review. Works,* Vol. IV, p. 119.

CHAPTER 3

p. 54 "own words in between them." "Bad Lawyers or Good?"
Fortnightly, 1870. *Works,* Vol. V, p. 69

p. 56 Mr. Estlin. Presumably her brother-lin-law who was a
distinguished oculist in Bristol.

p. 56 and mysteries. *Life,* p. 145.

p. 57 out of the way corners. *Life,* p. 192.

p. 59 "will hold his own." *Life,* pp. 194-6.

p. 60 political beliefs. "Letters on the French *coup d'état* of
1851," *The Inquirer, Works,* Vol. I.

p. 62 behind their actions. Edward Hyams (trans.), *Taine's*

Notes on England (London: Thames and Hudson, 1957), p. 164.

p. 63   "because of the Empire." In reviewing Louis Napoleon's *Life of Julius Caesar. The Economist,* 1865.

p. 64   saving her country. Crabb Robinson Letters. Dr. Williams' Library.

CHAPTER 4

p. 66   French Revolution. See G. Kitson Clark, "The Romantic Element 1830-50," *Studies in Social History* (London: Longmans, 1955).

p. 68   the parish clergy. Elie Halévy, *History of the English People* (London: Benn, 1951), Vol. IV, p. 363.

p. 69   "for the encounter." G. M. Young, *Portrait of An Age, Early Victorian England* (London: Oxford University Press, 1934), Vol. II.

p. 70   average county bank. Stuckey's had developed in a quite different way from most of the other joint stock banks in England. When the Act of 1826 extended the joint stock principle to banking Vincent Stuckey was a partner in four or five other small West Country banks. He immediately made the partners in the other banks into shareholders in his bank, and their institutions into branches of Stuckey's, instead of founding a central joint stock bank and then slowly extending branches. The Manchester bankers thought his bank was not the genuine thing, according to their memorandum of 1832, but their criticism did not perturb Vincent Stuckey who expressed himself well content with the arrangement. Sir John Clapham, *An Economic History of Modern Britain* (London: Cambridge University Press, 1926), Vol. I, p. 279, Vol. II, p. 341.

p. 72   or tomorrow but soon. *Life,* pp. 211-4.

p. 73   much spare mind. *Lombard Street. Works,* Vol. VI, p. 279.

p. 73   five years earlier. W. B. to H. Crabb Robinson, August

17th, 1853. "You do not know of any lucrative literary employment just now in the market? It is not for myself (which would be too absurd) but for a much sounder man, my friend Mr. R. H. Hutton." Crabb Robinson Letters.

p. 75   "for clever padding." *Ibid.*, February 8th, April 5th, 1855.

p. 75   "on the other." J. Drummond, *Life of James Martineau* (London: Nisbet, 1902), Vol. I, p. 269.

p. 77   "of human things." "Wordsworth, Tennyson and Browning," (1864) *Works,* Vol. IV, p. 268.

p. 78   "wherein they were thought," *Works,* Vol. I, p. 203.

p. 80   "Shelley" and "Béranger," *Works,* Vol. II, Vol. III.

p. 82   technique and temperament. *Works,* Vol. III.

p. 83   "he praised them." "Wordsworth, Tennyson and Browning," (1864) *Works,* Vol. IV, p. 284.

p. 85   "mid-nineteenth century poetry." *History of Criticism,* Vol. III, p. 543.

p. 86   "The First Edinburgh Reviewers" (1855), *Works,* Vol. II.

p. 87   and lonely prophet. *Works,* Vol. II, p. 77. The first words of Jeffrey's famous review of "The Excursion" are "This will never do."

p. 87   "author behind it." William Irvine, *Walter Bagehot* (London: Longmans, 1939), p. 133.

p. 90   "quite the best." Herbert Read, *The Sense of Glory* (London: Cambridge University Press, 1929).

p. 90   "study of character." Oliver Elton, *A Survey of English Literature 1830-80* (London: Arnold, 1920), Vol. I, p. 106.

p. 91   "Walter Bagehot." *History of Criticism,* Vol. III, p. 542.

p. 91   many of them wrong. Forrest Morgan (ed.), *The Works of Walter Bagehot* (Hartford, Conn.: Traveller's Insurance Company, 1889), preface.

CHAPTER 5

p. 92   was individual. *Life,* pp. 230-1.

p. 93   "shortness of sight." *Memoir (Works),* Vol. I, p. 29.

p. 93   done so already. Unpublished letter, January 4th, 1853.

p. 97   the dominant theme. *The Economist, 1843-1943* (London: Oxford University Press, 1943).

p. 97   "to the House." William F. Monypenny and George Earle Buckle, *Life of Disraeli* (London: Murray, 1910), Vol. IV, p. 198.

p. 98   only a vegetable. *Works,* Vol. IV, p. 199.

p. 99   he makes of it. G. S. Hillard (ed.), *Life, Letters and Journals of George Ticknor* (Boston: Houghton Mifflin Co., 1876), Vol. II, pp. 363-4.

p. 100   "tarried." *The Love Letters,* p. 16.

p. 100   in her diary. Quoted from the biography of James Wilson. Mrs. Barrington, *The Servant of All* (London: Longmans, 1927), Vol. II, p. 9.

p. 101   commitments in Britain. One of the relatively few serious casualties of this panic was Franklin Delano Roosevelt's grandfather.

p. 101   North Country houses. Sir John Clapham, *The Bank of England: A History* (London: Cambridge University Press, 1944), Vol. II, p. 231.

p. 102   the way of that. This and the ensuing extracts are all drawn from *The Love Letters.*

p. 108   Bayswater that night. "Fitzjames Stephen was there. He came out from Bayswater and *back*!! He was pleasant; he is angular and has a rather aggressive development of conscience, but he talks sense and is agreeable." *Ibid.,* January 14, 1858.

p. 109   "her aberrations." *Life,* p. 266.

p. 109   "however formed." Quoted in K. B. Smellie, *A Hun-*

dred Years of English Government (London: Duckworth, 1950, rev. ed.).

p. 111   "deciding classes." *Works,* Vol. III, pp. 117-8.

p. 113   elaborate refinements. "Memoir of the Right Honourable James Wilson," *Works,* Vol. III.

p. 114   must be judged. *Works,* Vol. II.

p. 116   man of opposition. *Works,* Vol. II.

p. 117   on William Pitt (1861), *Works,* Vol. IV.

p. 118   political failure. *Works,* Vol. IV.

p. 118   Lord Althorp. *Works,* Vol. VII.

p. 119   "quite wrong." *Works,* Vol. VII, p. 289.

p. 119   grinding it down. *Works,* Vol. II, p. 79.

p. 120   within its groove. *Works,* Vol. IX, pp. 55-9.

p. 120   a great statesman. *Works,* Vol. IX, p. 9.

CHAPTER 6

p. 122   "and are resigned." "Lady Mary Wortley Montagu," *Works,* Vol. IV, p. 75.

p. 122   "converse with them." *Life,* p. 350.

p. 123   has today. This was a fair circulation in those days. Greenwood's *Pall Mall Gazette* which had a far more general appeal, was thought to be doing well with 4,000.

p. 124   specialized paper. In the possession of *The Economist* and quoted with the permission of the Editor.

p. 127   "and impartiality." Quoted in *The Economist, 1843-1943.*

p. 129   "I hope." "The Chances for a long Conservative Regime in England," *The Fortnightly Review. Works,* Vol. VII, p. 76.

p. 129   a phrase from Professor W. L. Burn, "The Age of Equipoise," *The Nineteenth Century* (London: October, 1949).

p. 130   superficial impression. *Memoir (Works),* Vol. I, p. 50.

p. 130   necessarily induced. "Sterne and Thackeray," (1864) *Works,* Vol. IV, p. 262.

p. 130   "to begin." *The Economist,* July 6th, 1861.

p. 131   English classes. *Ibid.,* May 31st, 1862.

p. 132   "a great shade." *Ibid.,* March 2nd, 1867.

p. 133   *The National, Works,* Vol. III.

p. 135   "political force." *The Economist,* November 4th, 1871.

p. 135   engraving of him. *Works,* Vol. IV, p. 187.

p. 137   "national costume." *The Economist,* July 2nd, 1859.

p. 137   "all along." *Ibid.,* March 9th, 1867.

p. 138   "the nation itself." *Works,* Vol. VII, p. 36.

p. 138   "what is to come." *The Economist,* December 4th, 1869.

p. 139   "to entertain in." *Life,* p. 367.

p. 139   "plates and descriptions." *The Economist,* February 7th, 1874.

p. 140   politicians. *Ibid.,* June 17th, 1865.

p. 142   for Bridgwater. "On the Emotion of Conviction," (1871) *Works,* Vol. V, p. 100.

p. 142   personal corruption. A. Patchett Martin, *Life and Letters of the Rt. Hon. Robert Lowe, Viscount Sherbrooke* (London: Longmans, 1893), Vol. II, p. 352.

p. 142   more intolerable. *The Economist,* February 7th, 1874.

p. 143   "public affairs." Mountstuart Grant Duff, *Out of the Past* (London: Murray, 1903), Vol. II, p. 7.

p. 144   embittered. *The Economist, 1843-1943,* p. 84.

p. 144   "of France." *The Economist,* January 11th, 1873.

p. 144   "hated us." *Ibid.,* October, 1870.

p. 144   against us. *Life,* p. 400.

p. 145   than a ship. "Count your Enemies and Economise your Expenditure," (1862) *Works,* Vol. IV, pp. 41-2.

p. 147   acting powers. *Memoir (Works)*, Vol. I, pp. 38-9.

p. 148   he called it. *The Economist*, December 15th, 1860.

p. 148   "village lawyer." *The Economist*, April 25th, 1863. *Works*, Vol. IV, pp. 227-8.

p. 149   and determined. *The Economist*, April 29th, 1865.

p. 150   "without champions." *Works*, Vol. III, pp. 368 and 381.

p. 150   at home. *Works*, Vol. I, pp. 64-5.

CHAPTER 7

The quotations in this chapter are from *The English Constitution, Works,* Vol. V, except where I have indicated other sources.

p. 151   "strong objections." Gordon S. Haight, *The George Eliot Letters* (New Haven, Conn.: Yale University Press, 1954).

p. 152   "the already known." Leslie Stephen, *Studies of a Biographer* (London: Duckworth, 1898), Vol. III, p. 176.

p. 152   Norman St. John-Stevas, *Walter Bagehot* (Bloomington: Indiana University Press, 1959).

p. 157   "to survive." *The Economist*, April 15th, 1871, and January 10th, 1874.

p. 159   for the future. L. S. Amery, *Thoughts on the Constitution* (London: Oxford University Press, 1953), p. 21.

p. 160   "consistent faithfulness." Sir Harold Nicolson, *King George V* (London: Constable, 1952), p. 62.

p. 162   "invigorated race." *Portrait of an Age, Early Victorian England*, Vol. III, p. 486.

p. 164   "in the land." *Ibid.*, p. 85.

p. 165   "not be obeyed." "Quiet Reasons for Quiet Peers," *The Economist*, June 12th, 1869. *Works*, Vol. IX, p. 66.

p. 165   Noel Annan (ed. J. H. Plumb), *Studies in Social History* (London: Longmans, 1955), Chapter VIII.

p. 168   English politics. "Mr. Gladstone and the People," *The Economist,* November 4th, 1871. *Works,* Vol. IX, p. 92 and 96.

p. 169   become impossible. "Not a Middle Party, but a Middle Government." *The Economist,* January 17th, 1874. *Ibid.,* p. 126.

p. 169   "influence of Parliament." "Lord Althorp and the Reform Act of 1832." *Works,* Vol. VII.

p. 170   "political work." "Dull Government," *The Saturday Review,* Feb. 16th, 1856. *Works,* Vol. IX, p. 240 *et seq.*

p. 170   "could not understand." "Average Government," *The Saturday Review,* March 29, 1856. *Ibid.,* p. 244 *et seq.*

p. 171   by demagogy. "Inconvincible Government," *The Saturday Review,* June 21st, 1856. *Ibid.,* p. 259.

p. 171   "the general sympathy." House of Commons. May 7th, 1782.

p. 175   "Tarpeian Rock." Quoted from Lionel Trilling, *Matthew Arnold* (London: Allen and Unwin, 1934), p. 278.

p. 176   "is solved." *Life,* p. 394.

p. 178   "are to be obeyed." "Lord Althorp." *Works,* Vol. VII, p. 68.

p. 178   cynical and unrealistic. For a difficult but rewarding analysis of this aspect of Bagehot's thought, see "Walter Bagehot and Liberal realism" by David Easton. *The American Political Science Review,* April, 1949.

CHAPTER 8

The quotations in this chapter are from *Physics and Politics, Works,* Vol. VIII, except where I have indicated other sources.

p. 180   "can define it." *Physics and Politics,* p. 59.

p. 183   *Mendelsohn. Thyrsis* by Matthew Arnold. *The Espousal* by Patmore.

p. 185   "facts of matter." Sir Ernest Barker, *Political Thought in England* (London: Home University Library, 1915), p. 149.

p. 186   Sir Herbert Read, *The Sense of Glory,* p. 184.

p. 187   had been asked. See the most informative study by C. H. Driver, "Bagehot and the Social Psychologists," *Social and Political Ideas of the Victorian Age* (London: Harrap, 1933), and in particular his examination of the ideas of Thomas Rowe Edmond, *Practical, Moral and Political Economy* (London, 1828), which anticipated some of Bagehot's ideas.

p. 196   "to act less." *Memoir (Works)*, Vol. I, p. 38.

p. 196   "appreciate." *New Republic,* April 18th, 1955.

p. 197   Reform Bills. But only to a certain extent, for the introduction to the second edition of *The English Constitution* which is instinct with his fear that English politics would degenerate into a scramble for the working class vote was written after he had finished *Physics and Politics.*

p. 199   other writings. *The Westminster Review,* whose reviewer had clearly only skimmed the book, reproved Bagehot for examining "scientific propositions which nowadays no-one calls in question, and it is doubted if much is to be gained by further dwelling on them."

p. 199   their source. Gabriel Tarde, *Les Lois de l'Imitation* (Paris, 1890) and Gustave LeBon, *Les Lois Psychologiques de l'Evolution des Peuples* (Paris, 1894).

p. 201   "primitive desiring being." *Works,* Vol. II, p. 104.

p. 201   "demoralises society." Noel Annan, *Leslie Stephen* (London: McGibbon and Kee, 1951), p. 172.

p. 202   "transcendentalist." *Memoir (Works),* Vol. I, p. 15.

p. 204   of religion. *Life,* p. 274; *Love Letters,* p. 82.

p. 204   as well. *Works,* Vol. I, pp. 273-4.

p. 204   sensitive young. "Adam Smith as a Person," (1875) *Works,* Vol. VII, p. 30.

p. 205   the Church. The first verse begins:
>   The lamp of faith is brightly trimmed,
>   Thy eager eye is not yet dimmed,
>   Thy stalwart step is yet unstayed,
>   Thy words are well obeyed.

p. 205   "his notice." I am indebted to Mr. Robert H. Tener, who is at work on a study of R. H. Hutton, for unearthing this.

p. 206   the Pope. "Bishop Butler," *The Prospective Review*, 1854. *Works*, Vol. I, p. 269.

p. 206   "insuperable." *Works*, Vol. I, p. 278.

p. 207   "showy tournaments." Frederic William Maitland, *Life and Letters of Leslie Stephen* (London: Duckworth, 1906), p. 263.

p. 207   without them. *Works*, Vol. V, p. 110.

p. 207   room to himself. "Shakespeare—the man," (1853) *Works*, Vol. I, p. 241.

CHAPTER 9

p. 209   even faster. Sir Walter Layton and Geoffrey Crowther, *The Study of Prices* (London: Macmillan, 1934, 3rd ed.). *Portrait of an Age, Early Victorian England,* Vol. I.

p. 210   "half a century." *The Economist, 1843-1943,* p. 41.

p. 210   averting. Gladstone Papers.

p. 211   *attainable. The Economist,* January 7th, 1865. Macaulay had held the same views twenty years earlier and Dalhousie had put them into effect as Viceroy of India.

p. 212   adopted it. *Works*, Vol. VI, p. 255.

p. 212   should be. George Sampson, Introduction to Everyman edition, *Literary Studies* (London: Dent, 1932)

p. 212   desk and papers. *Works*, Vol. VII, p. 138.

p. 213   "superficial sentiment." *Economic Studies. Works,* Vol. VII, p. 277.

p. 213   "determining mind." *Ibid.,* p. 137.

p. 214   "democratic endeavour." *The New Republic,* January 22nd, 1916.

p. 214   "mass of the people." W. S. Jevons, *Methods of Social Reform* (London: 1878), quoted in K. B. Smellie, *A Hundred Years of English Government* (London: Duckworth, 1937), p. 92.

p. 216 *"better than we are." Works,* Vol. II, p. 331.

p. 217 W. W. Rostow, *British Economy in the Nineteenth Century* (London: Oxford University Press, 1948), pp. 161-78.

p. 218 "brief periods." *The Economist,* 1863.

p. 218 "their business." *The Economist,* July 15th, 1865. In contrast to the other leading City paper, *The Banker's Magazine,* welcomed this as the "greatest triumph of limited liability." W. T. C. King, *History of the London Discount Market* (London: Routledge, 1936).

p. 219 "impassable." *The Times,* May 12th, 1856.

p. 219 "better." *Lombard Street, Works,* Vol. VI, p. 21.

p. 219 the loans began. "Bagehot as an Economist," *Fortnightly,* 1880.

p. 219 inactive and intense. *Works,* Vol. II, p. 283.

p. 220 susceptible. *The Economist,* p. 141, 1867.

p. 220 basic fourteen million pounds. I have used the word "basic" because the Act also gave the Issuing Department the right to add to this two thirds of the note issue of any private bank whose right issue lapsed through bankruptcy or merger.

p. 220 panics. See Chapter 2.

p. 221 "executive government." *Works,* Vol. II, p. 355.

p. 221 "community at large." Quoted in *The Bank of England: A History,* Vol. II, p. 285.

p. 223 "many figures." "Bagehot as an Economist."

p. 223 the world. The Act of 1844 had allowed the issues of the existing private banks outside the London area to continue though not to increase. The privilege fell into gradual disuse during the latter part of the century, partly because of the rise of the new joint stock banks who did not have the privilege, and partly because of the check system which the new banks fostered for this very reason. Since the right of issue lapsed on merger as well as on bankruptcy, the great era of bank amalgamations before the First World War brought it to a natural close before it was legally terminated. Stuckey's, which had retained the largest note issue of the private banks, thus lost its privilege on amalgamation with Parr's in 1907.

p. 224   "as any other." *Lombard Street,* Chapter II, p. 51.

p. 224   "proposing them." *Ibid.,* Chapter XIII, p. 199.

p. 225   "if possible." *Ibid.,* Chapter II, p. 32.

p. 225   "neocracy." *Ibid.,* Chapter VIII.

p. 225   "demoralised it." *Ibid.,* Chapter IV.

p. 226   "the Ministry." *Ibid.,* Chapter VIII.

p. 226   "liability of others." *Ibid.,* Chapter II.

p. 227   "are destructive." *Ibid.,* Chapter XII.

p. 227   gave it credit for. Notably W. T. C. King, *History of the London Discount Market* and Sir John Clapham, *The Bank of England: A History.*

p. 228   the reserve. R. S. Sayers, *Central Banking After Bagehot* (London: Oxford University Press, 1957), p. 15.

p. 229   "ephemeral fact." *The Banker,* March, 1926.

p. 229   "the opportunity." *Economic Journal,* September, 1915.

p. 229   "employments sake." *Lombard Street,* Chapter IX.

p. 230   "hereditary government." *Ibid.,* Chapter X.

p. 230   "England . . ." *Ibid.,* Chapter I.

p. 230   Bagehot. Gladstone Papers.

p. 231   the Prime Minister. *Ibid.*

p. 232   "Mr. Bagehot." *Life,* pp. 22-3.

p. 234   almost complete. Quoted by S. G. Checkland, "Economic Opinion as Jevons found it," *The Manchester School,* May, 1951.

p. 234   never since accepted. See Chapter 2.

p. 236   *every* society. *Works,* Vol. VII, p. 105.

p. 236   "abstraction." *Ibid.,* p. 106.

p. 237   "hard and fast" sense. *Ibid.,* p. 135.

p. 238   "political economy." *Ibid.,* p. 178.

p. 238   "or not enough." *Ibid.,* Vol. I, pp. 107-8.

p. 238   important errors. *Ibid.,* pp. 15-17.

p. 238 "worthy of its powers." R. F. Harrod, *John Maynard Keynes* (London: Macmillan, 1951), p. 467.

p. 239 in that trade. *Works,* Vol. VII, p. 226.

p. 239 "should do so." *Ibid.,* p. 228.

p. 239 "real things." *Ibid.,* pp. 229 and 232.

p. 239 economic thought. It would be foolhardy for someone who is not a professional economist to appraise the parts of "Economic Studies" that deal with economic theory. The best critique of these is still the Preface to the first two chapters which were published as, Alfred Marshall, *Postulates of English Political Economy* (London: Longmans, 1885).

CHAPTER 10

p. 241 the front rank. Earl of Oxford and Asquith, *Memories and Recollections* (London: Cassell, 1929), Vol. I, p. 37.

p. 241 living novelist. When George Henry Lewes died the year after Bagehot, Eliza's cook, on getting a letter from George Eliot's cook describing the demonstrative grief of her mistress, remarked acidly, "As they say in our part of the country, it's the bawling cow that misses its calf the least." *Ibid.,* Vol. I, p. 37.

p. 242 "principle of liberty." Viscount Morley, *Recollections* (London: Macmillan, 1917), Vol. I, p. 79.

p. 242 striking genius. *Life,* p. 6.

p. 242 "declamation." Letter to Hutton. *Life,* p. 358.

p. 243 "in the chase." Letter to Mrs. Barrington, *Life,* p. 35.

p. 244 boiled egg. Mr. Guy Barrington of Taunton, now 91 years of age.

p. 244 Mrs. St. Loe Strachey. The granddaughter of Nassau Senior, whose mother was an intimate friend of the Wilson sisters.

p. 246 "battalions." Keith Feiling, *Sketches in Nineteenth Century Biography* (London: Longmans, 1930), p. 147.

p. 247   work of philosophy. *Works,* Vol. VII, p. 301.

p. 248   aver him to be. G. M. Young, *Today and Yesterday* (London: Hart-Davis, 1948), pp. 240-1.

p. 250   and travel. *Works,* Vol. II, p. 97.

p. 250   "imperial manner." *Works,* Vol. II, p. 161.

p. 250   "with variety." *Works,* Vol. II, p. 118.

p. 251   their local "constituency." David Reisman, Nathan Glazer, Reuel Denney, *The Lonely Crowd* (New Haven, Conn.: Yale University Press, 1950).

p. 251   "great places." *Works,* Vol. IV, pp. 246-7.

p. 251   "as we now see it." *Physics and Politics,* p. 63.

p. 252   brevity. F. L. Lucas, *Style* (London: Cassell, 1955).

p. 255   "liberal temper," in *Social and Political Ideas of the Victorian Age,* p. 100.

INDEX